7m

7g~
10—

D0772496

First Principles

First Principles

The Jurisprudence of Clarence Thomas

Scott Douglas Gerber

NEW YORK UNIVERSITY PRESS

New York and London

NEW YORK UNIVERSITY PRESS
New York and London

Library of Congress Cataloging-in-Publication Data
Gerber, Scott Douglas, 1961–
First principles : the jurisprudence of Clarence Thomas / Scott
Douglas Gerber.
p.   cm.
Includes index.
ISBN 0-8147-3099-X (cloth : alk. paper) ISBN 0-8147-3100-7
(pbk. : alk. paper)
1. Thomas, Clarence, 1948–   2. Law and politics. 3. Political
questions and judicial power—United States. 4. United States.
Supreme Court.—Officials and employees—Selection and appointment.
5. Judges—United States—Biography.   I. Title.
KF8745.T48 G47 1998
347.73'2634—ddc21   98-25524
                                    CIP

New York University Press books are printed on acid-free paper,
and their binding materials are chosen for strength and durability.

Manufactured in the United States of America

10 9 8 7 6 5 4 3 2 1

For my parents: Sandra McDonald,
Stanford Gerber, and Kenneth McDonald, Jr.

Because the majority fundamentally misunderstands the notion of "reserved" powers, I start with some first principles.
—Thomas, J., dissenting in *U.S. Term Limits, Inc. v. Thornton* (1995)

Contents

Acknowledgments

This book could not have been written without the support I have received on this and other projects from Niko Pfund, my editor and now the director of New York University Press. This is my third book with Niko and his fine staff. I hope it will not be my last.

Many other thanks are due. I owe special thanks to Justice Clarence Thomas, who graciously provided me with copies of his articles and speeches. For financial support, I thank the Earhart Foundation and the Social Philosophy and Policy Center of Bowling Green State University. Tony Sullivan, secretary and director of program for the Earhart Foundation, supported this project from the beginning. I always will be grateful for that. Fred Miller, Ellen Paul, Jeff Paul, Kory Swanson, Harry Dolan, Mary Dilsaver, Tammi Sharp, Terri Weaver, Carrie Ann Biondi, James Taylor, and Kelly Spinnati—the administration and staff of the Social Philosophy and Policy Center—provided me with a congenial atmosphere in which to complete this book. If there is a more constructive environment in the academy in which to work, I do not know where it is.

An earlier version of Chapter 1 appeared in the *Journal of Black Studies* 27 (November 1996): 224–59. An earlier version of Chapter 3 appeared in the *Southern University Law Review* (fall 1997). I thank the editors of those journals for permission to reprint. I also would like to thank the managing and editorial boards of volume 8 of the *Journal of Law and Politics* for publishing my first essay about Clarence Thomas. That occurred during the fall of 1991, when I was a graduate student at the University of Virginia. Three books and eleven essays later, my experience working with the *Journal of Law and Politics* still ranks among the highlights of my professional career.

A number of people offered valuable feedback over the years on various parts of this manuscript. Those people are: Henry Abraham, George Billias, Carrie Ann Biondi, Michael Clemons, Bill Daniels, Matt Franck, Stanford Gerber, Gary Glenn, Bill Groff, Sandra McDonald, Gary

McDowell, Lawrence Morehouse, Bill Morrow, Keeok Park, Steve Presser, Roger Smith, Dick Stevens, and Kory Swanson. Charles Kromkowski was generous enough to read the entire manuscript, and he offered a number of insightful suggestions. Ellen Paul, the superb editor of the highly regarded journal *Social Philosophy and Policy*, gave the manuscript the "hard edit" it needed. The book is much improved as a result.

Introduction

"The mere passing of a decade may be no excuse for bursting into print with a collection of his utterances from the bench; but the period covered is long enough to justify the effort even from the standpoint of time, considering especially the highly articulate and prolific person who is their author." So wrote Samuel J. Konefsky in the introduction to his 1949 book about Felix Frankfurter's first ten years on the Supreme Court of the United States.[1]

The same may be said of Clarence Thomas. Although most people may not want to believe it, my research has convinced me, at any rate, that Justice Thomas is both articulate enough and prolific enough to warrant a book-length study of his first *five* years on the Supreme Court (1991–1995 terms). And I'm a liberal (at least a classical liberal).

Political science also recommends an early look at Justice Thomas's jurisprudence: judicial behavioralists have come to identify the first five years of a Supreme Court justice's tenure as a unique time in that justice's service on the Court—the so-called "freshman" or "acclimation" period (see Appendix I).[2] Justice Thomas agrees. He says that it takes "five years to become fully adjusted to the Court"[3] and that his "rookie years" were of special significance to his development as a justice.[4]

This said, the Supreme Court is not, and should not be, the exclusive province of judicial behavioralists.[5] The public at large likely will find an acclimation-period book about Justice Thomas to be of interest. After all, Justice Thomas has fascinated the American people like no other Supreme Court justice ever has. A Lexis-Nexis computer search of the newspaper database reveals that Justice Thomas was mentioned in 32,377 newspaper stories between July 1991 and December 1997. The next closest member of the Rehnquist Court in terms of newspaper references is Chief Justice William H. Rehnquist with 19,487, and that was for a much longer period of time—July 1972 to December 1997. The intense public interest in Justice Thomas also is reflected by the fact that there already have been over a dozen books written about him, although, as I describe in Chapter 1, all of those books have focused on his confirmation battle with Anita Hill.

The most important reason for writing a book-length study of Justice Thomas's early years on the Supreme Court is, however, this: unless such a study is undertaken—and undertaken dispassionately—his views are likely to be consistently misrepresented in the years to come. I document throughout this book how Justice Thomas's record is almost always judged against the benchmark of partisanship. As someone who tries to approach Justice Thomas's record as a scholar should—in other words, objectively—I find the substance of what he has to say to be too important for the kind of partisanship that has prevailed to date. This is especially the case when there is a major rethinking of public law issues underway (e.g., affirmative action, religious liberty, federal-state relations), a rethinking which Justice Thomas is helping to shape. Put directly, by understanding Justice Thomas's performance to date, we can better appreciate his impact in—and on—the future.

That, then, is *why* it is important to write a biography about Justice Thomas now. The next question that needs to be addressed is *what* type of biography this will be.

There are five main types of judicial biography. The first type is the "Life and Correspondence of . . ." collection, which is usually written by a member of the justice's family or a close associate. This type of judicial biography is not nearly as common as it used to be. A prominent example from the past is Gordon J. McRee's two-volume collection about James Iredell, a justice who served on the Supreme Court during the early days of the American republic.[6]

The second type of judicial biography is the personal biography, in which the subject's life and public career are presented, but his (and now her) work on the Supreme Court receives little or no treatment. Several biographies of Oliver Wendell Holmes, Jr., are good illustrations of this type.[7]

The third type of judicial biography is the published doctoral dissertation, or study by a more experienced historian, lawyer, or political scientist, that focuses on the legal philosophy of the justice. Charles F. Hobson's *The Great Chief Justice: John Marshall and the Rule of Law* (1996) is a recent example of this still popular type.[8]

The fourth, and most common, type is the full-scale judicial biography (or autobiography) in which the justice's entire life and career are chronicled. Obviously, this type of biography must wait until the justice has left the bench. Tinsley E. Yarbrough's biographies of Justice John Marshall Harlan I (1833–1911) and Justice John Marshall Harlan II (1899–1971) are fine examples of this type.[9]

The four types of judicial biography just described are quite broad. The fifth and final type is quite specific. It is this more specific type that Richard A. Posner, the Chief Judge of the U.S. Court of Appeals for the Seventh Circuit and one of the most influential legal scholars of the twentieth century, advocated in his keynote address to the 1995 National Conference on Judicial Biography. According to Posner, encyclopedic treatments of a justice's life or career are unlikely to bear much relation to what should be the primary function of judicial biography: "to illuminate the judicial process." Rather, a "judicial study" that focuses on a particular aspect of a particular justice's tenure "holds greater promise" for informing readers about how the judicial process *really* works.[10] *First Principles: The Jurisprudence of Clarence Thomas* was written with Posner's recommendation in mind.

There are several recent examples of this more focused type of judicial biography. Hadley Arkes's *The Return of George Sutherland: Restoring a Jurisprudence of Natural Rights* (1994), which argues for a "return" to the sort of higher law judicial decisionmaking practiced by Justice Sutherland in the 1920s and 1930s, and Christopher E. Smith's *Justice Antonin Scalia and the Supreme Court's Conservative Moment* (1993), which attempts to explain Justice Scalia's unexpected irrelevance on the Rehnquist Court, are two.[11] However, the judicial study most similar, conceptually, to this book is Nancy Maveety's *Justice Sandra Day O'Connor: Strategist on the Supreme Court* (1996).[12]

Maveety structures her book around the obvious, though surprisingly neglected, question: Why is her particular justice significant? To Maveety, Justice O'Connor is *not* significant—at least not *lastingly* significant—because of her status as a "famous first"—the first woman appointed to the Supreme Court—but rather because of her ability to influence the Court's decisions. And what makes Maveety's book so valuable for understanding the judicial process is her sophisticated use of social science techniques for demonstrating precisely how Justice O'Connor is able to exert her influence.

In the case of Justice Thomas, he is significant because of the debate he sparks (both among his colleagues on the Rehnquist Court and in the intellectual community at large), and because he provides a compelling case study of the anti-formalist thesis that "LAW IS POLITICS, pure and simple."[13] To make the point another way, no matter what Justice Thomas has to say about a particular area of the law, both his fellow justices and those who write about the justices for a living (i.e., journalists and academics) always seem to have something provocative to say in response. And while many justices and Court watchers still may prefer to believe that both judging and writing about judging are "neutral" activities unaffected by the political preferences of a given justice or commentator, an examination of Justice Thomas's acclimation period on the Supreme Court reveals—perhaps better than an examination of any other justice could—that judging and writing about judging are inherently political activities.

To illuminate best this particular aspect of the judicial process—the political aspect—*First Principles* is divided into three parts. Part I, "Politics," concerns "politics" in both the partisan and philosophical senses of the word. More specifically, Chapter 1 examines the partisan way in which Justice Thomas has been assessed to date—including during his controversial appointment process—whereas Chapter 2 explores Justice Thomas's political philosophy.* Part II, "Law," turns to the three major areas of public law about which Justice Thomas has spoken most forcefully in his Supreme Court opinions: civil rights (Chapter 3), civil liberties (Chapter 4), and federalism (Chapter 5). In keeping with the overall theme of the book, Part II also surveys the debate that Justice Thomas's opinions have generated. My focus is on Justice Thomas's *opinions*, because it is his opinions that have made him a significant member of the Rehnquist Court. His votes, also worthy of study, are discussed in Appendices I and II. Finally, Part III, "Law and Politics," attempts to tie together the findings of Parts I and II in a way that allows readers to appreciate what the phenomenon that is Justice Thomas has to say about the judicial process.

The research materials used in this book are Justice Thomas's articles, speeches, confirmation hearings testimony, and judicial opinions and

---

*Political scientists classify as a political "liberal" someone who advances pro-minorities and pro-women positions on civil rights matters; pro-defendant positions on criminal justice matters; pro-individual (versus the government) positions on First Amendment, due process, and privacy matters; and pro-national government positions on federalism matters. A political "conservative" is said to take the opposite positions. I adopt this convention here. See, for example, Lee Epstein, Jeffrey A. Segal, Harold J. Spaeth, and Thomas G. Walker, *The Supreme Court Compendium: Data, Decisions, and Development*, 2d ed. (Washington, DC: CQ Press, 1996), 455.

votes, and the reactions to each of these in the popular press and the law reviews. I take my analysis through the 1995 Supreme Court term: the final term of Justice Thomas's acclimation period on the nation's highest court.

Absent from my sources of information are interviews with Justice Thomas and his law clerks. I do not know if Justice Thomas would have agreed to such interviews. (He did provide me with copies of his speeches and articles.) I thought long and hard about whether I should ask him— and I was encouraged to ask by my editor and by a scholar who anonymously reviewed a grant proposal for this book—but I decided against it because (1) I believe it is important to let Justice Thomas's record speak for itself and (2) I distrust interviews. Although many social scientists place great stock in interviewing as a method for gathering information, I have come to believe that interviews are far too vulnerable to manipulation by both the interviewer and the subject to be of much use.[14] To mention but one example, what Supreme Court justice is going to say that she or he does not respect precedent?

I would like to close this Introduction with a personal note about some of the reaction I already have received concerning this book. Inevitably, most of the reaction has been political. Some of the politics were fairly innocuous. What springs most quickly to mind in this regard is an e-mail I received from a law student who was scheduled to introduce me at a talk I was asked to give about my then work-in-progress. The law student wrote: "I have been asked to introduce you next week. Please provide me information regarding the substance of your discussion. Are you supporting Clarence Thomas? Are you against him?"

Conspicuously absent from this law student's way of thinking was a willingness to believe that someone might be writing a book about Justice Thomas because he finds him interesting—nothing more, nothing less (more on this in Part III). Indeed, the law student's e-mail is a perfect illustration of the theme of this book: that almost everything about Justice Thomas, including how people view the debate surrounding him, is political.

More troubling is an e-mail I received from a colleague who has shown a friend's interest over the years in the progress of my career. Upon learning of my then work-in-progress, my friend wrote: "I think it is a very worthwhile venture, but one fraught with potential problems." What "potential problems" could there be? I asked myself upon reading this. After all, I had managed to secure a publishing contract with a top-tier university press and two sizable research grants on the basis of a brief prospectus. The "potential problems," my friend informed me, were that unless I write a "very, very critical" book about Justice Thomas, my "own career may be damaged by the Thomas curse!"

Has academe really come to this? Have academics become so political that we are now required to write partisan pamphlets rather than scholarly treatises? I surely hope not. Note that this does not mean that I am "supporting Clarence Thomas." It does mean, however, that I am not "against him."

PART I

Politics

1

Judging Thomas

No new justice has ever before done so much damage so quickly.
        —Nat Hentoff in the *Village Voice* (1992)

He is going back to first principles . . . and writing about the most
fundamental change in the structure of government. I agree with
him that most of what the federal government does is mischievous
and wrong.   —Richard A. Epstein in the *Los Angeles Times* (1995)

From Pin Point, Georgia, to the Supreme Court of the United States

Clarence Thomas was born in 1948 in the dirt-poor town of Pin Point,
Georgia, the second child and first son of Leola Williams and M. C.
Thomas. Clarence's father abandoned the family when Clarence was two
and his mother was pregnant with his younger brother. When Clarence
was six, he and his brother were sent to live with his maternal grandpar-
ents in Savannah.

Justice Thomas invariably acknowledges his maternal grandfather,
Myers Anderson, as the person who most influenced his life.[1] In a time
when Blacks were forced to live in a segregated society, Anderson decided
that the only way to overcome racism was to work for himself. He delivered wood, coal, ice, and heating oil from the back of a pickup truck, and
he was successful enough to be able to provide his grandsons with a comfortable home. He worked very hard, and he expected his grandsons to do
so as well—especially in school.

Thomas received an excellent formal education at a variety of private
schools, all of which, with the exception of Yale Law School, were predominately, and in some cases exclusively, Catholic. His educational experience was not entirely positive, however. At St. John Vianney Minor
Seminary, a Catholic boarding high school just outside of Savannah,

Thomas's White* classmates would tease him at lights out, saying, "Smile, Clarence, so we can see you."[2] At Immaculate Conception Seminary in northwestern Missouri, where Thomas enrolled to prepare for the priesthood, he overheard a White classmate's delight at hearing the news that Martin Luther King, Jr., had been assassinated. Thomas was so upset by this particular display of racism—the most egregious among many that he encountered at Immaculate Conception—that he left the seminary.

Thomas worked for a while before matriculating in 1968 to the College of the Holy Cross in Worcester, Massachusetts. Among Thomas's most notable achievements in college was his role in helping to found the school's Black Student Union. He graduated in the spring of 1971 with an honors degree in English. The day after graduation he married Kathy Grace Ambush, with whom he later had a son, Jamal. (Thomas and Ambush divorced in 1984.)

In the fall of 1971 Thomas enrolled at Yale Law School, having been accepted, in part, under the institution's affirmative action plan to recruit qualified minorities. Thomas was troubled by this policy. He later said, "You had to prove yourself every day because the presumption was that you were dumb and didn't deserve to be there on merit."[3] He specialized in tax and antitrust law, rather than civil rights and constitutional law, in order to distance himself as much as possible from subjects he regarded as stereotypically "Black."

His first job after graduating in 1974 was in the office of then–Missouri Attorney General John C. Danforth. Thomas's association with Danforth would later prove to be the most important in his professional career. Thomas requested to work on tax law issues, rather than civil rights cases, and Danforth honored his request. When Danforth was elected to the U.S. Senate in 1977 Thomas went to work as a corporate lawyer for Monsanto, a St. Louis–based chemical firm. Two and a half years later, Thomas rejoined Danforth's staff—this time in the nation's capital. He specialized in energy and environmental matters for the senator.

Civil rights work was not far off on the horizon, however. In 1981 Thomas, who had become active in the Black conservative movement

---

*Many of today's scholars of color capitalize "Black" but not "white." See, for example, Neil Gotanda, "A Critique of 'Our Constitution Is Color-Blind,'" *Stanford Law Review* 44 (November 1991): 1–68, 4 n. 12. I concur with the view that equality requires that both (or neither) be capitalized. See Bryan K. Fair, "Foreword: Rethinking the Color Blindness Model," *National Black Law Journal* 13 (spring 1993): 1–82, 1 n.

shortly after arriving in Washington in 1979, was named assistant secretary for civil rights in the U.S. Department of Education by President Reagan. Ten months later, he was named chairman of the U.S. Equal Employment Opportunity Commission (EEOC). It was at the EEOC that Thomas established his reputation.[4]

During his eight years at the EEOC, Thomas was credited with improving morale and making the agency more efficient. However, he was criticized by Democrats and civil rights groups for shifting the agency away from its traditional group-based approach in civil rights to an individual-based approach (see Chapter 2 for more on the philosophical basis for this shift), and for abandoning the traditional remedies to discrimination—numerical goals and timetables—in the process. He also was taken to task for largely forsaking the use of class action suits that relied upon statistical evidence to prove discrimination and for letting approximately nine thousand age discrimination complaints lapse.

It was during his long tenure at EEOC that Thomas became a much sought-after speaker on law school campuses and in conservative circles. (He also met and married his current wife, Virginia Lamp Thomas, at this time.) Few were surprised, then, when President Bush nominated Thomas in 1989 to the U.S. Court of Appeals for the District of Columbia Circuit. Thomas was confirmed in March of 1990, after an uneventful—especially in the light of future events—confirmation hearing.* On July 1, 1991, President Bush nominated the then-forty-three-year-old Thomas to be an associate justice of the Supreme Court of the United States. The nomination was made possible by the retirement of Thurgood Marshall, the first Black ever appointed to the Supreme Court and one of the most famous and influential civil rights lawyers of all time.[5] The rest, as they say, is history.

The Thomas-Hill Hearings

Clarence Thomas's Supreme Court confirmation process was arguably the most dramatic and divisive ever conducted. For instance, the National

---

*In one of the great ironies of American politics, Thomas replaced Robert H. Bork on the D.C. Circuit. Bork, of course, was himself the subject of a heated confirmation process. (His nomination was defeated.) See generally Robert H. Bork, *The Tempting of America: The Political Seduction of the Law* (New York: Free Press, 1990).

Association for the Advancement of Colored People (NAACP)—the preeminent civil rights organization in the United States—took the highly
unusual step of opposing an African-American nominee to the federal
bench when it sought to block Thomas's nomination on the ground that
his record on civil rights was "reactionary."[6] Likewise, the People for the
American Way—an influential liberal interest group—claimed that
Thomas had shown an "overall disdain for the rule of law" while chairman of the EEOC and assistant secretary for civil rights at the Department of Education.[7] Others objected as well, most notably to Thomas's
apparent willingness to invoke natural law in constitutional interpretation[8] and to his seeming opposition to *Roe v. Wade*, the 1973 Supreme
Court decision that legalized abortion.[9]

These issues received considerable attention in Thomas's confirmation
hearings (see Chapter 2). However, the issue that made all others pale in
comparison was the allegation by then–University of Oklahoma law professor Anita Hill that Thomas had sexually harassed her during their
tenure together at the Department of Education and at the EEOC.*
Thomas categorically denied Hill's charges. He even went so far as to
characterize the process that gave rise to those charges—his nationally
televised confirmation process—as a "high-tech lynching for uppity-
blacks who in any way deign to think for themselves."[10]

The Thomas-Hill hearings galvanized the nation. Hill's sexual harassment allegations—which were leaked to the press, and thereby resulted in
the highly public hearings[11]—were "an unprecedented event" in the history of the Supreme Court appointment process.[12] The Senate and the
nation alike were deeply divided over whom to believe. And the debate
rages on: well after Clarence Thomas took his seat on the most powerful
court in the world. There have been no fewer than fifteen books written
about the Thomas-Hill hearings, not to mention a flood of articles in pe-
riodicals ranging from the *Journal of Feminist Studies in Religion* to *Playboy*. A survey of the most important of that literature, that which has appeared in the law reviews and in books, provides insight into the cultural
phenomenon that Clarence Thomas has become.[13]

By my count, there have been seventeen law review articles about the
Thomas-Hill confirmation battle, as well as two symposia. The sheer

---

*Chronologically, the controversy surrounding Anita Hill's sexual harassment allegations
took place after the debate over Thomas's political views. However, in terms of defining who
Thomas is in the political culture, the Hill controversy took—and still takes—primacy.

number of the law review articles about the hearings is not surprising; the vitriolic tone of the overwhelming majority of them is. Most of the law review articles read more like partisan political tracts than objective legal analyses. For example, in the only article unabashedly defending Justice Thomas, conservative U.S. Court of Appeals Judge Laurence H. Silberman—a close friend and former colleague of Thomas's—called for the Bar to "rise up in righteous wrath" about the way the appointment process in Thomas's case was converted into an election process, especially by the press.[14]

The partisan nature of the law review articles was not unique to Silberman's pro-Thomas piece. The editor's introduction to a *Southern California Law Review* symposium about the hearings illustrates how one-sided the commentary from the pro-Hill side was as well:

> Anita Hill made a selfless and brave decision to come forward with evidence that was highly relevant to the confirmation of a Supreme Court Justice. In return, she was silenced with an impossible burden of proof, an accusation of racism, and the baseless claim that she was nothing but a hysterical woman whose unrequited love had made her delusional.[15]

Most of the law review articles focused on two related themes: (1) that Thomas was lying (a surprising number of authors came right out and said this), and (2) that the appointment process had broken down and needed to be reformed. I could discuss numerous articles addressing these themes, but two examples should suffice. The first is an article by USC law professor Erwin Chemerinsky in the symposium issue of the *Southern California Law Review*. Chemerinsky, who had prepared a position paper opposing Thomas's natural law views before Hill's allegations were made public,[16] asserted that "the tragedy of October 1991 was that a man was confirmed for the Supreme Court with quite dubious credentials, with extremely conservative views about crucial issues, and with, at a minimum, a serious doubt that he committed perjury before a national audience."[17] Gary J. Simson, a Cornell law professor, was equally straightforward in his *Cornell Law Review* article about the hearings. He declared that "Thomas's appointment was so indefensible that the process must be fundamentally flawed."[18]

Post-confirmation commentary about the Thomas-Hill hearings has not been limited to the law reviews. As mentioned above, at least fifteen books have been published on the subject, two of which—David Brock's *The Real Anita Hill: The Untold Story* (1993) and Jane Mayer and Jill

Abramson's *Strange Justice: The Selling of Clarence Thomas* (1994)—achieved the status of bestsellers. One of the principals, Anita Hill, even has penned a memoir on the subject. The politics involved in assessing the Thomas-Hill hearings are as evident in the books as they were in the law reviews. The manner in which the books have been reviewed also reeks of politics, especially with respect to Brock's and Mayer and Abramson's books. With the exception of Anita Hill's 1997 memoir, *Speaking Truth to Power*,[19] which is discussed separately in Chapter 6, this section analyzes the most important of the books about Thomas-Hill.[20]

Timothy M. Phelps of *Newsday* and Nina Totenberg of National Public Radio were the journalists who broke the Anita Hill story. Phelps continued to make his presence felt in the post-confirmation commentary with the publication of *Capitol Games: Clarence Thomas, Anita Hill and the Story of a Supreme Court Nomination* (1992), cowritten with Helen Winternitz. *Capitol Games* is an intriguing account of the Clarence Thomas story, from Thomas's roots in Pin Point, Georgia, to his first year on the Supreme Court. At the heart of the book, however, is Anita Hill. Like virtually all of the post-confirmation commentators, Phelps and Winternitz seemingly were obsessed with putting their own "spin" on the sexual harassment phase of the confirmation process. And the authors left little doubt that they believed it was Anita Hill who was telling the truth. In fact, in the book's prologue, Phelps and Winternitz suggested that Justice Thomas should be impeached and removed from the Court for perjury.[21]

Nina Totenberg continued to make her presence felt as well. In her case it was by way of an introduction she wrote for the "complete" transcripts of the Thomas-Hill hearings. Demand for copies of the official transcripts was so great that the Government Printing Office quickly sold out. With *The Complete Transcripts of the Clarence Thomas–Anita Hill Hearings: October 11, 12, 13, 1991* (1994), Academy Chicago Publishers rushed in to fill the void. Although Totenberg's introduction is only four pages long, her take on the hearings is not difficult to discern: She, too, sided with Anita Hill. She also made clear her opinion about several of the other books about the hearings. Totenberg wrote:

> In the publishing world, books about the hearing continue to proliferate. Both *Newsday* reporter Tim Phelps and Sen. Paul Simon wrote interesting volumes. Conservative polemicist David Brock caused quite a stir with his book, *The Real Anita Hill*, a work that, although well-reviewed in some places by journalists who covered the hearings, is riddled with factual er-

rors. Eagerly awaited is an investigative book in the works by two first-rate *Wall Street Journal* reporters, Jill Abramson and Jane Mayer.[22]

Phelps and Totenberg, like most members of the media, are political liberals,[23] and their interpretations of the Thomas-Hill controversy were plainly influenced by their political views. However, the most overtly partisan of the books about the hearings came from the conservative end of the political spectrum. That book, *Clarence Thomas: Confronting the Future* (1992),[24] is a collection of one-sided excerpts from the hearings, with an equally biased introduction by L. Gordon Crovitz, the conservative Supreme Court reporter for the *Wall Street Journal*. The book's warm reception by the conservative *National Review* says it all: "This book allows us to rediscover the true Mr. Thomas, and to examine the Judiciary Committee's dog-and-pony show at our leisure."[25] The book was published by Regnery Gateway, a publishing house with a reputation for publishing conservative manuscripts.

Four of the Thomas-Hill books are essay collections. The sheer number of essays in these collections makes it impossible to discuss more than a couple of them. By discussing only a few, I do not mean to minimize the significance of the rest. Indeed, the collections were events in themselves. Ronald Dworkin, himself no fan of Justice Thomas,[26] made this point well in a *New York Times Book Review* essay about the two collections that were published shortly after the hearings concluded, *Race-ing Justice, En-Gendering Power: Essays on Anita Hill, Clarence Thomas, and the Construction of Social Reality* (1992) and *Court of Appeal: The Black Community Speaks Out on the Racial and Sexual Politics of Thomas vs. Hill* (1992).[27] Dworkin wrote:

> The fact that so many of [the essays] react as passionately and eloquently as they do, yet interpret the events and their importance so differently from one another, is itself an important event in the history of race and gender in the United States. *Race-ing Justice, En-gendering Power* and *Court of Appeal* are thus among the rare books that are themselves events in the history they interpret.[28]

Most of the nineteen essays that constitute *Race-ing Justice, En-Gendering Power* are reactions to "An Open Letter to Justice Clarence Thomas" by A. Leon Higginbotham, Jr., which opens the collection.[29] More specifically, most of the essays are reactions to what Higginbotham—a highly respected liberal authority on the history of civil rights law who at the time of the letter was a senior judge on the U.S. Court of

Appeals for the Third Circuit—appears to fear most: the declining consensus in the African-American community about how to approach civil rights. Revealingly, Toni Morrison, the Nobel Prize–winning novelist and critic who edited *Race-ing Justice, En-Gendering Power,* stood virtually alone in insisting that Higginbotham was wrong to fear Justice Thomas's appointment. Morrison wrote:

> Regardless of political alliances, something positive and liberating has already surfaced. In matters of race and gender, it is now possible and necessary, as it seemed never to have been before, to speak about these matters without the barriers, the silences, the embarrassing gaps in discourse. It is clear to the most reductionist intellect that black people think differently from one other; it is also clear that the time for undiscriminating racial unity has passed.[30]

Reaction to the book was mixed—and fell almost exclusively along partisan lines. As noted, Ronald Dworkin, one of the leading liberal theorists of the second half of the twentieth century, praised the collection. Others, like John O'Sullivan, editor of the conservative *National Review,* condemned it. The tone of O'Sullivan's review was particularly bitter. He railed about the "politically correct" nature of the essays and their apparent lack of interest in seeking to discover what really happened between Thomas and Hill. O'Sullivan wrote:

> [The] contributors are not concerned with facts in any such vulgar sense. None of them tries to assemble the evidence for Miss Hill and against Mr. Thomas, and certainly not vice versa. They assume Mr. Thomas's duplicity and Miss Hill's rectitude and, that done, go on to consider deeper questions.[31]

Court of Appeal was more even-handed than *Race-ing Justice, En-gendering Power.* In his introduction to the collection, political scientist Robert Chrisman emphasized that the forty-one essays included in the volume span "the full sociopolitical spectrum—from ultraconservative to liberal to radical, and from both women and men."[32] Not surprisingly, those on the conservative end of the sociopolitical spectrum were pro-Thomas and those on the liberal end were pro-Hill. For example, in "Race, Gender, and Liberal Fallacies," Orlando Patterson, a prominent Black conservative, characterized Thomas's comments to Hill—assuming arguendo that they were made—as a "down-home style of courting," whereas Ronald W. Walters, a liberal, wrote in "Clarence Thomas and the Meaning of Blackness" that "Thomas and his supporters are not politi-

cally Black and have no right, either based on history nor, just as important, on any demonstrated validity of their ideas, to change the political
standard." Other essays in the collection bore provocative titles such
as "The Gang Rape of Anita Hill and the Assault upon All Women
of African Descent" and "'Them against Us': Anita Hill v. Clarence
Thomas," but perhaps the most telling contribution of all was by Maya
Angelou. Angelou, an acclaimed poet and author, wrote that she supported Thomas's confirmation because she "dare[d] to hope" that he
would remember where he came from and become a liberal.[33] A person
cannot be more straightforward than that in terms of the standard by
which he or she judges the success or failure of a Supreme Court nominee: politics.

Several years elapsed before the next edited collection appeared. That
collection was 1995's *African American Women Speak Out on Anita
Hill–Clarence Thomas.*[34] It was the first book about the hearings written
exclusively by Black women. The editor, Geneva Smitherman, is a soci-
olinguist who specializes in African-American speech, something that illustrates dramatically how many of the essays written about Thomas-
Hill—in Smitherman's volume and elsewhere—were attempts to decon-
struct what (if anything) was *said* between the two parties, as well as at
the hearings. Smitherman, for example, in her own essay concluded from
her examination of the hearings transcripts that Hill's arid professional
verbal style, in contrast to Thomas's "exploitation" of African-American
rhetoric, lost her support among Blacks. "African-American women must
fashion a language, building on and rooted in the African American Experience, that speaks to the *head* and the *heart* of African America,"
Smitherman explained.[35]

Almost to a woman, the contributors to *African American Women
Speak Out* supported Anita Hill. From the perspective of politics, the
most important of the essays was Linda F. Williams's "Anita Hill, Clarence
Thomas, and the Crisis of Black Political Leadership." Williams, who is a
political liberal, argued that the "traditional" civil rights leadership—
people like Benjamin Hooks, Benjamin Chavis, and Leon Higginbotham—were not well-suited to face the challenge that Justice Thomas
represented: the challenge of Black conservatism. The simple fact that
Thomas was *confirmed* by the Senate proved this, Williams maintained.[36]

The year 1995 also witnessed the publication of Anita Hill and Emma
Coleman Jordan's *Race, Gender, and Power in America: The Legacy of the
Hill-Thomas Hearings.*[37] This book is a collection of essays written for a

conference at Georgetown University Law Center that convened one year to the day after the Thomas-Hill hearings adjourned. As with the other collections, the intersection of race and gender in American politics was the thread that held the book together. Essays from many of the same authors who contributed to *Race-ing Justice, En-gendering Power* and *Court of Appeal* were included, but the most important contribution was made by Anita Hill herself.

Hill argued in her essay—her first published reflection on the hearings—that her lack of a patron and of a husband made it impossible for her to establish her credibility. (The irony that perhaps Thomas—and Hill referred to him as "Thomas," rather than as "Justice Thomas" or "Clarence"—was her patron was not discussed by Hill.) Hill wrote:

> The ease with which I was transformed from respected academician to malicious psychotic in the eyes of the public illustrates the tenuousness of my association with power. In sum, my license to speak before the committee as a credible witness was revoked by the tribunal and the process. I was cast as just another African American woman who was not to be trusted to describe her own experiences truthfully and who had no place in the decidedly political arena of the moment. To paraphrase Adele Logan Alexander's [another contributor to the collection] discussion, I was no law professor; I was a "niggress."[38]

It should come as no surprise to learn that the contributors to Hill and Jordan's collection deified Hill and demonized Thomas. In fact, Jordan—who was one of Hill's lawyers during the Thomas-Hill hearings—wrote, "The contributors to this book became a kind of family whose lives have been touched by the hearings and Anita Hill's testimony."[39]

Reaction from the political right to the Hill-Jordan collection was fast and furious. Journalist Ramesh Ponnuru provided a particularly scathing review for the *National Review*, a periodical which, along with the *American Spectator*, is a popular outlet for defenders of Clarence Thomas. Ponnuru wrote:

> The contributors to this book do not argue that Clarence Thomas was guilty as charged and should have been rejected for the Supreme Court. They simply assume these premises—indeed, the idea that an accusation of sexual harassment could ever be false has evidently never occurred to them—and try to explain the cultural pathologies that in 1991 kept most Americans from grasping the obvious. This approach has its advantages: none of the authors need mention, let alone try to refute, David Brock's

The Real Anita Hill. . . . All in all, there's nothing wrong with this book that a lighted match couldn't fix.[40]

Thomas's political allies did not limit their support of the justice to vitriolic reviews of pro-Hill books. In *Resurrection: The Confirmation of Clarence Thomas* (1994), Senator John Danforth—Thomas's former employer and his sponsor during the Supreme Court confirmation process—offered a book-length defense of the justice. Danforth, an ordained minister, characterized Thomas's confrontation with Hill as one of "good vs. evil" and what happened to Thomas as a "crucifixion" and then a "resurrection." Danforth's identification of Thomas with Jesus Christ could not have been more plainly stated. As Danforth wrote in an especially evocative passage:

> During the summer of 1991, Clarence lived in fear that people would kill him. In all but the strictly physical sense, the person I saw on Wednesday afternoon, October 9 was dead.
> Less than forty-eight hours later, on the morning of the third day, Clarence Thomas walked into the Senate Caucus Room, took his seat at the witness table, and commenced his testimony. Clarence had risen.
> Alleluia![41]

Shorn of its religious imagery, *Resurrection* is a behind-the-scenes account of how flawed Danforth believed the confirmation process had become by the time Thomas was nominated to the Supreme Court. In fact, Danforth admitted that *he* stepped over the line when, despite his staff's admonitions, he attempted to undermine Hill's credibility by collecting testimony from her students regarding her sexual practices and by suggesting that she suffered from erotomania (the delusion some women have that men in power have a romantic interest in them).

Perhaps because of the reservoir of bipartisan good will that Senator Danforth had accumulated over the years, reviews of *Resurrection* were far more temperate than they were for the other books about Thomas-Hill. There were exceptions, however. Jeffrey Rosen, the legal affairs editor for the (usually) liberal *New Republic* said that with Danforth's book, "The Oprah-izing of the Supreme Court is now complete." And in the spirit of the cliché "with friends like these who needs enemies," Rosen wrote: "Although it purports to be 'a story of friendship and faith,' John Danforth's defense of Thomas is even more of a blow to the justice's reputation than Mayer and Abramson's full-frontal attack."[42] Rosen was referring to Danforth's vivid description of Thomas sobbing to friends and writhing in pain on his bedroom floor during the peak of the controversy surrounding Hill's allegations.*

For readers who still harbor doubts about how pervasive politics were in the published accounts of the hearings and the reactions to them, an examination of David Brock's *The Real Anita Hill: The Untold Story* (1993) and Jane Mayer and Jill Abramson's *Strange Justice: The Selling of Clarence Thomas* (1994) should erase them.[43] These two books should be read together. Typically, that was how they were reviewed in the subliterature that made the reviews described above seem kinder and gentler (to borrow a phrase that President Bush made famous during his inaugural). Both books were bestsellers, which attests to how strong the interest in Clarence Thomas and Anita Hill was—and, with the publication of Hill's 1997 memoir, apparently still is.

David Brock is an investigative reporter who contributes regularly to the *Washington Times* and the *American Spectator*, two of the most conservative publications in the nation.[44] In *The Real Anita Hill* Brock accused Hill of fabricating her sexual harassment charges against Thomas. Early in the book, Brock advanced a fairly benign theory regarding the origins of Hill's charges: Hill simply failed to correct her friend Susan Hoerchner's false impression that it was Thomas whom Hill had accused some ten years earlier of sexually harassing her. Later in the book, however, Brock posited a more sinister thesis: Hill, aided by feminist law professor Catherine MacKinnon and other well-placed liberals set on defeating Thomas's nomination, intentionally misled Hoerchner and other corroborating witnesses into identifying Thomas as her harasser. Importantly, Brock claimed that Hill never really "came forward" on her own, but rather was "drawn forward" by these liberals.[45] Hill, in other words, was merely a pawn of liberal activists—including several Senate staffers—who were out to "bork" Thomas's nomination, no matter what the cost to Thomas and to the nation.

---

*As with a Shakespearean tragedy, the Thomas-Hill hearings had moments of comedy. Who can forget, for example, Senator Orrin Hatch's claim that Hill had to be lying because her testimony that Thomas had made a remark about finding pubic hair on his Coke can closely resembled a scene in *The Exorcist* about pubic hair in a drink? Garry Wills nicely captured the absurdity of this scenario when he wrote, "If she had said Thomas called her a bug, Hatch would presumably have proved that the exchange did not take place by brandishing Kafka's *Metamorphosis*." Garry Wills, "Thomas's Confirmation: The True Story," *New York Review of Books*, 2 February 1995, 36–43, 42.

The Real Anita Hill initially was praised by liberals and conservatives alike. Warm reception from conservatives was not surprising. Thomas Sowell, for one, called *The Real Anita Hill* a "carefully researched book" that "vindicates" Justice Thomas, while George F. Will declared the book "persuasive to minds not sealed by the caulking of ideology."[46] The favorable response Brock's book initially received from liberals was surprising, however. To mention but two examples, David J. Garrow, the Pulitzer Prize–winning biographer of Martin Luther King, Jr., found Brock's evidence against Hill's version of events "highly plausible" in *Newsday*, while feminist cartoonist and commentator Signe Wilkinson wrote in the *New York Times Book Review* that Brock "effectively demolish[es] the assertions of the witnesses who supported [Hill]. . . . He badly damages her case."[47]

The consensus of favorable opinion about *The Real Anita Hill* was shattered by a devastating review essay in the *New Yorker* by Jane Mayer and Jill Abramson.[48] In that essay, Mayer and Abramson—who were working on *Strange Justice* at the time—offered a point-by-point rebuttal of most of Brock's important factual claims (e.g., that MacKinnon was a driving force behind Hill's allegations, and that Hoerchner had misunderstood that it was Thomas about whom Hill was originally complaining).[49] Mayer and Abramson's rebuttal itself led to a counterrebuttal by Brock—an eight-page single-spaced letter of complaint to the *New Yorker*, which the magazine refused to print. The editors of the *National Review* charged that the *New Yorker*'s refusal to print Brock's reply showed that the magazine was "determined to discredit Clarence Thomas."[50] However, the *American Spectator* did publish Brock's reply,[51] and the shouting match about one of the most divisive events in Supreme Court history continued—most notably in the reviews of Mayer and Abramson's own book.*

In their 1994 *Strange Justice*, liberal journalists Mayer and Abramson portrayed Justice Thomas as an extremely ambitious man who was willing to ingratiate himself with the conservative establishment in order to one day attain a seat on the Supreme Court. More importantly, they also

---

*Brock himself delivered a set speech on several college campuses around the nation in which he accused the "liberal media" of attempting to silence him. The text of the speech was reprinted as an afterword in the revised edition of Brock's book. See David Brock, *The Real Anita Hill: The Untold Story*, rev. ed. (New York: Free Press, 1994), 389–402.

portrayed him as a liar and a sexual harasser with a strong yen for pornography. The sources for the details of Thomas's personal life were several witnesses who were not heard from at the confirmation hearings. These witnesses were apparently ready to testify that Thomas had sexually harassed them too. (Why the witnesses did not testify is itself a subject of much political controversy.)

Few books have received the media attention that *Strange Justice* got. First, there was a massive excerpt in the *Wall Street Journal*. This was followed by an hour-long edition of ABC's *Turning Point* devoted to the book and extensive coverage by *Nightline*, *Larry King Live*, and a host of morning news shows. There were also lengthy articles in magazines ranging from *Newsweek* to *Mirabella*—not to mention a National Book Award nomination *before* the book was published. However, and almost certainly because Brock's *The Real Anita Hill* was already in print, praise for *Strange Justice* came almost exclusively from the liberal end of the political spectrum. Jeffrey Rosen, for example, wrote in the *New Republic* that "Mayer and Abramson deserve real credit for removing the Thomas-Hill episode from the realm of unreason," while Mark V. Tushnet, a law professor, declared in the *George Washington University Law Review* that *Strange Justice* "establishes . . . beyond a reasonable doubt . . . that Clarence Thomas lied during his confirmation hearings."[52]

Conservatives were equally unambiguous in their evaluations of the book. The *National Review*'s John O'Sullivan referred to the book's authors as "hackettes," and the *American Spectator*'s R. Emmett Tyrell, Jr., named them the "winners of the 1995 J. Gordon Coogler Award for the Worst Book of the year . . . for their inept and tedious defamation of Supreme Court Justice Clarence Thomas."[53]

David Brock also had a word or two to say about *Strange Justice*. That "word or two" was actually a twenty-two-thousand-word review essay for the *American Spectator* in which he declared that Mayer and Abramson's book relied "on fake evidence, doctored quotes, and unreported hearsay." Brock called the book "the publishing hoax of the decade."[54]

Clearly, there were more than enough ad hominem attacks to go around. And the attacks did not end with Brock's review; Mayer and Abramson sent a letter to Brock, subsequently published in the *American Spectator*, that read:

> Your purported "re-reporting" of our book consisted of trying to bully our sources into recanting. When that failed, you then made up negative statements that they tell us they never made. Your review is built on the errors

that have become your hallmark. There are such a dizzying number that it is fruitless to enumerate them all—particularly since you have already told us that *The American Spectator* has no intention of printing our rebuttal. . . . This is sham journalism. But it's exactly the kind of faux investigative reporting that we've come to expect from you and *The American Spectator*.[55]

These personal attacks aside, the "factual" accounts of Thomas-Hill presented in *The Real Anita* and *Strange Justice* could not have been more different. A letter to the editor of the *American Spectator* from a nonparticipant (i.e., an ordinary reader of both books) made this point well:

> The gap between his [Brock's] account of the Anita Hill affair and that of his opponents has passed anything that can be explained in terms of differing opinions about who ought to be believed. . . . I think the time has come for you or Mr. Brock to reassure those who have trusted him by bringing legal action. Surely *somebody* here is knowingly telling lies or being maliciously indifferent to the truth, so a libel action ought to be possible.[56]

No such libel action has been filed. Consequently, the vitriolic tenor of the interpretations of the Thomas-Hill confirmation battle undoubtedly will continue. With the publication of Anita Hill's *Speaking Truth to Power*, it has, in fact, continued to this day. As now will be seen, the vitriol has not been confined to the confirmation controversy.

Justice Thomas's Performance on the Supreme Court

Now that Clarence Thomas is, like it or not,[57] a U.S. Supreme Court justice, we have entered upon what can only be described as "round two" of the national obsession with scrutinizing him and his actions. (Who would ever have imagined a Supreme Court justice being the subject of cover stories in both *People* magazine and the style section of the *Washington Post*?)[58] The conventional wisdom about Justice Thomas's first few years on the Court was that his opinions were shallow and poorly reasoned, he did little work, and he was a clone of conservative Justice Antonin Scalia with few ideas of his own.[59] More recently, the conventional wisdom appears to be changing. Justice Thomas is said by some to have emerged, in the words of one Supreme Court correspondent, "as a right-wing intellectual force in his own right, a radical conservative capable of spinning out bold, well-researched legal essays in clear, provocative prose."[60]

Justice Thomas's performance on the Court is viewed much differently by liberals than it is by conservatives. African-American leader Reverend Al Sharpton, to name one prominent liberal, led a people's crusade in October 1995 to Justice Thomas's house "to pray for Thomas's Black soul." Sharpton and his six hundred fellow protestors had been outraged by Justice Thomas's decisions on affirmative action.[61] Conservatives such as political columnist Robert Novak, by contrast, have gone to the other extreme and called Justice Thomas's opinions "brilliant."[62] The vast majority of the more lengthy evaluations of Justice Thomas's performance on the Court have been affected—some might say *in*fected—by political considerations as well. This section examines those evaluations.

The first thing that sprang to mind when I was reading the evaluations of Justice Thomas's Supreme Court performance was how quickly they began to appear. Interest in the cultural phenomenon that is Justice Thomas has been so intense that commentators could not wait the five years believed necessary by political scientists for a justice to become acclimated to the Court.[63] Many could not wait until Justice Thomas's first term was over. Less than five months after he was confirmed, every major newspaper had seemingly chimed in with a judgment. First out of the blocks was the *Los Angeles Times*, which decided after all of three months that Justice Thomas showed "signs of being a conservative hard-liner ready to sharply restrict the protections of the Constitution." Next came the *Wall Street Journal*, whose chief law correspondent wrote that Justice Thomas's early opinions made it clear why liberals had "wanted to stop him." The *Washington Post*, the *New York Times*, and the *Christian Science Monitor* were a bit more cautious: They waited an additional six weeks before they declared Justice Thomas to be, in effect, a right-wing ideologue.[64]

Somewhat more patience was exhibited in the professional journals—perhaps because of lags in publication or perhaps because, as journalist Eric Severeid once remarked, many academics are "slow journalists." In the winter 1992 edition of the *Howard Law Journal*, I submitted a detailed review of Justice Thomas's first-term freshman effect behavior, his opinions, and his voting record on the Court. I concluded that Justice Thomas showed no early signs of being disoriented, uncertain, or vacillating, and that his opinions and voting record rivaled that of Justice Scalia's for the 1991 term's most conservative performance. I also, however, fell victim to the same temptation to prognosticate that overcame the nation's leading newspapers when I declared that there was "nothing in Justice Thomas's first term performance, nor in his previous and extensive public record," to suggest that he would remember from whence he had come and in the future would moderate his views, as many liberals hoped he would.[65]

Political scientists Christopher E. Smith and Scott Patrick Johnson issued similar findings about Justice Thomas's first-term performance in a December 1992–January 1993 *Judicature* article. Smith and Johnson added also an interesting twist in their evaluation: Justice Thomas's solidly conservative performance during his first term "may tarnish his image with the public." The authors explained why they believed this possibility to be true:

> Thomas's confirmation hearing testimony before the Senate Judiciary Committee was premised on the theme that he had not thought deeply about and therefore had not prejudged controversial issues. . . . Because Thomas was so explicitly assertive in the opinions that he wrote and implicitly assertive by endorsing strident language in the opinions that he joined, especially the ones authored by Justice Scalia, he did little to diminish th[e] skepticism about his veracity during the confirmation process.[66]

The vast majority of the assessments of Justice Thomas's early performance on the Court were more overtly partisan than the two just described.[67] Indeed, the authors of most assessments made Justice Thomas's willingness to embrace the liberal "activist" vision of the courts the measure of his alleged success or failure. For instance, in an article comparing Justice Thomas's initial votes on the Court to his confirmation hearings testimony and his early life experiences, law professor Donald P. Judges assailed Justice Thomas's early performance as being devoid of any sensitivity to the values of fairness, privacy, and liberty. Those were values, Judges insisted, that Justice Thomas claimed to respect during his testimony and now should respect—and promote from the Court—given his life experiences. Judges's disdain for Justice Thomas's conservative voting record was thinly veiled at best:

> Perhaps Clarence Thomas learned nothing from the confirmation process after all about what privacy, liberty, and fairness might mean to other people. In retrospect, however, other people are learning something about what those values mean to him. And perhaps the lesson for all of us is that what matters is not *how* we choose our Justices, but *whom* we select. At present, at least with respect to sensitivity to the values of fairness, privacy, and liberty so passionately invoked by Justice Thomas in his confirmation hearings, there appears substantial room for improvement.[68]

Commitment to the liberal vision of the courts also was the benchmark for one legal commentator who originally supported Thomas, but who subsequently has changed his mind. Rodney K. Smith, then-dean of the Capital University Law and Graduate Center, testified on Thomas's behalf during the confirmation hearings. One reason he did so was his belief that Thomas's prior speeches and writings showed a clear commitment to protecting individual rights via the judicial process. In a *St. John's Journal of Legal Commentary* article, Smith explained why he had come to regret testifying for Thomas:

> My initial delight has largely been supplanted with doubt, disappointment, and dismay: doubt, because Justice Thomas's activity on the Court has caused me to have significant second thoughts regarding the conclusions I drew during the course of my testimony; disappointment, because I have been saddened by Justice Thomas's unwillingness to adhere to views that I had believed he held prior to his ascendancy to the Court; and dismay, because I am concerned that Justice Thomas has fallen under the sway of Justice Scalia and the allure of what I have referred to as "deferentialism" [deference to the government in cases involving individual rights].[69]

On one occasion the tenor of what was said about Justice Thomas went too far to merit publication. I am referring to a no-holds-barred attack on Justice Thomas by law professor Craig Bradley that proved too hot for even *Reconstruction* magazine—whose credo is "robust, wide-open debate"—to handle. In his proposed essay, Bradley suggested that Justice Thomas cast a surprising vote with the majority to reverse the conviction of a man charged with illegally purchasing child pornography because he likes to watch X-rated videos. Bradley also said that Justice Thomas's controversial dissenting opinion in a prisoner beating case showed that the justice "is about as warm to the plight of criminal suspects and prisoners as that frosty can of Coke on his desk at E.E.O.C." Of course, what Bradley was alluding to with this last statement was Anita Hill's confirmation hearings testimony that Thomas had once told her that he had found a pubic hair on a can of Coca Cola he was drinking. It was allusions like these that caused Randall Kennedy, the editor of *Reconstruction*, to reject Bradley's article on the grounds of "smarminess."[70]

A bit more restraint—but only a bit—was shown by Ronald Suresh Roberts in *Clarence Thomas and the Tough Love Crowd: Counterfeit Heroes and Unhappy Truths*, published in 1995 by New York University Press. Although Roberts's book is actually a series of essays criticizing several prominent Black neoconservatives (e.g., Shelby Steele, Stephen Carter, V. S. Naipaul), the chapter devoted to Justice Thomas's first year on the Supreme Court is quite detailed. It also is quite unflattering—as the title to that chapter, "Justice Thomas's Sins," suggests. In short, Roberts characterized Justice Thomas as a right-wing ideologue who believes that "justice is apparently someone else's work."[71]

Two current or former federal judges have also written articles about Justice Thomas's early performance on the Court. The first was Julian Abele Cook, Jr., Chief Judge of the U.S. District Court for the Eastern District of Michigan. Cook, who is both Black and liberal, "arbitrarily" (his word) examined three cases from Justice Thomas's first two terms that addressed the issues of capital sentencing, the Eighth Amendment, and federal habeas corpus relief. Cook concluded that "it is indisputable that the fundamental philosophies of Thurgood Marshall and Clarence Thomas are diametrically opposed." It was not difficult to discern whose philosophy Cook preferred. He wrote:

> Although it may be too early to accurately assess the impact Clarence Thomas has made, and will make, on the issues before the Supreme Court, there is nothing in his record to suggest that he will modify his extremely conservative philosophy or change his views regarding civil rights. . . . Time will only tell if Clarence Thomas, the 106th justice to sit on the Supreme Court, will stay the course of his present philosophy or whether he will venture into the land of judicial activism that has now been vacated by his distinguished predecessor, Thurgood Marshall.[72]

Leon Higginbotham, Chief Judge Emeritus of the U.S. Court of Appeals for the Third Circuit (retired), was the other federal judge to write about Justice Thomas's early performance on the Court. (Readers will recall that it was Higginbotham who wrote the widely read "Open Letter" to Justice Thomas shortly after the confirmation hearings concluded.) Higginbotham was much tougher on Thomas than Cook was. Indeed, the tone of Higginbotham's analysis of Justice Thomas's first two years on the Court is remarkably confrontational. Two passages merit singling out: one, where Higginbotham wrote that "Justice Thomas's . . . views are for the 1990s at times the moral equivalent of the views of the shameful majorities in the nineteenth century Supreme Court cases of *Plessy* and *Dred Scott*," and the other where Higginbotham wrote that "I can think of only one Supreme Court Justice during this century who was worse than Justice Clarence Thomas—James McReynolds, a white supremacist who referred to Blacks as 'niggers.'"[73]

What was the explanation for Justice Thomas's "immoral" and "shameful" performance? "Racial self-hatred," concluded Higginbotham. And what was the basis for Higginbotham's psychoanalytic conclusion? "Conversations with my daughter, who has her doctorate in clinical psychology, and with her friends, who are trained in clinical psychology and social work," wrote Higginbotham.[74]

Higginbotham was not alone in offering a psychoanalytic interpretation for Justice Thomas's performance on the Court. In fact, journalist Jeffrey Toobin was the first to offer the "anger angle," at least in print. Toobin, a lawyer, emphasized Justice Thomas's ire in a September 27, 1993, article in the *New Yorker*: an article quoted at length by Higginbotham.[75] As Craig Bradley attempted to do with his article that was rejected by *Reconstruction*, Toobin portrayed Justice Thomas as a vindictive and possibly psychologically disturbed individual whose performance on the Court is driven by deep anger, rather than by reason.

What makes Toobin's article significant is not simply the bold charges he leveled against Justice Thomas (e.g., that some of Justice Thomas's speaking engagements on behalf of conservative groups may have violated the law), but also how the article has been attacked in conservative circles. Of course, the conservatives' response is reminiscent of the continuing debate over Thomas's confirmation battle with Anita Hill. The editors of the *National Review*, for one, called Toobin's article more evidence of the *New Yorker*'s apparent obsession with discrediting Justice Thomas.[76]

Justice Thomas's alleged anger was also emphasized in other analyses of his Supreme Court record. The subtitle to a *Playboy* profile of Justice Thomas by Lincoln Caplan, for instance, was "How Clarence Thomas Came to Be the Angriest Man on the Supreme Court," and a controversial *Time* essay by Jack E. White, "Uncle Tom Justice," declared that "the most disturbing thing about Thomas is not his conclusions, but his twisted reasoning and bilious rage."[77] Jeffrey Rosen, who has written a number of articles about the justice, echoed this sentiment in the *New Republic*, albeit in a slightly less vicious tone. Rosen wrote:

> Thomas's own voice—radical, angry, interestingly perverse—has emerged clearly in important cases. He seems to relish taking positions that are, legally, just beyond the pale, for the sole purpose of sticking it to his familiar opponents—the liberals, the interest groups, Congress.[78]

Finally, *Emerge* magazine's treatment of Justice Thomas clearly falls into a category of its own. Most notable in this regard was the November 1996 issue of this self-proclaimed "Black America's Newsmagazine." In that issue Justice Thomas was depicted on the cover as a grinning lawn jockey under the headline, "Uncle Thomas: Lawn Jockey of the Far Right." Accompanying the cover story inside was a caricature of Justice Thomas as a be-robed shoe-shine boy polishing the footwear of Justice Scalia. George E. Curry had this to say about the matter in the editor's note that opened the issue:

> I apologize. Exactly three years ago, shortly after I took over as editor of *Emerge*, we ran a cover illustration of U.S. Supreme Court Justice Clarence Thomas, resplendent with an Aunt Jemima–like handkerchief on his head. In retrospect, we were far too benevolent. Hence, this month's cover with Clarence appropriately attired as a lawn jockey. Even our latest depiction is too compassionate for a person who has done so much to turn back the clock on civil rights, all the way back to the pre–Civil War lawn jockey days.[79]

Curry apparently accomplished his apparent objectives: The November 1996 issue sold many copies and received much attention. However, plenty of people felt that *Emerge* had crossed the line—and they were not all conservatives.[80] I include myself among them. As I stated in the Introduction, I am neither "for" Justice Thomas nor "against" him: I simply find him an interesting case for analysis. But I felt enough was enough. I sent *Emerge* the following letter, my first and only *personal* comment about anything involving Justice Thomas (including Anita Hill):

> I was troubled to encounter the caustic tone of your November cover story, "Uncle Thomas: Lawn Jockey for the Far Right." I was even more troubled by your Editor's Note "We Were Too Kind" in which you essentially challenged Justice Thomas to a fight. Has journalism come to this? Is America now so mean-spirited that we have come to this?
>
> In the most recent issue of the academic periodical *Journal of Black Studies* (November 1996) I address the question that is at the heart of your cover story: Why is Justice Thomas assessed in a vituperative fashion? Simply put, it is one thing to criticize a public figure such as Justice Thomas, it is quite another to do so with the contempt he is shown. The debate over the future of minority rights is too important to be overwhelmed by vitriol. Perhaps we should start *talking* to each other and stop *yelling* at each other. Who knows, Justice Thomas might listen then.

Curry published my letter in the December 1996 issue of his magazine, albeit after editing it down to two sentences (the two following the colon in the second paragraph) and crediting the letter to "Morton Hall"—the name of the building where my office was located at the time.

Conclusion

The modern Supreme Court is an institution of enormous power. Indeed, Alexander Hamilton's retort in *Federalist* No. 78 that the judicial would be "the least dangerous branch" of the national government[81] is one of the most conspicuous errors of prognostication in the history of American politics. From questions involving the relationship of the individual to the government, to disputes about the distribution of authority and responsibility among the branches of the national government and between the national government and the state and local governments, the Supreme Court, as Justice Oliver Wendell Holmes, Jr., once observed, is a "storm centre" of political controversy.[82] And in a world that knows that an individual's political values shape her or his positions on the leading issues of the day, it should be expected that Court watchers would have strong opinions about those individuals who sit on the highest court in the land.

In Clarence Thomas's case, however, the assessments of his performance—both during his confirmation process and as a Supreme Court justice—have been, with only a few exceptions, unusually vitriolic. There are a number of explanations for this phenomenon. The first is grounded in race and ethnicity. We should not forget that Thurgood Marshall, Justice Thomas's predecessor on the Supreme Court, and the first African-American appointed, was also sharply criticized during his appointment process and in his early days on the Court.[83] The fact that Justice Thomas is Black has undoubtedly played a similar role in how he has been assessed, no matter how much we may hate to admit it.

A second explanation for the vitriolic nature of the commentary is that, as a conservative, Justice Thomas strongly opposes much of what the civil rights movement and liberals in general have worked hard to achieve—most notably, affirmative action. To paraphrase Lloyd Bentsen's famous quip to Dan Quayle during the 1988 vice presidential debate, "Clarence Thomas is no Thurgood Marshall." Given that Justice Thomas is Black, his approach to civil rights is particularly offensive to many. This is obvious both in the ad hominem attacks about "Uncle Tom Justice" and in the more in-depth critiques of his record. In fact, the underlying premise behind the most prominent of those evaluations—that of Higginbotham—is that Justice Thomas has an "unavoidable obligation" to support the liberal agenda of the civil rights movement.[84] Justice Thomas himself identifies his political views as the primary reason why he has been treated harshly by his critics. As he puts it in an often-repeated passage:

> Cleverly, the purveyors of the "new intolerance" claim legitimacy in the name of fostering "tolerance," "sensitivity," or a "sense of community." Yet, in my experience, these popular buzzwords are merely trotted out as justifications in an attempt to intimidate and silence those who dare to question popular political, social or economic fads. To defend this turf from criticism, competing ideas and points of view are ignored and the jugular of the dissenter vengefully slashed at. Does a black man instantaneously become "insensitive," a "dupe" or an "Uncle Tom," because he happens to disagree with the policy of affirmative action? Is it any more justified to hurl invectives at him for what he believes, than to call him names for the color of his skin? In both instances a man's reputation is disparaged and his name sullied.[85]

Another explanation for the "disparaging" and "sullying" manner in which Justice Thomas has been assessed is the explosive nature of the accusation that damaged him most: sexual misconduct. Sex is an extremely sensitive subject. Witness, for example, Justice Thomas's unwillingness "to put [his] private life on display for a prurient interest or other reasons" during his confirmation hearings.[86] The weight of the sexual misconduct charge is most plainly seen in the plethora of essay collections about Thomas-Hill. Here readers should note not simply the confrontational titles of many of the individual essays (e.g., "The Gang Rape of Anita Hill and the Assault upon All Women of African Descent," "The Message of the Verdict: A Three-Act Morality Play Starring Clarence Thomas, Willie Smith, and Mike Tyson"), but also the focus of the collections themselves—gender and power. A careful review of these collections shows that many of the essays address the concern that women—especially Black women—do not have power and, consequently, are exploited by men—especially for sexual purposes. Anita Hill's own essay on the confirmation hearings, in which she maintained that she was mistreated by the Senate Judiciary Committee because she was unmarried and lacked a powerful male benefactor, is representative of this perspective on the intersection of sex and power in America.

A final explanation for the vituperative way Justice Thomas has been assessed is that many people consider him, quite frankly, a liar and a hypocrite. More specifically, many people believe that Justice Thomas lied during his confirmation hearings, not only about Anita Hill, but about other matters, including his positions on abortion, prayer in the public schools, and natural law theory. They view him as a hypocrite because he opposes affirmative action and if it were not for affirmative action he would not be where he is today. Commentators as a result are tougher on him than they otherwise might be. Justice Thomas's alleged hypocrisy about affirmative action is a particularly common—and particularly vigorous—criticism of his record to date. Higginbotham makes the point most dramatically:

> In 1984, the *Washington Post* reported that you had criticized traditional civil rights leaders because, instead of trying to reshape the Administration's policies, they had gone to the news media to "bitch, bitch, bitch, moan and moan, whine and whine." If that is still your assessment of these civil rights organizations or their leaders, I suggest, Justice Thomas, that you should ask yourself every day what would have happened to you if there had never been a Charles Hamilton Houston, a William Henry Hastie, a Thurgood Marshall, and that small cadre of other lawyers associated with them, who laid the groundwork for success in the twentieth-century racial civil rights cases? Couldn't they have been similarly charged with, as you phrased it, bitching and moaning and whining when they challenged the racism in the administrations of prior presidents, governors, and public officials? If there had never been an effective NAACP, isn't it highly probable that you might still be in Pin Point, Georgia, working as a laborer as some of your relatives did for decades?[87]

Have we had enough? Has Justice Thomas been subjected to enough vitriol to last a lifetime? No less a figure than Kweisi Mfume—the Black former congressman who replaced Benjamin Chavis as president of the NAACP in 1996—believes so. In an interview previewing the 1997 annual meeting of the board of directors of the NAACP, Mfume declared that he did not believe "we can ever change Clarence Thomas" and that he did not wish to spend any more of his time or that of the NAACP trying to do so. "I think we must end the Clarence Thomas fixation in our community and use that energy to change things around us," Mfume insisted.[88]

Whether Mfume's call for a change in orientation will be heeded remains to be seen. Indications are that it will not.[89] Why is this issue important? Because, in my view, it suggests how difficult it is to write an "objective" or "impartial"—pick your synonym for "neutral"—analysis of Justice Thomas's jurisprudence. I attempt to do precisely that in the pages that follow. Whether I succeed is left for the readers to decide.

2

The "Natural Law Thing"

Well, Judge, I don't know why you are so afraid to deal with this natural law thing.　　　　　　—Senator Joseph R. Biden, Jr., during the
Clarence Thomas Confirmation Hearings (1991)

As the declaration of independence established so eloquently, our government is founded on the idea that "all men are created equal, that they are endowed by their creator with certain unalienable rights—that among these are life, liberty, and the pursuit of happiness."　　　　　　—Justice Clarence Thomas, Speech to the
New England School of Law (1996)

　　　　The previous chapter concerned "politics" in the partisan sense of the word. There, I explained how partisan politics was at the heart of the unusually vitriolic reaction to Justice Thomas, both during his confirmation hearings and during his early years on the Supreme Court. This chapter concerns "politics" in the philosophical sense of the word. My objective here is to explain Justice Thomas's political philosophy. This, in turn, requires an investigation into what Justice Thomas means by "natural law." Joseph R. Biden, Jr. (D-DE), chairman of the Senate Judiciary Committee during Thomas's confirmation hearings, was well aware of the importance of Thomas's natural law views: He opened the confirmation hearings by proclaiming that understanding the nominee's writings and speeches about natural law was "the single most important task of this committee."[1]

　　　Natural law has deep roots in the history of political philosophy: Its origins trace to Plato (427?–347 B.C.) and the ancients, it permeates the writings of St. Thomas Aquinas (1225–1274 A.D.) and the medieval scholastics, and it speaks to the legitimacy of the modern Western nation-state itself—including the United States of America. Defining natural law is no easy task however, because it has meant, and continues to mean, different things to different people. For Plato, for example, natural law concerned man's place in the proper order of the universe. For St. Thomas Aquinas, it represented nothing more—nor less—than God's will. For America's Founders, and John Locke (1632–1704) before them, most scholars would say, natural law delineated what rights a man (and now a woman) was endowed with by virtue of being human.[2] The Declaration of Independence (1776) states: "We hold these truths to be self-evident, that all men are created equal, that they are endowed by their Creator with certain unalienable Rights, that among these are Life, Liberty and the pursuit of Happiness."

In order best to understand what *Clarence Thomas* means by the often abstruse concept of natural law, this chapter is divided into four parts. The first part examines the relationship between political philosophy and constitutional interpretation, both in general terms and in terms of what Thomas's confirmation hearings have to say about the matter in particular. The second part discusses Thomas's controversial position on the relationship between the political philosophy of the Declaration of Independence and the Constitution of the United States. The third part moves from the general interpretive issues discussed in the first two parts to Thomas's philosophical views about specific rights. Finally, the conclusion assesses what the debate over Thomas's natural law views has to say about the appointment process itself.

The sources of information for this chapter are Thomas's confirmation hearings testimony, his writings, and his speeches (both before he was nominated to the Supreme Court and after he was confirmed).[*] Because, in my judgment, it is important to let Thomas's record speak for itself, I quote extensively from that record. Justice Thomas endorses this type of approach. When asked after a 1997 speech to comment upon some of the criticism he has received, Justice Thomas stated: "I told my brother that if someone criticizes me, ask them a stunning question, and that will end the criticism: Have you read the [record]? That will take care of 99.9 percent of the criticism."[3]

Although Justice Thomas undoubtedly was being facetious when he stated that "99.9 percent" of the criticism would dissipate if his opponents actually read what he wrote, this chapter makes plain that there is

---

[*]Readers will recall from the Introduction that Part II examines Justice Thomas's judicial opinions. Part III ties together his judicial opinions with his political philosophy.

more—*much* more—to Thomas than whether he sexually harassed Anita Hill. Hill and Thomas may be forever linked in American political history, but Thomas's natural law views are unquestionably more significant for understanding his jurisprudence, no matter how vociferously A. Leon Higginbotham, Jr., and other prominent liberals may promote the "anger angle."

The Politics of Interpretation

The Constitution of the United States is not self-interpreting, nor does it specify *how*—broadly? narrowly?—it should be interpreted. History reveals, however, that judges, scholars, and partisans alike have not been shy about expressing how *they* believe the Constitution should be read. Michael J. Gerhardt and Thomas D. Rowe, Jr., make this point well in their preface to *Constitutional Theory: Arguments and Perspectives* (1993):

> Theoretical debates about constitutional adjudication are as old as the Constitution itself, draw from and may at times inform the disputes among Supreme Court Justices about proper constitutional interpretation, and provide the intellectual justifications for the directions that different political forces or interest groups intend for constitutional law.[4]

Readers understandably overwhelmed by the confirmation hearings controversy over whether Clarence Thomas sexually harassed Anita Hill may find it difficult to remember that Thomas, like Robert H. Bork before him, was questioned intensely about his theory of constitutional interpretation before Hill's allegations became public. While Bork attempted, unsuccessfully, to defend his previously articulated theory that the Constitution should be interpreted as the Framers would have interpreted it,[5] Thomas attempted, successfully, to distance himself from his previously articulated theory that the Constitution should be read in light of the political philosophy of the Declaration of Independence. When pressed about his many speeches and articles which seemed to suggest that, as Thomas himself phrased it in one of those articles, "a 'plain reading' of the Constitution . . . puts the fitly spoken words of the Declaration of Independence in the center of the frame formed by the Constitution,"[6] the nominee replied that statements such as that were merely the musings of "a part-time political theorist."[7]

Thomas went on to testify that his approach to judging was, and would continue to be if confirmed to the Supreme Court, unaffected by his philosophical beliefs—conservative or otherwise. As he put it in response to a question from Senator Dennis DeConcini (D-AZ):

> *Judge Thomas.* Senator, I think it is important for judges not to have agendas or to have strong ideology or ideological views. That is baggage, I think, that you take to the Court or you take as a judge.
>
> It is important for us, and I believe one of the Justices, whose name I cannot recall right now, spoke about having to strip down, like a runner, to eliminate agendas, to eliminate ideologies, and when one becomes a judge, it is an amazing process, because that is precisely what you start doing. You start putting the speeches away, you start putting the ideology away. You begin to decline forming opinions in important areas that could come before your court, because you want to be stripped down like a runner. So, I have no agenda, Senator.[8]

Here, and elsewhere during his confirmation hearings,[9] *nominee* Thomas was affirming his commitment to one of the cardinal maxims of Anglo-American constitutional theory: judicial neutrality. Indeed, if the vast majority of the theories of constitutional interpretation that have been advanced over the years have but one thing in common, it is the ideal that judges should remain nonpartisan and unbiased when deciding cases.

Justice Thomas reaffirmed his commitment to judicial neutrality in arguably the most important speech he has delivered since joining the Supreme Court of the United States: an April 8, 1996, address to the University of Kansas School of Law in which he criticized scholars and partisans who promote the idea that law is nothing more than politics.[10] Justice Thomas's remarks, which read like a polished version of his understandably more spontaneous confirmation hearings testimony, are worth quoting at length:

> If we are to be a nation of laws and not of men, judges must be impartial referees who are willing at times to defend constitutional principles from attempts by different groups, parties, or the people as a whole, to overwhelm them in the name of expediency. . . . Life tenure and an irreducible salary are not good policies in their own right. They exist only to help judges maintain their independence and, hence, their *impartiality*. It is the value that the critical theorists and the political interest groups wish to destroy in their arguments on judicial decision-making. But in my mind, impartiality is the very essence of judging and of being a judge. A

judge does not look to his or her sex or racial, social, or religious background when deciding a case. It is exactly these factors that a judge must
push to one side in order to render a fair, reasoned judgment on the
meaning of law. In order to be a *judge*, a person must attempt to exorcise
himself or herself of the passions, thoughts, and emotions that fill any frail
human being. He must become almost pure, in the way that fire purifies
metal, before he can decide a case. Otherwise, he is not a judge, but a leg-
islator, for whom it is entirely appropriate to consider personal or group
interests.[11]

How, then, did Thomas avow to remain true to the ideal of judicial
neutrality? By applying, he testified during his confirmation hearings,
the "traditional tools of constitutional interpretation or adjudication, as
well as statutory construction"[12] (e.g., text, framers' intent, precedent).
Thomas stated repeatedly during the hearings that those of his speeches
and articles that generated controversy were *political* speeches that had
nothing to do with his approach to *judging*. "The only point I am making is that, to the extent that those are political statements or policymaking statements, I don't think they are relevant in my role as a judge," he
said in response to a question from Senator Herbert Kohl (D-WI).[13]

Why would Thomas strive so fervently to distance himself from his
"plainly" stated position about the role of the Declaration of Independence in constitutional interpretation[14]—a position so "plainly" stated, in
fact, that many of the Democratic senators on the Judiciary Committee
accused him of undergoing a "confirmation conversion" during the hearings?[15] Partisan politics once again provides the most likely answer.
Thomas apparently believed it necessary to distance himself from his
writings and speeches about natural law because several of his most strident liberal critics were making alarmist claims about the implications of
his natural law views. For example, Laurence H. Tribe of Harvard Law
School—perhaps the most prominent liberal law professor in the nation—wrote in a widely read op-ed in the *New York Times* shortly after
Thomas was nominated by President Bush that Thomas, if confirmed,
likely would use natural law (1) to allow "employers to conduct business
free of health and safety regulations and minimum wages laws," as a conservative Court did at the beginning of the twentieth century, (2) to restrict women to their "'noble and benign offices of wife and mother,'" as a
conservative Court attempted to do in the second half of the nineteenth
century, and (3) to criminalize abortion.[16] What Thomas's critics failed

adequately to appreciate, however, as Thomas himself pointed out during some off-the-cuff remarks at a photo session for the *Legal Times*, was that political giants such as Martin Luther King, Jr., Abraham Lincoln, and the Founders of our nation believed that the Constitution should be interpreted in light of natural law.[17]

This said, it is difficult to take seriously Thomas's attempts during the hearings to distance himself from his prior statements about the role of natural law in constitutional interpretation. The title of one of Thomas's law review articles, "Toward a 'Plain Reading' of the Constitution—The Declaration of Independence in Constitutional Interpretation," could not be "plainer" on the matter, nor could his other pre–confirmation hearings speeches and articles.[18]

However, this does not mean that Thomas lied during his confirmation hearings about his approach to constitutional interpretation. In fact, he expressly stated during questioning by Senator Biden that natural law must play a role in constitutional interpretation:

> *The Chairman.* As a starting point. So at least, Judge will you not acknowledge you conclude that natural law indirectly impacts upon what you think a phrase in the Constitution means?
>
> *Judge Thomas.* To the extent that it impacts, to the extent that the Framers' beliefs comport with that. . . .
>
> *The Chairman.* So, you are going to apply, at least in part, the Framers' notion of original intent of natural law, right?
>
> *Judge Thomas.* As a part of the inquiry.[19]

The exchange on natural law between Biden and Thomas continued throughout the hearings. Here is perhaps the most illuminating, and perhaps the most colorful, exchange:

> *The Chairman.* Well, Judge, I don't know why you are so afraid to deal with this natural law thing. I don't see how any reasonable person can conclude that natural law does not impact upon adjudication of a case, if you are a judge, if you acknowledge that you have to go back and look at what the Founders meant by natural law, and then at least in part have that play a part in the adjudication of . . .
>
> *Judge Thomas.* I am admitting that.
>
> *The Chairman.* Pardon me?
>
> *Judge Thomas.* I am admitting that.
>
> *The Chairman.* Oh, you are admitting that?
>
> *Judge Thomas.* I have. I said that to the extent that the Framers . . .

The Chairman. Good. So, natural law does impact on the adjudication of cases.

Judge Thomas. To the extent the Framers believed.[20]*

Of course, the reason that Thomas's views about the relationship between the Declaration of Independence and the Constitution of the United States are important is because his views impact upon how he decides specific cases. *Justice* Thomas's concurring opinion in the 1995 affirmative action case *Adarand Constructors, Inc. v. Peña* illustrates the point. He wrote:

> There can be no doubt that the paternalism that appears to lie at the heart of this [affirmative action] program is at war with the principle of inherent equality that underlies and infuses our Constitution. See Declaration of Independence ("We hold these truths to be self-evident, that all men are created equal, that they are endowed by their Creator with certain unalienable Rights, that among these are Life, Liberty, and the pursuit of Happiness").[21]

The fact that Thomas's political values impact upon how he decides specific cases should come as no surprise to students of the law. After all, one does not need to proceed far down any recommended reading list of Supreme Court cases or legal theory books and articles to appreciate that it is *impossible* to divorce the interpretation of a law—including the Constitution—from the political values the interpreter brings to that law. It is not just a coincidence, in other words, that—be she or he judge, senator, activist, or scholar—the interpreter's interpretive method almost always leads to the policy results she or he prefers.

Several members of the Senate Judiciary Committee emphasized the interconnectedness of political values and legal interpretation during

---

*Thomas testified in a similar fashion in his less widely publicized U.S. Court of Appeals confirmation hearings:

> But recognizing that natural rights is a philosophical, historical context of the Constitution is not to say that I have abandoned the methodology of constitutional interpretation used by the Supreme Court. In applying the Constitution, I think I would have to resort to the approaches that the Supreme Court has used. I would have to look at the texture of the Constitution, the structure. I would have to look at the prior Supreme Court precedents.

As quoted in Roy M. Mersky, J. Myron Jacobstein, and Bonnie L. Koneski-White, eds., *The Supreme Court of the United States: Hearings and Reports on Successful and Unsuccessful Nominations of Supreme Court Justices by the Senate Judiciary Committee, 1916–1991*, vol. 17A, Clarence Thomas (Buffalo, NY: William S. Hein and Co., 1995), 1417.

their questioning of Thomas. Senator Paul Simon (D-IL) made the point most dramatically:

> When you say you have no agenda or when you say you are not a policy-maker, the reality is you become a policymaker on the U.S. Supreme Court. If I may quote from Justice Frankfurter, "It is the Justices who make the meaning," talking about the law and the Constitution. "They read into neutral language of the Constitution their own economic and social views. Let us face the fact that five Justices of the Supreme Court are molders of policy, rather than the impersonal vehicles of revealed truth."[22]

To summarize, Justice Thomas may be sincere in his commitment to judicial neutrality—to the separation of law and politics in judicial decisionmaking—but history—even Thomas's *own* history—reveals that it is impossible to effectuate this commitment in practice.

Thomas's Natural Law Views

Just prior to the commencement of the Senate Judiciary Committee's hearings on Thomas's nomination to the Supreme Court, Senator Biden published a lengthy essay in the *Washington Post* titled "Law and Natural Law: Questions for Judge Thomas." In that essay Biden previewed the most important questions he planned to ask Thomas about his natural law views: "Would he place 'natural law above the Constitution'?" "Is natural law a 'moral code' or is it 'a protector of personal freedom'?" "Is the nominee's vision of natural law a static one or an evolving one?" "Would Judge Thomas employ natural law to limit government's ability to respond in changing circumstances, or does he see it as permitting the government to adjust to new social challenges?"[23]

Several of those questions were answered in the previous section. For example, we saw that Thomas does not place natural law "*above* the Constitution," but rather considers it as providing *context for* the Constitution.

This section endeavors to flesh out the specifics of Thomas's natural law views—that is, to go beyond the bare bones of his argument about the use of natural law as an exegetical tool.[24] After doing so, perhaps Thomas's natural law views will be less "murky."[25]

To understand best the specifics of Thomas's natural law views, it is necessary to understand the origins of his interest in natural law. To do that, there is no better person to whom to turn than Ken Masugi, a former student of the Straussian political theorist Harry V. Jaffa[26] and, more important for present purposes, the former EEOC "scholar in residence" who played a major role in helping to shape Thomas's natural law views.[27]

"It is manifestly appropriate," Masugi wrote shortly after Thomas was confirmed,

> that Thomas turned to natural right political thinking. Earlier, Thomas had found libertarian thought and even that of Ayn Rand appealing. But his moral, religious character insisted on principles and objective standards, which he found lacking in those doctrines. The willfulness of much of traditional conservative thought, with its genuflection toward states' rights and Southern sympathies, appalled him. He questioned whether original intent theory did more than "skim the surface." He heard talk about "realignment," but little about the principles that historically have defined realignments. Although he regarded some conservatives (as well as some liberals) as racist, he saw their political and economic programs as ultimately to the advantage of Black Americans in particular. He wanted a positive, principled civil rights policy that was also consistent with a political and social agenda that respected individual liberty. He sought a political philosophy that would reflect the man who altered and formed his life—his grandfather. Although focused on race, he was not overwhelmed by it. A natural Aristotelian, he wanted to combine splendor with justice, in a manner very much consistent with the American Founding generation and, above all, with Abraham Lincoln. Thus, the references to natural right (in the form of natural law or, somewhat more frequently, natural rights) would occur in conjunction with mentions of American statesmen such as Lincoln, Jefferson, or Martin Luther King. Natural right was the perfect expression of his desire to transcend his concerns for race and civil rights, in the sense that it preserved his care for the fate of Black Americans while it enabled him to speak intelligently and in a principled fashion about politics and society in general. Natural right refined his love of his own.[28]

Masugi's characterization of the origins of Thomas's natural law views is consistent with Thomas's own statements on the matter. Thomas testified as follows in response to a question from Senator Orrin Hatch (R-UT):

> *Judge Thomas.* Senator, as I noted, my interest particularly in the area of natural rights was as a part-time political theorist at EEOC who was looking

for a way to unify and to strengthen the whole effort to enforce our civil rights laws, as well as questions about people like my grandfather being denied opportunities. Those were important questions to me.[29]

Those "questions" were so important to Thomas that he sought—it appears, unsuccessfully—to reorient the Republican party to his way of thinking about natural law.[30] Thomas himself made this point in an impassioned 1987 speech to the Heritage Foundation:

[The natural law] approach allows us to reassert the primacy of the individual, and establishes our inherent equality as a God-given right. This inherent equality is the basis for aggressive enforcement of civil rights laws and equal employment opportunity laws designed to protect individual rights. Indeed, defending the individual under these laws should be the hallmark of conservatism rather than its Achilles' heel.[31]

As these remarks make clear, at the heart of Thomas's philosophical value system is the primacy of the individual and the concomitant importance of protecting individual rights. Indeed, Thomas testified at his confirmation hearings that his concerns for individuals and individual rights were what tied together his scores of public law speeches and articles. He made this point unequivocally in response to a question from Senator Howard M. Metzenbaum (D-OH), arguably Thomas's most unwavering opponent on the Judiciary Committee:[32]

Judge Thomas. Senator, I think that I have not [had] an opportunity to go back and review that speech in detail. I have looked at it and don't know exactly where that quote [that America is "careening with frightening speed toward a statist, dictatorial system"] appears in it. But the point I think throughout these speeches is a notion that we should be careful about the relationship between the Government and the individual and should be careful that the Government itself does not at some point displace or infringe on the rights of the individual. That is a concern, as I have noted here, that runs throughout my speeches.[33]

Thomas made this point elsewhere during his confirmation hearings, most notably when he defended a speech in which he praised Justice Antonin Scalia's controversial dissenting opinion in *Morrison v. Olson* (1988).[34] In that opinion Justice Scalia called into question, on separation of powers grounds, the constitutionality of the federal independent counsel law. Thomas responded as follows to a barrage of questions on the matter from Senator Edward M. Kennedy (D-MA):

Judge Thomas. The point that I was making was very simply that it wasn't that it should not be determined or that wrongdoing should not be ferreted out, nor did I indicate that perhaps there could not be—that the executive could necessarily totally oversee itself. I don't think that was my point.

My point was that the individual, when an independent body was involved in the investigation and conducted the investigation, that there wasn't that responsiveness directly to either one of the three branches, and that that concern led to a view that an individual—that that lack of accountability could actually undermine the individual freedom of the person who is being investigated. That was the totality of that point. And that is, I think, an important point, and it was one that I made in the context of a speech about individual freedom.[35]

Thomas's professed commitment to the twin pillars of individualism and individual rights sometimes led him to disagree in his early speeches and writings with modern strands of conservative thought. His critique of prevailing notions of Borkean originalism—regarded by almost all conservatives as sacrosanct[36]—is particularly noteworthy in this regard. Note again in the following passage from "Notes on Original Intent" Thomas's emphasis on the primacy of the individual and the concomitant importance of protecting individual rights:

The young [Alexander] Hamilton defended American rights against a Tory by arguing "the fundamental source of all your errors, sophisms, and false reasonings is a total ignorance of the natural rights of mankind." This could apply to virtually any judge or dare I say any teacher of law today. . . . I would advocate . . . a true jurisprudence of original intent, one which understood the Constitution in light of the moral and political teachings of human equality in the Declaration. Here we find both moral backbone and the strongest defense of individual rights against collectivist schemes, whether by race or over the economy. Morality and political judgment are understood in objective terms, the Founders' notions of natural rights.[37]

In short, Thomas adopted a *classical* liberal interpretation of America's founding moment. He stated in his speeches and articles that "John Locke['s] political philosophy informs our Declaration of Independence,"[38] and his emphasis on the individual and on protecting individual rights is consistent with a Lockean reading of the Founding in general and of the Declaration of Independence in particular.[39] The Lockean orientation of Thomas's interpretation of the American Founding is clear beyond cavil in the following response to a question from Senator Howell Heflin (D-AL):

> *Judge Thomas.* The point there is that, in our regime, if you notice, I speak to the higher law political philosophy of the Founders. Their philosophy was that we were all created equal and that we could be governed only by our consent, and that we ceded to the Government only certain rights, and that, to that extent, the Government had to be and was a limited government.[40]

Justice Thomas continues to hold a Lockean view of the American regime. He said in a 1996 speech to the New England School of Law:

> Our democracy is founded on the idea that each individual is an equal, autonomous actor in our political system—each individual has an equal vote and each individual has an equal (though perhaps somewhat attenuated) voice in the decisions of the government. As the declaration of independence established so eloquently, our government is founded on the idea that "all men are created equal, that they are endowed by their creator with certain unalienable rights—that among these are life, liberty and the pursuit of happiness." For the collective self-governance that our democracy relies upon to work, each individual must be given equal respect and must receive equal recognition of his or her rights and responsibilities in society.[41]*

Thomas's Views about Specific Rights

Clarence Thomas has spent almost his entire professional life in government service. Consequently, unlike an academician, he has not had the occasion, nor perhaps seen the need, to offer a systematic account of his political philosophy.[42] This was apparent in the preceding sections, in which I had to piece together Thomas's confirmation hearings testimony

---

*Intriguingly, Justice Thomas has expressed his commitment to conservative (a.k.a. Borkean) originalism in several of the speeches he has delivered since joining the Supreme Court. See, for example, Clarence Thomas, "Judging," *University of Kansas Law Review* 45 (November 1996): 1–8, 6–7. As will be seen in Part II, he likewise has alternated between what I have elsewhere called "liberal originalism" and conservative originalism in the opinions he has written on the Court. "Liberal originalism" maintains that the Constitution should be interpreted in light of the political philosophy of the Declaration of Independence. "Conservative originalism," in contrast, maintains that the Constitution should be interpreted as the Framers themselves would have interpreted it. See Scott Douglas Gerber, *To Secure These Rights: The Declaration of Independence and Constitutional Interpretation* (New York: New York University Press, 1995), introduction.

and his various articles and speeches to explain his philosophical views about constitutional interpretation and natural law, respectively. The same holds true for his philosophical views about specific areas of the law: Here, too, I must piece together his confirmation hearings testimony and his writings and speeches to explain his views.

Civil Rights

Given that most of Thomas's government service prior to his appointment to the Supreme Court involved civil rights, it should be expected that he would have said more about civil rights than about any other issue. His philosophical views about civil rights are profoundly influenced by his commitment to the ideal of inherent equality that is at the heart of the Declaration of Independence. Thomas made this point on several occasions during his confirmation hearings. One such occasion was during an exchange with the strongly pro-Thomas Senator Alan K. Simpson (R-WY):

> *Senator Simpson.* . . . So my final question for you, do you believe that that passage that I just moments ago quoted from the Declaration of Independence has meaning, perhaps the meaning I attached to it? Is the belief that all men are endowed with certain inalienable rights one that you would consider well accepted within the judicial mainstream and consistent with most Americans' values and principles?
>
> *Judge Thomas.* Senator, I think that most Americans, when they refer to the Declaration of Independence and its restatement of our inherent equality, believe that. And I believe that our revulsion when we think of policies such as apartheid flow from the acceptance of our inherent equality.[43]

Thomas tied civil rights enforcement to the concept of equality that is at the heart of the Declaration in a much less friendly exchange with Senator Biden: an exchange—one of many during the hearings—concerning Thomas's apparent praise for a pro-life article by conservative activist Lewis Lehrman. Thomas testified:

> *Judge Thomas.* . . . I felt that conservatives would be skeptical about the notion of natural law. I was using that as the underlying approach. I felt that they would be conservative and that they would not—or be skeptical about that concept. I was speaking in the Lew Lehrman Auditorium of the Heritage Foundation. I thought that if I demonstrated that one of their own accepted at least the concept of natural rights, that they

would be more apt to accept that concept as an underlying principle for being more aggressive on civil rights. My whole interest was civil rights enforcement.[44]

Thomas's articles are replete with similar statements. He wrote, for instance, in "Toward a 'Plain Reading' of the Constitution—The Declaration of Independence in Constitutional Interpretation," that "the proper way to interpret the Civil War amendments is as extensions of the promise of the original Constitution which in turn was intended to fulfill the promise of the Declaration."[45] This "promise," Thomas continued, requires that the Constitution be interpreted in a "color-blind" fashion.[46] That is to say, for Thomas, as noted above, rights are *individual* rights and the Constitution protects every individual's rights equally, regardless of skin color. As he put it, "this approach allows us to reassert the primacy of the individual, and establishes our inherent equality as a God-given right."[47]*

In many of his speeches and writings, Thomas has been critical of the modern Supreme Court's civil rights jurisprudence. He starts at the beginning, with *Brown v. Board of Education* (1954), a case that he contends was decided on the basis of "dubious social science," rather than "reason and moral and political principles, as established in the Constitution and the Declaration of Independence."[48] Thomas does say that the result reached in *Brown*—that "separate but equal" is unconstitutional—is correct, but he argues that it should have been reached by interpreting the Constitution in a colorblind fashion.

Thomas also has expressed disagreement with *Green v. County Board of Education* (1968),[49] a case in which the Court held that the "freedom of choice" school assignment systems that were used by many school districts to circumvent desegregation were incompatible with *Brown*. Thomas objects to what he calls *Green's* requirement of "school integration" (the mandate that Blacks and Whites must attend school together), as opposed to *Brown's* requirement of school desegregation (the mandate

---

*The (post-) Civil War Amendments—the Thirteenth (1865), Fourteenth (1868), and Fifteenth Amendments (1870)—were designed to ameliorate the plight of Blacks by remedying the constitutional silence on federal protection of civil rights. The scope of these amendments, especially the Fourteenth, has been a frequent source of debate among judges, partisans, and scholars. Thomas is not alone in maintaining that they embody the philosophical principles of the Declaration of Independence. Several egalitarian liberals even share this view. See, for example, David A. J. Richards, *Conscience and the Constitution: History, Theory, and Law of the Reconstruction Amendments* (Princeton: Princeton University Press, 1993).

that Whites not prohibit Blacks from attending school with Whites, if Blacks so desire).[50] Finally, Thomas has criticized, albeit in passing, the "disastrous series of cases requiring busing and other policies that were irrelevant to parents' concern for a decent education."[51]

Thomas's critique of the Supreme Court's school desegregation decisions illustrates perhaps better than anything could that what motivates his approach to civil rights and the post–Civil War Amendments is his conception of civil rights as an *individual* rather than a *group* concern. In his most detailed examination of the subject to date, a 1988 essay titled "Civil Rights as a Principle versus Civil Rights as an Interest," Thomas wrote that it is an "error" to focus on groups rather than individuals, "for it is above all the protection of *individual* rights that America, in its best moments, has in its heart and mind."[52] And it is because of this "error" in constitutional politics, Thomas concluded, that "civil rights [has] become entrenched as an interest-group issue rather than an issue of principle and universal significance for all individuals."[53]

Thomas's philosophical conception of civil rights as an individual rather than a group concern also explains his views on voting rights. In a 1988 speech to the Tocqueville Forum, he argued:

> In both the judicial and the legislative branches we find growing acceptability in treating blacks as a separate group. This is not only to the long term disadvantage of black Americans, but it reflects as well on the health of our politics in general. The critical weakness in Congress is traceable to the decline of the notion of a common good or public interest above and beyond the desires of interest groups. . . . The Voting Rights Act of 1965 certainly was crucial legislation. It has transformed the policies in the South. Unfortunately, many of the Court's decisions in the area of voting rights have presupposed that blacks, whites, Hispanics, and other ethnic groups will inevitably vote in blocs. Instead of looking at the right to vote as an individual right, the Court has regarded the right as protected when the individual's racial or ethnic group has sufficient clout.[54]

Thomas's criticism of the Supreme Court's Voting Rights Act cases put him in hot water during his confirmation hearings, most notably with Senator Kennedy, one of the principal sponsors of the extension of the Act. Thomas was pressed so relentlessly by Kennedy that he apparently felt compelled to say at one point, "I absolutely support the aggressive enforcement of voting rights laws and certainly support the results in those cases."[55]

However, elsewhere during his confirmation hearings Thomas remained (more or less) committed to his earlier views as expressed at the Tocqueville Forum. The following exchange with Senator Arlen Specter (R-PA) is particularly illuminating:

Senator Specter. . . . My question to you is: Don't you think, aside from the generalization of individualism, that there is some very important objective to be reached through the Voting Act to have a group with an adequate meaningful participation in the political process?

Judge Thomas. . . . My attitude was that if, indeed, there is proportional representation that that presupposes—I think that is the word I used in that speech—that presupposes that all minorities would vote alike or all minorities thought alike. And that is something that I have—those kinds of stereotypes are matters that I have felt in the past were and continue to feel are objectionable.[56]

Thomas's philosophical conception of civil rights as an individual rather than a group concern also informs his most well-known policy position: his opposition to affirmative action.* Thomas has criticized at one time or other virtually every decision the Supreme Court has issued in favor of affirmative action, including, by name, *Regents of the University of California v. Bakke* (1978) (invalidating a set-aside of sixteen slots for racial minorities in a class of one hundred, but approving race as one factor in admissions decisions), *United Steel Workers v. Weber* (1979) (upholding a private, consensual affirmative action plan to reserve 50 percent of training slots for minorities because previously only 1.8 percent of skilled workers were Black in a community that was 39 percent Black), *Fullilove v. Klutznick* (1980) (upholding a federal set-aside program of 10 percent of federal public works monies to local governments for minority-owned businesses), *Local 28, Sheet Metal Workers Union v. EEOC* (1986) (upholding a court-ordered affirmative action plan to remedy in-

*Justice Thomas is well aware of the notoriety surrounding his views about affirmation action. In a question-and-answer session following a 1997 speech, he stated: "I think you pretty much know what my view is. As a matter of policy and as a matter of constitutional analysis, I've written very clearly, and my opinion said it's a racial classification." Clarence Thomas, Speech to the Savannah, Georgia, Bar Association, Savannah, Georgia, 1997, broadcast on C-SPAN. Thomas was actually somewhat supportive of affirmative action during an early stage of his tenure at the EEOC. Even then, however, he was committed to the ideal of protecting *individual* rights. See, for example, Clarence Thomas, Speech to the General Meeting of Women Employed in Chicago, Illinois, 30 March 1983.

tentional racial discrimination by setting a goal that 29 percent of the union, the percentage of Blacks in the community, would eventually be Black), *Local 93, Firefighters v. Cleveland* (1986) (holding that Title VII does not require that an individual be the actual victim of an employer's discriminatory practice to benefit from a consent decree), *United States v. Paradise* (1987) (upholding a one-Black-for-one-White police department promotion requirement, where the state was guilty of deliberately circumventing an earlier court order to integrate), and *Johnson v. Transportation Agency, Santa Clara County, California* (1987) (approving a state-ordered affirmative action plan for women seeking skilled trade jobs that selected women over men with higher test scores).[57]

What is the philosophical basis for Thomas's opposition to affirmative action? It is the same as it was for his opposition to the Supreme Court's *Brown*-era desegregation and Voting Rights Act decisions: a philosophical commitment to individualism and to protecting individual rights. As Thomas put it in a *Yale Law and Policy Review* article on the subject:

> Class preferences are an affront to the rights and dignity of individuals—both those individuals who are directly disadvantaged by them, and those who are their supposed beneficiaries. I think that preferential hiring on the basis of race or gender will increase racial divisiveness, disempower women and minorities by fostering the notion that they are permanently disabled and in need of handouts, and delay the day when skin color and gender are truly the least important things about a person.[58]

Thomas was more cautious about opposing affirmative action during his confirmation hearings than he was in his speeches and articles. For example, in response to a question from Senator Hatch, he stated that "society had an obligation to include those individuals who had been left out in our society, in the economy, in our schools, our educational programs, et cetera,"[59] and he told Senator Biden that "I said that from a policy standpoint I agreed with affirmative action policies that focused on disadvantaged minorities and disadvantaged individuals in our society."[60] He went on to add, "I am not commenting on the legality or the constitutionality. I have not visited it from that standpoint, Senator."[61]* *Justice* Thomas has continued to criticize the *policy* of affirmative action

*As a U.S. Court of Appeals judge Thomas wrote a majority opinion striking down on *constitutional* grounds an FCC gender affirmative action policy. The opinion was not released until after he was confirmed to the Supreme Court. See *Lamprecht v. FCC*, 958 F.2d 382 (D.C. Cir. 1992).

in several of the speeches he has delivered since joining the Supreme Court.[62]

It should be emphasized here that Thomas is not unconcerned about discrimination. Indeed, he stated repeatedly while he was chairman of the EEOC that his agency would vigorously defend *anyone* who could show that she or he was *personally* discriminated against.[63] This said, he believes that most people do not need government help to succeed, they only need to apply themselves. He frequently cites his own rise from poverty as an example that self-help works. In a 1987 review of sociologist William Julius Wilson's book about poverty and public policy, Thomas spoke from personal experience:

> Those of us who have ascended from the ranks of "the truly disadvantaged" through the strength of those who raised us would have been crippled by the [redistributionist] program Mr. Wilson sets forth. . . . It is precisely through self-help, with attention to both cultural and class traits of the underclass, that the most reliable progress can be made.[64]

Thomas has continued to emphasize self-help as a remedy to discrimination, and the lessons he learned from his grandfather in this regard, in the speeches he has delivered since becoming a Supreme Court justice.[65] Several commentators have gone so far as to opine that Thomas's views regarding self-help make him the Booker T. Washington to Thurgood Marshall's W. E. B. Du Bois. Washington was a proponent of a philosophy of Black self-help; Du Bois was an exponent of a strategy of Black protest and agitation for reform.[66]

Economic Freedom

Thomas was profoundly influenced by his grandfather on another rights matter: economic freedom. His most detailed discussion of economic freedom, an August 10, 1987, speech to the Pacific Research Institute, is replete with stories depicting how his grandfather's actions helped to shape his thinking on the subject. Here is an especially evocative passage:

> Bear with me a minute as I reflect back on my early life. Picture a poorly educated, recently married young Black man during the Depression in Savannah, Georgia. Envision him starting a wood-delivery business then adding coal, then adding ice, then moving to fuel oil. Picture him getting only two or three hours sleep per night. Go forward in time with him as he

builds his own house with his own hands and as he acquires a modest amount of property. That is the brief encapsulated story of my own grandfather who during the most repressive period of Jim Crow law and racial bigotry was able to gain some financial and economic security because there was at least some economic liberty, some economic freedom, even though political and social freedom were denied. . . . Do you think this man would raise his grandsons to ignore economic freedom as a major part of their lives?[67]

It was not stories such as this that concerned Senator Biden—who opened the confirmation hearings by waving in the air copies of libertarian scholars Richard A. Epstein's and Stephen Macedo's respective books about property rights and constitutionalism and then questioning Thomas about whether he subscribed to their contents[68]—among others. It was statements—in the very same speeches—such as:

> Today, we are comfortable referring to civil rights. But economic rights are considered antagonistic to civil rights—the former being venal and dirty, while the latter is lofty and noble. This, as I have noted, is not the way I was taught. After all, aren't free speech and work both means to a higher end? . . . Natural law when applied to America means not medieval stultification but the liberation of commerce.[69]

Of course, the concern of Senator Biden and other liberals was that, if confirmed, Thomas would work to abandon the so-called "double standard," under which the Supreme Court assesses governmental restrictions on economic rights more leniently than it does governmental restrictions on "personal" rights (e.g., political speech, religious worship). In some of his pre–confirmation hearings speeches and writings Thomas did appear to question the propriety of the double standard. For example, he told the Business Law section of the American Bar Association, "What we need to emphasize is that the *entire* Constitution is a Bill of Rights; and economic rights are protected as much as any other rights."[70] It was statements such as this that led Laurence Tribe to warn, in his now-famous *New York Times* op-ed opposing Thomas's confirmation to the Supreme Court, that Thomas would return the Court to the *Lochner* (1905) era—an era in which the Court was accused of sacrificing the health and safety of American workers at the altar of laissez-faire capitalism.[71]

Thomas specifically rejected a return to *Lochner* during his confirmation hearings. He testified as follows in an exchange with Senator Hatch:

Judge Thomas. . . . I think that the post-*Lochner* era cases were correct. I
think that the Court determined correctly that it was the role of Congress, it was the role of the legislature to make those very, very difficult
decisions and complex decisions about health and safety and work
standards, work hours, wage and hour decisions, and that the Court
did not serve the role as superlegislature to second-guess the legislature.

I think that those post-*Lochner* era cases were correctly decided, and
I see no reason why those cases and that line of cases should have been
or should be revisited.[72]

Later in the hearings, this time in an exchange with Senator Biden,
Thomas explicitly rejected the idea that the Court should jettison the
double standard.[73]

All of this said, Thomas continued to stress during his confirmation
hearings that "there should be a recognition of property rights—economic rights" in America.[74] He presses this point as well in the speeches
about self-help that he has delivered since becoming a Supreme Court
justice.[75] Apparently, then, Thomas has a strong philosophical commitment to economic rights, but he is reluctant—at least in his philosophical
statements on the subject—to jettison the approach to those rights that
the Court has been employing since 1937, when the *Lochner* era came to a
close.[76]

Abortion

With the notable exception of Anita Hill's allegations, the most hotly
debated issue during Thomas's confirmation process was abortion. If I
count correctly, Thomas was questioned seventy-one times on the matter.
This was undoubtedly because he had a track record: He had participated
in a White House working group that called for the reversal of *Roe v.
Wade*, the 1973 Supreme Court decision that constitutionalized the right
to choose;[77] he had criticized *Roe* in a footnote to a 1989 *Harvard Journal
of Law and Public Policy* article about the privileges or immunities
clause;[78] he had singled out abortion in a newspaper article condemning
judicial activism;[79] and, most problematically for the nominee, he had
praised as a "splendid example of applying natural law" an April 1987
essay by conservative activist Lewis Lehrman that discussed what the natural law political philosophy of the Declaration of Independence had to
say about abortion.[80]

Lehrman's essay, "The Declaration of Independence and the Right to Life: One Leads Unmistakably from the Other," argued that *Roe* was a "coup" against the Constitution. Equating the current struggle to ban abortion with Abraham Lincoln's struggle to ban slavery, Lehrman characterized the Supreme Court's unwillingness to protect a "child-about-to-be-born (a person)" as a "holocaust" that was fundamentally inconsistent with the "expressly stipulated right to life, as set forth in the Declaration and the Constitution."[81]

The implications of Lehrman's interpretation of the Declaration and the Constitution as protecting the unborn child from the moment of conception extend further than the overruling of *Roe v. Wade*. Abortion would be *constitutionally prohibited:* states would not even have the authority that existed before *Roe* to permit abortion, if they so chose. This fact was not lost on pro-choice interest groups and senators. For instance, Eleanor Curti Smeal, testifying on behalf of the Fund for the Feminist Majority, said:

> There is nothing—*not a paragraph, not a sentence, not a word*—in Thomas's writings that indicates a willingness to protect reproductive freedoms and women's lives. To the contrary, *Thomas may well be the first Justice in American history even willing to prohibit states from allowing abortion.*[82]

As far as pro-choice senators were concerned, Senator Kennedy, to mention but one notable example, argued in his opening statement that

> on the right to privacy, Judge Thomas has strongly commended an article entitled "The Declaration of Independence and the Right to Life." One leads unmistakably from the other. That article refers to the constitutional right to abortion in *Roe v. Wade* as a conjured right with not a single trace of lawful authority. According to the article, which Judge Thomas has called "splendid," abortion is the constitutional equivalent of murder.
>
> If this view is accepted by the Supreme Court, not only Roe v. Wade will be overruled, neither the Congress nor any State legislature will have the power to protect a woman's right to choose an abortion in cases of rape or incest. And Federal and State governments will have an engraved invitation to invade other basic aspects of individuals' private lives.[83]

Thomas's approach to the abortion controversy during his confirmation hearings was, bluntly stated, to duck it.[84] He claimed, for instance, never to have read the "White House Working Group Report on the Family" that he had signed and, with respect to the Lehrman essay, to have been issuing an offhand remark in the Lewis Lehrman Auditorium aimed at establishing a rapport between himself and a hitherto alien, conservative audience. Thomas went so far as to testify that he had never discussed abortion generally, or *Roe v. Wade* specifically, with anyone ever, and that he had an open mind on the subject.[85] However, that did not prevent him from voting to overturn *Roe* the very first time the question came before him as a Supreme Court justice.[86] He also had this to say in response to a question following a 1997 speech: "I have dissented in all the abortion cases because I don't think there's a constitutional right but, with that said, if there was a constitutional right that gave the right to an abortion, then I can't frustrate that."[87] Clearly, *Justice* Thomas is far more certain of his position on abortion than *nominee* Thomas led the Senate to believe he would be. I offer a possible explanation for this state of affairs in the conclusion to this chapter.

Privacy

The right of privacy has been the subject of intense political debate in the United States since at least 1965, when the Supreme Court decided *Griswold v. Connecticut*.[88] At issue in *Griswold* was a Connecticut statute that barred the distribution and use of contraceptive devices. The Court, in a 7-to-2 vote, held that the statute was an unconstitutional infringement on marital privacy. Writing for the majority, Justice William O. Douglas declared that while there was no "right of privacy" mentioned in Constitution, such a right could be inferred from the existence of "penumbras" that were formed by "emanations" from other provisions of the Bill of Rights that recognized "zones of privacy."[89]

Justice Douglas's opinion for the Court instantly became one of the most controversial in the Court's history. In addition to the stinging dissents of Justices Hugo Black and Potter Stewart in *Griswold* itself,[90] Robert Bork wrote that "the protection of marriage was not the point of *Griswold*. The creation of a new device for judicial power to remake the Constitution was the point."[91] Indeed, the Court's decision in *Griswold* that there is a right of privacy in the Constitution was a principal cause of the call, by Bork and other conservatives, for a jurisprudence of original intention.

Not surprisingly, then, the right of privacy received considerable coverage during Thomas's confirmation process. Thomas testified that "there is a right of privacy in the 14th Amendment."[92] The Fourteenth Amendment provides, in pertinent part, that no state may "deprive any person of . . . liberty . . . without due process of law." However, Thomas equivocated on the question of whether a right of privacy is also found in the Ninth Amendment, as many liberals have long maintained.[93] The Ninth Amendment states: "The enumeration in the Constitution, of certain rights, shall not be construed to deny or disparage others retained by the people." Thomas told Senator Simon that "I would not foreclose it, Senator, but with respect to the privacy interest, I would continue to say that the liberty component of the due process clause is the repository of that interest."[94]

Several liberal interest groups that opposed Thomas's nomination to the Supreme Court argued that Thomas's pre-confirmation hearings, speeches, and writings evidenced an unwillingness on Thomas's part to give the Ninth Amendment substantive content.[95] The record supports this interpretation of Thomas's position. Thomas's pre-confirmation hearings speeches and writings adopted Bork's position on the Ninth Amendment, a position that, as will be explained in a moment, *rejects* the idea that the Ninth Amendment protects unenumerated rights.[96] As Thomas wrote in a 1988 essay for the Cato Institute, "I daresay the great majority of those who were berating Judge Bork for slighting the ninth amendment were scarcely proponents of limited government."[97] According to Thomas, reading the Ninth Amendment as recognizing unenumerated rights would give the Court "a blank check. . . . Far from being a protection, the ninth amendment w[ould] likely become an additional weapon for the enemies of freedom."[98]

In a well-known argument, Bork—whose own nomination to the Supreme Court was rejected in 1987 in part because of his views about privacy—maintains that the Ninth Amendment was designed solely to ensure that rights already held by the people under state law would remain with the people and that the enumeration of rights in the federal Constitution did not change this fact.[99] Again, Thomas appears to agree, at least in his philosophical statements. "To add a series of amendments that would explicitly deny to the national government certain powers over various subjects would imply," Thomas wrote in his essay for the Cato Institute, "that those subjects, and perhaps others besides, could be regulated in other, unspecified ways."[100]

Religion

Thomas's views about religious freedom also received a great deal of attention during his confirmation process. The First Amendment contains two religion clauses, the Establishment Clause and the Free Exercise Clause. The Establishment Clause expressly forbids the creation of a national church; it separates church and state. The Free Exercise Clause guarantees that individuals may worship as they please. Unfortunately, the apparent dictates of these two clauses often point in opposite directions. For example, does prohibiting prayer in the public schools on Establishment Clause grounds violate the right of students to free exercise of religion? Moreover, each of the two religion clauses, when examined separately, is rife with ambiguity. Does all state aid to religious schools constitute an establishment of religion? Religious *beliefs* are protected by the Free Exercise Clause, but how far may the government go in prohibiting certain religious *practices*? The confusion raised by the two religion clauses is not helped by the fact that the Supreme Court's decisions in this area are themselves confusing, and often contradictory.[101]

Thomas was questioned about both Establishment Clause issues and Free Exercise Clause issues during his confirmation hearings. His answers were sometimes at odds with his pre-hearings statements. For example, when asked in a 1985 symposium to comment upon then-President Reagan's public school prayer initiatives, Thomas said: "As for prayer, my mother says that when they took God out of the schools, the schools went to hell. She may be right. Religion certainly is a source of positive values and we need to get as many positive values in the schools as we can get."[102] While it is difficult to discern much from this cryptic remark, it seems to indicate that Thomas was willing to sanction substantially greater government involvement in religion than Supreme Court precedent allows (even muddled Supreme Court precedent). Thomas's confirmation hearings testimony was 180 degrees the reverse. He testified that "I have no personal disagreement with the [Lemon] tests" and "I think the wall of separation is an appropriate metaphor."[103] The *Lemon* test is a three-part test articulated by the Court in 1971 to guide Establishment Clause decisions. The "wall of separation between Church and State" is a phrase penned by Thomas Jefferson in 1802 and often has been used by the Court as a metaphor in Establishment Clause cases—especially when the Court has decided that a particular government practice *violates* the Establishment Clause.[104]

In at least one speech delivered since joining the Supreme Court, Justice Thomas appears to have returned to the accommodationist inclinations of his pre-confirmation hearings pronouncements.* Thomas told the 1996 graduating class of Liberty University, a Christian college founded by the Reverend Jerry Falwell, "We cannot turn our backs on the essence of our current sanctity and well being. We cannot turn our backs publicly or privately."[105] He also is reported to have told his friend Armstrong Williams, a conservative political commentator, that "God's law required him to vote against affirmative action."[106] In short, *Justice* Thomas appears quite comfortable in his speeches and writings with marrying religion and public affairs.

Thomas also was quizzed during his confirmation hearings about the Free Exercise Clause. The context was a series of questions concerning Justice Scalia's controversial opinion for the Court in *Oregon v. Smith* (1990), which held that an otherwise valid law does not violate the Free Exercise Clause if it incidentally affects religious practices.[107] The Court had previously held, since *Sherbert v. Verner* (1963), that if a government policy was challenged on free exercise grounds, the government had to demonstrate a compelling interest for the policy to survive judicial scrutiny.[108] Put more directly, *Sherbert* was widely regarded as being more protective of religious liberty than *Smith* was, and Thomas was asked which test he preferred. Thomas responded as follows to a question from Senator Biden (who preferred *Sherbert*):

> *Judge Thomas.* . . . And I guess my point is our concerns are the same, that any test which lessens the protection I think is a matter of concern. The point I am making, though, in not being absolutist is that I think it is best for me, as a sitting Federal Judge, to take more time and to think that through, but my concern about the approach taken by Justice Scalia is that it may have the potential and could have the potential of lessening protection, and I think the approach that we should take certainly is one that maximizes those protections.[109]

---

*An "accommodationist" holds that government may aid or extend benefits to religion as long as it does not prefer one religion over another. Government aid to religion is much easier to justify under an accommodationist position than it is under a "high wall" position. Political conservatives tend to be accommodationists. See, for example, Robert L. Cord, *Separation of Church and State: Historical Fact and Current Fiction* (New York: Lambeth Press, 1982); Stephen B. Presser, *Recapturing the Constitution: Race, Religion, and Abortion Reconsidered* (Washington, DC: Regnery, 1994); *Wallace v. Jaffree*, 472 U.S. 38, 91–114 (1985) (Rehnquist, J., dissenting).

Justice Thomas has yet to address the Free Exercise Clause in any of the speeches he has delivered since joining the Supreme Court. Consequently, it remains to be seen whether he is still as committed, philosophically, to a pro-rights position on the Free Exercise Clause as he was during the hearings. If he is, then he, too, would appear to have fallen victim to the confusion that perhaps inevitably follows from there being *two* religion clauses in the First Amendment.

Criminal Justice

Thomas said more about criminal justice during his confirmation hearings than about almost any other subject. His emphasis was on the importance of *protecting* defendants' rights. First, of course, there was his memorable "But for the grace of God there go I" response to a question from Senator Kohl about why he wanted to serve on the Supreme Court.

> *Judge Thomas*. . . . You know, on my current court, I have occasion to look out the window that faces C Street, and there are converted buses that bring in the criminal defendants to our criminal justice system, busload after busload. And you look out, and you say to yourself, and I say to myself almost every day, But for the grace of God there go I.
>
> So you feel that you have the same fate, or could have, as those individuals. So I can walk in their shoes, and I can bring something different to the Court. And I think it is a tremendous responsibility, and it is a humbling responsibility; and it is one that, if confirmed, I will carry out to the best of my ability.[110]

Thomas continued this pro–defendants' rights posture throughout the confirmation hearings when he was questioned about specific areas of criminal justice law. For instance, he offered support for *Miranda v. Arizona* (1966), which put strict limits on police conduct when interrogating suspects in custody,[111] and he expressed concern about *Payne v. Tennessee* (1991), which authorized the use of victim impact statements during the sentencing phase of death penalty cases.[112]

Thomas said a lot about the death penalty during his confirmation hearings. He clearly stated that he was not opposed to capital punishment, but he also said that "we [must] provide all of the available protections and accord all of the protections available to a criminal defendant who is exposed to or sentenced to" death.[113]

Thomas also expressed concern about the efforts by conservatives to limit habeas corpus relief for prisoners. The right of a prisoner who believes that she or he is being wrongfully detained by the government to petition a court for a writ of habeas corpus (Latin for "you have the body") is one of the most venerated of all Anglo-American rights. It also is expressly guaranteed in Article I, Section 9, of the Constitution of the United States. However, many conservatives believe that the vast majority of habeas corpus petitions are frivolous. Thomas testified as follows in response to a question from Senator Specter about congressional attempts to restrict habeas petitions:

> *Judge Thomas.* . . . The question as to whether or not 90 days is the appropriate time [limit for a habeas corpus petition], I don't know. My concern would be this: I know that there is the attitude that we must move on, that you must clear these cases from the docket. We feel that way. We certainly feel the pressure as judges. But I think there can be instances in which 90 days is not enough. There can be instances in which it may take more time to assure oneself that a particular defendant has been accorded all of his or her rights.
>
> I would be reluctant to say that I endorse a particular cookie-cutter approach, but at the same time, I have no alternative to offer as to what is an appropriate length of time. But my concern would always be that we do not put ourselves in the position of adopting an approach that would ultimately in some way curtail the rights of the criminal defendant.[114]

Thomas has spoken at length about criminal justice in his off-the-bench activities as a Supreme Court justice. Those speeches suggest that he has moved a long way from the concerns for the rights of criminal defendants he expressed at his confirmation hearings. More specifically, his speeches indicate that he has returned to the theme of individual responsibility that has been prominent throughout his life. His most detailed exegesis on the subject was a May 16, 1994, speech to the Federalist Society and the Manhattan Institute. He opened his speech by criticizing the "'rights revolution'—that is, the legal revolution of the past thirty or so years in creating and expanding individual rights."[115]

Presented by itself, this is a surprising statement. After all, Justice Thomas spent almost the entirety of the pre–Anita Hill phase of his confirmation hearings testifying about the sanctity of the individual and the concomitant importance of protecting individual rights. When read in context, however, Justice Thomas's remarks are consist-ent with a Lockean reading of the American regime. As he succinctly put it:

> I am convinced that there can be no freedom and opportunity for many in our society if our criminal law loses sight of the importance of individual responsibility. Indeed, in my mind, the principal reason for a criminal justice system is to hold people accountable for the consequences of their actions. Put simply, it is to hold people's feet to the fire when they do something harmful to individuals or society as a whole.
>
> Why is holding people accountable for harmful behavior important to us? Three reasons strike me as especially convincing: persuasion or deterrence, respect for the individual who violates the law, and payment of a debt to society.[116]

Lockean? Yes, because (1) one of Locke's main arguments for civil society was the more effective mechanisms for the rightful punishment of criminals that exist therein, and (2) Locke insisted, as Thomas did, that "justice on an offender"—treating an offender with the dignity that comes from recognizing his free will and moral responsibility—requires that the offender be held accountable for his actions.[117] To make the point in more accessible terms, Justice Thomas has a *different philosophical conception* of the rights of criminal defendants than did the liberal members of the Warren Court (1953–1969) who were largely responsible for the "rights revolution."

Justice Thomas is especially concerned about recognizing the criminal defendant's free will and moral responsibility, primarily because they touch upon the question of race. He closed his May 16, 1994, speech with the following provocative words:

> I have no doubt that the rights revolution had a noble purpose: to stop society from treating blacks, the poor, and others—many of whom today occupy our urban areas—as if they were invisible, not worthy of attention. But the revolution missed a larger point by merely changing their status from invisible to victimized. Minorities and the poor are humans—capable of dignity as well as shame, folly as well as success. We should be treated as such.[118]

Conclusion

From Senator Strom Thurmond (R-SC) to Senator Edward M. Kennedy (D-MA), and almost all those on the political spectrum in between, the members of the Judiciary Committee emphasized in their opening statements at Clarence Thomas's confirmation hearings the importance of any successful nominee to the Supreme Court's being committed to protecting individual rights.[119] Most of the questions Thomas faced reflected this fact. In nearly every instance, the nominee exhibited a pro-rights posture.[120] Indeed, when all was said and done, Thomas's interest in natural law was shown during the hearings to stem from a belief that the United States of America was founded to secure individual rights and that public policy should be made, and assessed, with this in mind.[121] This also was Thomas's position before he was nominated to the Supreme Court,[122] and it continues to be the position he articulates in his speeches and articles since joining the Court.[123] Certainly, several eminent historians have worked long and hard in recent decades to prove that the American regime was founded to cultivate civic virtue (at the expense of individual rights, if need be),[124] but the American people remain convinced that the primary purpose of government is to protect individual rights.[125] In the words of the Declaration of Independence, "to secure these rights, Governments are instituted among Men."[126]

Why, then, was there so much "sound and fury" expended during the confirmation process about Thomas and, to use Senator Biden's colorful phrase, the "natural law thing"? Perhaps it was because natural law is an unfamiliar concept to most Americans—our intuitive feeling that ours is "a culture of rights" notwithstanding.[127] Or perhaps it was because Thomas, being a government official and not an academician, was, and is, himself sometimes ambiguous—and inconsistent[128]—on the subject. Or perhaps it was—and this is what my reading of the record suggests to me—because of the unfortunate tendency in American politics to do anything one can, including distort the facts, to defeat someone who appears to disagree with one's policy goals. (Several of Thomas's strongest supporters maintain that this also explains Anita Hill's allegations.)

Of course, this does not mean that Thomas was any less result-oriented than many of his critics. Although only Justice Thomas *really* knows why he distanced himself from his controversial pre-confirmation hearings speeches and writings regarding civil rights, economic rights, abortion, privacy, religion, criminal justice—and even natural law itself—it is not unreasonable to suspect that a desire to be confirmed to the most powerful court in the world was the reason. In my view, that unfortunate circumstance speaks more to the corruption of the appointment process itself than it does to the veracity of a particular Supreme

Court nominee—including Clarence Thomas. This does not mean that Thomas's "artful dodging"[129] during the hearings was appropriate—indeed, it understandably may lead some people to question the credibility of his denials of Anita Hill's charges—but it was, sadly, seemingly inevitable in this era of attack politics. Politics is *everywhere* in the appointment process, even in "philosophical" debates about a subject as venerable as natural law. After all, although only the most avid followers of the Supreme Court appointment process may remember, many of the key participants in Thomas's confirmation process took the *opposite* position on natural law during Robert Bork's confirmation process than they did during Thomas's: liberals *criticized* Bork for rejecting a role for natural law in judicial decisionmaking, while conservatives *applauded* him for it. Principle, it seems, has little to do with confirmation hearings inquiries into political philosophy.

The remainder of this book is devoted to exploring the theme at the core of Part I: the proposition that law *is* politics, with "politics" being used in both the partisan and philosophical senses of the word. From this point forward, however, the focus will be on the opinions Justice Thomas has issued as a member of the Supreme Court of the United States.

PART II

Law

3

Civil Rights

The assumptions upon which our vote dilution decisions have been based should be repugnant to any nation that strives for the ideal of a color-blind Constitution.

—Thomas, J., concurring in *Holder v. Hall* (1994)

Modern color-blind constitutionalism supports the supremacy of white interests and must therefore be regarded as racist.

—Neil Gotanda in the *Stanford Law Review* (1991)

Gunnar Myrdal put it well some fifty years ago when he wrote that race has always been the "American dilemma."[1] As the previous chapter suggested, the Founders in the Declaration of Independence dedicated the "United States of America" in 1776 to the natural law principle "all men are created equal." Of course, many of these same Founders—including Thomas Jefferson, the Declaration's author—owned slaves, and many later recognized and protected slavery in the U.S. Constitution drafted in 1787.[2] Put succinctly, the history of American law reflects a regime struggling with what "equality" means. Although slavery was formally abolished with the Thirteenth Amendment in 1865, racial discrimination was not.[3] Indeed, the "story" of Clarence Thomas is a testament to the persistence of racism in American life: Clarence Thomas, who as a schoolboy was asked by his White classmates to smile so they could see him in the dark; Clarence Thomas, who as a young professional felt compelled to steer clear of civil rights work so as not to be labeled an affirmative action hire; Clarence Thomas, who as a Supreme Court nominee deemed it necessary to refer to his confirmation hearing as a "high-tech lynching"; and Clarence Thomas, who as a Supreme Court justice initially was barred from speaking at an elementary school graduation

ceremony because his views did not comport with those of the "traditional" civil rights community.

The Supreme Court of the United States has played a leading role—
perhaps *the* leading role—in defining what equality means in American
law. The Court's record on race has changed over the years. Here is how
the authors of a recent civil rights casebook capture the point:

> [O]ur analysis reveals that the Supreme Court's behavioral propensities in
> civil rights cases have varied over time. For instance, from 1801 to 1910, the
> Supreme Court constitutionalized racism, subordinated blacks and
> women, and fostered segregation in public education, public accommoda-
> tions, and housing. From 1910 to 1953, we identify a transitional shift in
> the Supreme Court's commitment to racial equality. The Supreme Court's
> institutional commitment to egalitarianism reached its peak during the
> Warren Court era (1953–1969), the period we refer to as the "modern era"
> with respect to civil rights. We also view the Burger Court (1969–1986) as a
> Court in transition, providing continuity with the Warren Court in some
> policy areas but becoming increasingly conservative in others. Finally, our
> analysis of the Rehnquist Court (1986–1995) indicates that it has substan-
> tially reduced its support for civil rights, compared with the previous
> Courts during the modern era.[4]

Clearly, the authors of this passage operate under the assumption that
there is a "correct" way to decide civil rights questions: namely, the way
the NAACP and other traditional civil rights groups would decide them.
In Part I we saw that Clarence Thomas, as a policymaker and as a "part-
time political theorist," challenged this monolithic view of civil rights.
This chapter explores what *Justice* Thomas has had to say about civil
rights during his acclimation period on the Supreme Court (1991–1995
terms).

Justice Thomas has issued two major opinions concerning desegregation, two major opinions concerning voting rights, and two major opinions concerning affirmative action during his first five years on the
Supreme Court.[5] Here I examine each in detail and each in context. With
respect to context, I chronicle not only what the other members of the
Rehnquist Court have had to say about Justice Thomas's positions, but
also where his positions fall on the political spectrum. I focus particularly
on juxtaposing Justice Thomas's positions with those taken by "Critical
Race Theorists." First, then, a few words about Critical Race Theory.

Cornel West, a leading African-American intellectual who currently
teaches at Harvard, calls Critical Race Theory "the most exciting develop-

ment in contemporary legal studies."[6] The origins of Critical Race Theory are in the *success* of the movement's inspirational leader, Derrick A. Bell, Jr.[7] In the 1970s Bell developed and taught a course called "Race, Racism, and American Law" at Harvard Law School.[8] Because of his stature in the legal academy, Bell was offered and accepted the deanship at the University of Oregon Law School in 1980. When the Harvard Law School administration declined to appoint a Black to replace Bell, a student protest, boycott, and organization of an alternative course on race and the law resulted. What originated as a protest flowered into a full-blown intellectual movement in the mid-1980s when "race-conscious scholars of color" participated in a number of leftist academic conferences, first under the auspicious of the Conference on Critical Legal Studies and then separately.[9] These conferences and the scholarship that accompanied them were devoted to reassessing the impact of race on American law and society. As of this writing (August 1998), Critical Race Theorists are among the legal academy's most prolific and influential scholars, as attested by the recent republication of *two* collections of the movement's key writings.[10]

Critical Race Theory's central premise is readily identifiable: American law reflects, promotes, and perpetuates White supremacist politics. Importantly, Critical Race Theorists are critical of both liberalism and conservatism. Their criticism of liberalism is manifested most dramatically by the movement's being driven in large part by a frustration over the slow pace of reform being achieved through the assumptions and tactics of the traditional civil rights community. Their criticism of conservatism is manifested most dramatically by their confrontational assessments of the Rehnquist Court in general and of Clarence Thomas in particular.

With respect to the Rehnquist Court, the editors of one of the two recent collections of Critical Race writings state in their introduction, "As this volume goes to press, the U.S. Supreme Court issued a series of decisions which effectively repeal the ideological 'settlement' struck during the civil rights era."[11] The decisions to which the editors refer are *Missouri v. Jenkins* (1995), *Miller v. Johnson* (1995), and *Adarand Constructors, Inc. v. Peña* (1995). These decisions involved desegregation, voting rights, and affirmative action, respectively. Justice Thomas has had much to say in each of these areas, as we will see. With respect to Justice Thomas, these same scholars maintain that racialist politics "installed" him on the Supreme Court,[12] but, perhaps because of space constraints, they do not grapple with what Justice Thomas has had to say once he took his seat.

However, other Critical Race Theorists have addressed Justice Thomas's jurisprudence head-on. As will be seen, they are more than a little "critical" of it.[13]

Desegregation

If one case symbolizes the quest for racial equality in America, it is *Brown v. Board of Education* (1954).[14] In *Brown*, of course, the Warren Court unanimously held that state-imposed segregated schools were "inherently unequal" and must be abolished. One year later, in *Brown* II (1955), the Court charged federal district courts with the responsibility of implementing the desegregation mandate of *Brown* I.[15]

Two views of the Court's 1954 *Brown* decision have emerged in recent years.[16] The first is the "traditional" view of *Brown* as one of the two or three most important cases in American history. According to this view, *Brown* fueled the modern civil rights movement, showed that courts can assert moral leadership, and stressed that Blacks are entitled to the same dignity and respect as Whites. The traditional view is expressed most systematically by Richard Kluger in *Simple Justice* (1976) and Juan Williams in *Eyes on the Prize* (1987).[17] The second view of *Brown* is a reaction to the first and, predictably, is termed the "revisionist" view. In the hands of scholars such as Gerald N. Rosenberg and Michael J. Klarman, *Brown* did not accomplish much.[18] Some revisionist scholars go further. Derrick Bell, for one, argues that *Brown* was counterproductive because it both stiffened the resistance of the opponents of racial equality and lulled civil rights activists into a false sense of security.[19]

After a flurry of *Brown*-inspired decisions by the Warren and Burger Courts—decisions asserting everything from the Supreme Court is the ultimate arbiter of the Constitution,[20] to busing is an appropriate remedy for eliminating racial imbalances[21]—school desegregation cases remained off the Court's docket during the early years of the Rehnquist Court (1986–). Beginning in 1990, however, the Court reentered the fray. Two cases, *Missouri v. Jenkins* (1990)[22] and *Board of Education of Oklahoma City Public Schools v. Dowell* (1991),[23] were decided before Clarence Thomas was nominated to the Supreme Court. A third case, *Freeman v. Pitts* (1992),[24] was argued before Thomas was confirmed and he did not participate in the disposition. However, he did not have to wait long to participate in a major school desegregation case: *United*

States v. Fordice (1992)[25] was decided during his initial term on the Supreme Court.

United States v. Fordice (1992)

Fordice found the Supreme Court addressing for the first time the question of the states' duty to dismantle the dual system of higher education that exists throughout the former de jure segregated South. The case began in 1975 when a group of Black plaintiffs filed an equal protection and Title VI civil rights lawsuit against the governor of Mississippi and the administrators of Mississippi's higher education system. The plaintiffs alleged that since the time of *Brown* the defendants had maintained a system of higher education in which there were separate institutions for Blacks and Whites and in which Black institutions were demonstrably inferior.

The defendants denied any wrongdoing. They argued that they had implemented a good faith nondiscriminatory admission and operation policy with respect to students, faculty, and staff. They further argued that this policy was designed to ensure equality of opportunity and that the continued existence of predominately White and predominately Black colleges and universities in the state was the result of students' freedom of choice.

Like many landmark public law cases, *Fordice* traveled a long and winding road to the Supreme Court. The U.S. District Court for the Northern District of Mississippi dismissed the plaintiffs' claims (after twelve years of pretrial preparation), a Fifth Circuit panel reversed the District Court, the Fifth Circuit en banc vacated the Fifth Circuit panel decision and affirmed the District Court, and finally the Supreme Court issued a decision.

The Supreme Court in an 8-to-1 decision written by Justice Byron White vacated the Fifth Circuit en banc decision and remanded the case to the lower courts with instructions to apply the following standard:

> If the State perpetuates policies and practices traceable to its prior system that continue to have segregative effects—whether by influencing student enrollment decisions or by fostering segregation in other facets of the university system—and such policies are without sound educational justification and can be practicably eliminated, the State has not satisfied its burden of proving that it has dismantled its prior system.[26]

In essence, the Court held that a state that once operated segregated institutions of higher education must do more than simply declare those institutions open to all races. The state must either justify any "constitutionally suspect" remnants of its prior segregated system or eliminate them. The Court identified a number of troubling practices by Mississippi: (1) higher admission standards for historically White institutions than for historically Black institutions, (2) program duplication, (3) inferior mission assignments for historically Black institutions compared to those of historically White institutions, and (4) continued operation of eight public universities (five predominately White, three predominately Black).[27] These practices, the Court maintained, had the segregative effect of channeling Black students to historically Black colleges and universities. Importantly, however, the Court rejected—or, more precisely, left for the lower courts to decide on remand—the plaintiffs' request that the defendants be made to rectify their constitutional violation by increasing the funds allocated to historically Black institutions to the same level as historically White institutions.

Justices Sandra Day O'Connor and Clarence Thomas issued separate concurring opinions. Justice Antonin Scalia filed a dissent. The debate in the separate opinions revolved around whether the majority had applied the standard set forth in *Green v. School Board of New Kent County* (1968)[28] or *Brazemore v. Friday* (1986).[29] *Green* held that a racially neutral admissions policy was an inadequate means of integrating segregated public primary and secondary schools and placed an affirmative duty on states to eliminate all vestiges of de jure segregation "root and branch." "Freedom of choice" was declared an inadequate means of compliance. *Brazemore* held that a state's policy was legitimate if the state had discontinued prior discriminatory practices and adopted a neutral admissions policy. The Court in *Brazemore* distinguished *Green* on the basis that the decision to join a state university–financed youth club (the issue before the Court in *Brazemore*) was voluntary, whereas the decision to attend primary and secondary school was not.

In *Fordice*, the District Court applied *Brazemore*, the Fifth Circuit panel applied *Green*, and the Fifth Circuit en banc applied *Brazemore*. Justice White's opinion for the Supreme Court was unclear on which standard—*Green* or *Brazemore*—the majority applied. Justice O'Connor said it was *Green*, and applauded it.[30] Justice Scalia said it was *Green*, and deplored it.[31] Justice Thomas said it was *Brazemore*, and the heart of his opinion was why it was imperative that it not be *Green*.[32]

Justice Thomas opened his concurring opinion with a quotation from W. E. B. Du Bois's 1917 essay, "Schools," about the importance of defending historically Black institutions against attack. (The irony that Justice Thomas, who has been described as the Booker T. Washington to Thurgood Marshall's Du Bois,[33] turned for support to Du Bois rather than to Washington should not go unnoticed.) Justice Thomas made clear at the outset his reason for writing separately:

> I write separately to emphasize that this standard [announced by the majority] is far different from the one adopted to govern the grade-school context in *Green v. School Bd. of New Kent County*, 391 U.S. 430, 88 S.Ct. 1689, 20 L.Ed. 716 (1968), and its progeny. In particular, because it does not compel the elimination of all observed racial imbalance, it portends neither the destruction of historically black colleges nor the severing of those institutions from their distinctive histories and traditions.[34]

To Justice Thomas, the continued existence of historically Black colleges and universities "as such"—albeit open for admission to all on a race-neutral basis—was essential because of the contributions these institutions had made, and still make, to Black pride, leadership, and upward mobility. He emphasized that these institutions had "survived and flourished" despite the nation's "shameful history" of racism.[35]

Justice Thomas closed his concurring opinion as forcefully as he had opened it: with a plea on behalf of historically Black institutions of higher education. He wrote:

> Although I agree that a State is not constitutionally *required* to maintain its historically black institutions as such, . . . I do not understand our opinion to hold that a State is *forbidden* to do so. It would be ironic, to say the least, if the institutions that sustained blacks during segregation were themselves destroyed in an effort to combat its vestiges.[36]

Fordice was widely praised. Then-Solicitor General Kenneth W. Starr, who argued the case for the federal government, called the decision "a magnificent victory for the United States."[37] Howard University law professor J. Clay Smith, Jr., who filed a brief for the Congressional Black Caucus and an alliance of Black colleges and universities, said, "This is a decision the Warren Court could have written. The spirit of Thurgood Marshall lives on this Court."[38] Concern was expressed, however, about the detrimental effect the decision likely would have on Black institutions of higher education.[39] With the notable exception of political columnist William Raspberry (no Clarence Thomas fan), who made Justice

Thomas's argument without mentioning the source,[40] Justice Thomas was afforded almost universal acclaim by political commentators for articulating in his concurring opinion this concern about the survival of historically Black colleges and universities.[41] Justice Thomas's opinion was equally well received by legal commentators.[42]

Of the numerous law review articles and case comments about *Fordice*, the most intriguing was by Alex M. Johnson, Jr., a law professor and Critical Race Theorist at the University of Virginia.[43] Johnson opened "Bid Whist, Tonk, and *United States v. Fordice*: Why Integrationism Fails African-Americans Again" with the self-consciously provocative claim, "*Fordice* was wrong because *Brown* was wrong."[44] Johnson's self-consciousness is illustrated by the following passage:

> Twenty to thirty years ago this Article would not have been written. The views presented herein would have been so far outside the mainstream that, frankly, they would have been unthinkable by an African-American scholar employed at a prestigious law school. Quite the contrary, the views expressed herein might have been more easily attributed to an avowed racist.[45]

Substantively, Johnson argued that *Fordice* and *Brown* were wrong because the Court in both landmark cases (and those decided in between) conflated the "process" of integration (i.e., commingling Blacks and Whites in the public education system) with the "ideal" of integration (i.e., ending racial discrimination). The former, wrote Johnson, perpetuated the dominance of White culture; the latter would have assimilated the best of White and Black cultures into a better society. Assimilation would take time and nurturance. Consequently, Johnson called for a "transitional" stage in which historically Black colleges and universities would play a central role in the cultural development of Black youth.[46] Herein lied the rub: Because the Court refused to mandate increased funding for historically Black institutions, Johnson feared that *Fordice* sounded the "death knell" for these institutions.[47]

Has the fear about the likely demise of historically Black colleges and universities expressed by Justice Thomas, Professor Johnson, and others[48] come to pass? On March 7, 1995, the District Court issued its decision on remand.[49] The district judge ordered Mississippi to apply the same admissions standards for historically White and historically Black institutions and to spend more money as part of a program to improve the historically Black institutions. At first blush, this is good news for proponents of historically Black schools. However, it must be added that the district judge directed that the increased monies be used primarily to increase *White* enrollment at historically *Black* institutions. This could dilute the unique mission of the Black schools. The district judge also declined to guarantee the survival of one of the three Black schools in question, Mississippi Valley State University, taking a wait-and-see approach to merging it with Delta State University (a predominately White school). In short, the final chapter on the future of state-financed historically Black institutions of higher education has yet to be written.

Missouri v. Jenkins (1995)

Missouri v. Jenkins (1995)[50] was the other major desegregation case in which Justice Thomas participated during his acclimation period on the Supreme Court. At issue was a district court's authority to impose the most ambitious and expensive public primary and secondary school desegregation plan in American history—that involving the Kansas City, Missouri, School District (KCMSD). The KCMSD was one of thirteen school districts in Kansas City, and it enrolled approximately thirty-seven thousand students. Through the intervention of the U.S. District Court for the Western District of Missouri, more than $1.5 billion was spent in the KCMSD between 1987 and 1995 to further the desegregation plan.

Jenkins, like *Fordice*, was in litigation for many years.[51] The case began in 1977 when the KCMSD, the school board, and two children of a school board member brought suit against the state of Missouri for allegedly causing and perpetuating a system of racial segregation in the Kansas City metropolitan schools. The KCMSD was realigned as a nominal defendant. The District Court then found that Missouri in general and the school district in particular were operating a segregated school system. (The District Court emphasized, among other things, that a provision of the Missouri Constitution that required the separation of the races in public schools was not repealed until 1976 and that Kansas City school district boundary lines were redrawn after *Brown* to create a single-race district.) Over the next several years the District Court entered a series of remedial orders aimed at eliminating the vestiges of segregation. The remedies included reducing class sizes, implementing a state-funded "effective schools" program, increasing salaries for instructional and noninstructional employees, and establishing a comprehensive magnet school and capital improvements plan for the district.

The defendants did not appeal the liability finding. They did appeal several of the remedial orders. In *Missouri v. Jenkins* (1990) (*Jenkins* II),[52] the Supreme Court considered whether the district judge had exceeded his remedial authority when he ordered a massive property tax increase to finance the creation of the multimillion-dollar magnet school program for inner Kansas City designed to draw students away from their neighborhood and private schools through distinctive curricula and high quality. The Supreme Court held 5 to 4 that the district judge could not order the tax increase himself, but that he could order the school board to raise the taxes.

Jenkins II was important for *Jenkins* III—the case in which Justice Thomas participated—because a question not granted certiorari in *Jenkins* II was what ultimately was decided in *Jenkins* III.[53] That question was "Whether a federal court, remedying an intradistrict violation, may require improvements to make the district schools comparable to those in surrounding districts?" This was the question that Justice Anthony Kennedy, joined by Chief Justice William Rehnquist and Justices O'Connor and Scalia, addressed in a separate opinion in *Jenkins* II, and this was the question that Chief Justice Rehnquist, joined by Justices O'Connor, Scalia, Kennedy, and Thomas, addressed in his opinion for the Court in *Jenkins* III. In fact, Chief Justice Rehnquist spent much of his opinion for the Court in the 1995 case, and Justice O'Connor spent much of her concurring opinion,[54] attempting to rebut Justice David Souter's lengthy argument in dissent, in which he was joined by Justices John Paul Stevens, Ruth Bader Ginsburg, and Stephen Breyer,[55] that the majority had reached out and decided the "foundational" issue of whether an "intradistrict" violation ever may make appropriate an "interdistrict" remedy. According to the dissenting justices, the issues before the Court were (1) the extent to which a district court may rely on students' test scores in determining whether a school district had attained partial unitary status and (2) whether the District Court in this case had the authority to order salary increases for instructional and noninstructional employees. According to the majority, these questions were indeed before the Court, but they could not be answered without considering the entirety of the District Court's remedial plan.

The Rehnquist-led majority threw out the remedial plan—all of it. The majority found that in devising a so-called plan of "desegregative attractiveness" the district judge had exceeded his remedial authority because that plan involved school districts that did not participate in the constitutional violation. Moreover, the majority chastised the district judge for failing to appreciate that under *Board of Education of Oklahoma City Public Schools v. Dowell* (1991) and *Freeman v. Pitts* (1992)[56] he should have endeavored to extricate himself from supervision of the Kansas City schools rather than immerse himself more deeply.[57]

Justice Thomas joined Chief Justice Rehnquist's opinion for the Court in *Jenkins* III, but he wrote separately to continue the exegesis on the Court's desegregation jurisprudence that he began in *Fordice*.[58] Justice Thomas's lengthy concurring opinion was in three parts: (1) a critique of *Brown*, (2) a critique of the Court's equity jurisprudence, and (3) a discourse on federalism and the separation of powers.

Justice Thomas in *Jenkins* III became the first Supreme Court justice to criticize *Brown* directly. It should be made clear at the outset, however, that Justice Thomas did not criticize *Brown*'s holding that intentional racial segregation of public schools was unconstitutional. He called state-mandated segregation "despicable."[59] Rather, Justice Thomas was concerned about the notion of Black inferiority that *Brown* had come to represent, and with the use of social science evidence to get there. Justice Thomas's opinion was replete with statements condemning the notion of Black inferiority. He opened, for example, by saying, "It never ceases to amaze me that the courts are so willing to assume that anything that is predominately black must be inferior."[60] Elsewhere in *Jenkins* III Justice Thomas returned to the theme he articulated in *Fordice*: separate Black schools might actually benefit Blacks because they "can function as the center and symbol of black communities, and provide examples of independent black leadership, success, and achievement."[61] Indeed, Justice Thomas faulted the District Court for failing to recognize that racial imbalances in the schools might be the result of voluntary demographic choices and that racial imbalances in and of themselves were not unconstitutional. He wrote:

> In effect, the [District] court found that racial imbalances constituted an ongoing constitutional violation that continued to inflict harm on black students. This position appears to rest upon the idea that any school that is black is inferior, and that blacks cannot succeed without the benefit of the company of whites. . . . The District Court's willingness to adopt such stereotypes stemmed from a misreading of our earliest school desegregation case.[62]

Justice Thomas then went on to discuss the mistake he believed the *Brown* Court made in relying on social science evidence—specifically, on the writings and studies of psychologists and sociologists who claimed that segregation made Black children "feel" inferior. At the heart of Justice Thomas's critique was his view that one can find a social science study to support almost any proposition.[63] Footnote 2 of Justice Thomas's opinion listed a string of social science studies that contradict the studies the *Brown* Court referenced in its famous footnote 11. Importantly, to Justice Thomas this was more than an academic debate because, in his judgment, it led to the District Court's erroneous conclusion that the existence of de jure segregation in the KCMSD prior to 1954 made the existence of de facto segregation in the KCMSD four decades later unconstitutional. According to Justice Thomas, this mistake would have been avoided if *Brown* had relied upon "constitutional principle" rather than social science. And that principle, wrote Justice Thomas, was that under the Equal Protection Clause "the Government must treat citizens as individuals, and not as members of racial, ethnic or religious groups."[64] State-sponsored segregation did not treat citizens as individuals, and that, Justice Thomas concluded, was what *Brown* truly was about.

The second part of Justice Thomas's concurring opinion in *Jenkins* III continued along the "major rethinking" lines he undertook in his reexamination of *Brown*. In the second part, Justice Thomas called into question the "expansive" equity powers the federal courts have employed in modern times, in desegregation cases and elsewhere. ("Equity" is justice administered according to fairness, as contrasted with strictly formulated rules of "law.") Justice Thomas's position is well captured by his remark, "The time has come for us to put the genie back in the bottle."[65]

Justice Thomas first pointed out that there was no general equitable remedial power expressly granted by the Constitution or federal statute. Consequently, as an "inherent" power the Court "ought to be reluctant to approve its aggressive or extravagant use."[66] Unfortunately, continued Justice Thomas, the Court, especially in desegregation cases, had permitted federal district judges to be "virtually boundless" in their use of equitable remedial power.[67] Although Justice Thomas understood why the Court had traveled down this road—foot-dragging by state and local officials opposed to desegregation—he disapproved of it. Indeed, he embarked in his concurring opinion on a lengthy originalist critique of "extravagant uses of judicial power."[68]

Justice Thomas recounted the debate between the Anti-Federalists and the Federalists over the scope of the federal courts' equitable powers. He discussed the Anti-Federalist concern expressed by the "Federal Farmer" and "Brutus," as well as by Thomas Jefferson (who, though not an Anti-Federalist, often shared their concerns), about the threat to popular government that unbridled equity power presented. According to Justice Thomas, this concern was met by Alexander Hamilton, writing as "Publius" in *The Federalist*, when he described Article III equity as a jurisdiction over certain types of cases (e.g., fraud, hardship) rather than as a broad remedial power. Justice Thomas went on to say that it was not until the desegregation litigation of the 1950s and 1960s that the equitable powers of the federal courts were used in the policymaking fashion exhibited by the district judge in *Jenkins* III.

Justice Thomas concluded his critique of the Supreme Court's desegregation jurisprudence with the reminder that under the Constitution's system of federalism and separation of powers federal judges may not do whatever they think wise, let alone whatever they want. (This was the portion of Justice Thomas's concurring opinion that Justice O'Connor was willing to endorse.) As Justice Thomas pithily remarked, "There simply are certain things that courts, in order to remain courts, cannot and should not do. . . . When we presume to have the institutional ability to set educational, budgetary, or administrative policy, we transform the least dangerous branch into the most dangerous one."[69]

Reaction to *Jenkins* III initially was muted by the uproar over the voting rights cases decided during the same term (see the next section).[70] A Lexis-Nexis computer search reveals that while the nation's major newspapers opined forcefully about *Fordice* in 1992, they were remarkably silent about *Jenkins* III in 1995. After the dust settled, however, there was a flood of political commentary on the Kansas City desegregation case. Most of that commentary was directed at Justice Thomas's concurring opinion. David J. Garrow, a liberal civil rights historian and author, wrote, for example, that it was "remarkable" that any justice, let alone a Black justice, would express misgivings about *Brown*, while journalist William H. Freivogel observed that the "main thing" that had changed between *Jenkins* II in 1990 and *Jenkins* III in 1995 was that "Justice Thurgood Marshall . . . has been replaced by Justice Clarence Thomas."[71]

Surprisingly, a Critical Race assessment of *Jenkins* III has yet to appear in the law reviews. The traditional civil rights community has had much to say, however. Most notable in this regard is the Harvard Project on School Desegregation's 1996 book *Dismantling Desegregation: The Quiet Reversal of Brown v. Board of Education.*[72] *Dismantling Desegregation* is a series of case studies that document, in the words of the NAACP's Elaine R. Jones, "how and why the promise of *Brown* is being eviscerated."[73] And while Justice Thomas participated in only one of the leading decisions on desegregation chronicled in the book—*Jenkins* III—his presence is everywhere felt. (*Fordice*, being a higher education case, was not chronicled.)[74]

The threads that hold together the case studies are two essays by Gary Orfield, director of the Harvard Project and coeditor (with Susan E. Eaton) of the book. In the first essay, "Turning Back to Segregation," Orfield advanced a "law is politics" thesis.[75] He argued that the "quiet reversal" of *Brown* was a consequence of political conservatives packing the Supreme Court and the lower federal courts with their ideological kin. Like so many in the traditional civil rights community, Orfield identified as the "starkest symbol" of the conservatives' triumph the replacement of Thurgood Marshall, who litigated *Brown*, with Clarence Thomas, who criticized it.[76]

If Orfield provided in his opening essay a useful, albeit partisan, road map to why the Supreme Court had "turned back to segregation" (and he did), he offered a disturbing (and some might say convincing) exegesis in "*Plessy* Parallels: Back to Traditional Assumptions" on the similarities between the "separate but equal" rationalizations of *Plessy v. Ferguson* (1896) and the "resegregationist" decisions of the Rehnquist Court (*Dowell*, *Pitts*, and *Jenkins* III).[77] In both sets of decisions, Orfield wrote, changes in electoral politics foreshadowed the decline in civil rights. That is to say, once changes in the electoral landscape were institutionalized in the Supreme Court via the appointment process, the positions promoted in the electoral arena were effectuated through judicial decisions. The most prominent of these positions was the importance of state and local power and the need to limit federal power. Of course, this was a position that Justice Thomas emphasized in his *Jenkins* III opinion.

One certainly can disagree with Orfield's confrontational summary of the holding in *Jenkins* III—"the Court majority said that rapid restoration of state and local authority was much more important than efforts to assure that educational remedies produced actual gains for minority children"[78]—but it is difficult to dismiss his larger concern about "*Plessy* Parallels." Orfield wrote:

The courts assume today, as the *Plessy* Court did, that local agencies with a history of treating blacks unfairly could now be trusted to treat them fairly with no outside supervision. This prediction—that local officials would ensure equality—was dead wrong in *Plessy*, and the research presented in later chapters of this book indicates that the assumption is still wrong.[79]

Although the jury still may be out on the future of desegregation in higher education in the United States, the case studies that constitute *Dismantling Desegregation* appear to indicate, as Orfield stressed, that America has turned back from *Brown*. On this point the positions of Thurgood Marshall and Clarence Thomas could not be more different: Justice Marshall fought for integration, Justice Thomas cautions against it.[80]

Voting Rights

Earl Warren wrote in his memoirs that the voting rights cases, not *Brown v. Board of Education* and its progeny, were the most important cases decided during his chief justiceship. Chief Justice Warren stressed the voting rights cases because he believed that once Blacks were allowed to participate freely and fairly in the electoral process they no longer would need to look to the judiciary for help.[81]

The voting rights cases are also central to Justice Thomas's Supreme Court tenure. Indeed, Justice Thomas's "breakthrough" opinion is often said to be his concurring opinion in *Holder v. Hall* (1994),[82] in which he called for a dramatic rethinking of the high Court's voting rights jurisprudence.

The history of voting rights in America is replete with discrimination, especially against Blacks.[83] The Fifteenth Amendment (1870) was, of course, the first major constitutional step toward enfranchising Blacks. It provides:

> Section 1. The right of citizens of the United States to vote shall not be denied or abridged by the United States or by any State on account of race, color, or previous condition of servitude.
>
> Section 2. The Congress shall have power to enforce this article by appropriate legislation.

The Fifteenth Amendment went largely unenforced until the Voting Rights Act of 1965. (Practitioners of discrimination in voting had resorted to a number of devices such as the "grandfather clause," the "White primary," the poll tax, interpretation clauses, and understanding clauses to deny Blacks the franchise.)[84] In the eyes of most voting rights scholars, the Voting Rights Act was "a revolutionary measure" that went a long way toward enforcing the promise of the Fifteenth Amendment.[85] The Act was designed to work on two levels. First, in Section 2, it prohibited discriminatory voting policies, practices, and procedures. Second, in Section 5, it subjected certain "covered" states—states that had been the most aggressive practitioners of discrimination in voting—to a "preclearance" requirement, which mandated federal approval of any change in voting policies, practices, or procedures.

The Voting Rights Act was construed broadly by the Warren Court during the so-called "first generation" of voting rights cases. In addition to *South Carolina v. Katzenbach* (1966), in which the Act was upheld against an immediate constitutional challenge,[86] the Warren Court in *Allen v. State Board of Elections* (1969) interpreted Section 5 to mean that "Congress intended to reach any state enactment which altered the election law of a covered State in even a minor way."[87] The Warren Court also invalidated a number of state-imposed literacy requirements to voting.[88]

The Voting Rights Act received a more mixed reception in the "second generation" of voting rights cases, decided by the Burger Court. Whereas first-generation voting rights litigation sought to remove direct impediments to minority voting (e.g., literacy tests), second-generation litigation challenged perceived efforts by some states to "dilute" minority voting strength through practices such as gerrymandering, annexations, at-large elections, multimember districts, decreasing the size of a governmental body, exclusive slating groups, and run-off primaries. Initially, in a string of decisions culminating in *City of Mobile v. Bolden* (1980), the Burger Court was unreceptive to voting rights challenges. In *Bolden* the Court held 6 to 3, over a strong dissent by Justice Marshall, that minority plaintiffs must prove *intent* to discriminate in vote dilution cases.[89] After Congress amended Section 2 in 1982 to overrule *Bolden* and the discriminatory intent requirement, the Burger Court became more receptive to claims of minority vote dilution. Most notable in this regard was a case decided during the final term of the Burger Court: *Thornburg v. Gingles* (1986).[90]

In *Gingles* the Supreme Court for the first time construed the amended Section 2.* The Court ruled 5 to 4 that a close examination of the "totality of the circumstances" of the North Carolina multimember districting structure at issue revealed that the political process was not open equally in North Carolina to minority voters to elect candidates of their choosing. *Gingles* announced a three-part test that made it easier for minorities to prevail in vote dilution cases. That test was: (1) the minority group was sufficiently large and geographically compact to constitute a majority in a single-member district; (2) the minority group was politically cohesive; and (3) the White majority was sufficient as a bloc to enable it to defeat, in a multimember system, the minority's preferred candidate.

The issue of minority-group representation is widely regarded as the most important issue confronting the Court in the 1990s.[91] Redistricting after the 1990 census led to record numbers of Blacks and Latinos being elected to office in 1992 throughout the South. Often, this was accomplished through the creation of racially adjusted districts urged and sanctioned by the U.S. Department of Justice to increase the number of minorities elected to political office. The first challenge to these new majority-minority districts came in the now-landmark case *Shaw v. Reno* (1993).[92]

In *Shaw* the Rehnquist Court ruled 5 to 4 that creating a majority Black congressional district might violate the constitutional rights of White voters under the Equal Protection Clause of the Fourteenth Amendment. Justice O'Connor wrote the majority opinion, in which Chief Justice Rehnquist and Justices Scalia, Kennedy, and Thomas joined.[93] At issue was a North Carolina redistricting plan—a plan that was redrawn in light of Justice Department objections that the state had not done enough in its first plan to ensure that Blacks would be better represented in electoral politics—that created two "bizarrely-shaped" majority-minority districts. Emphasizing the plan's irregular shape, the conservative majority concluded that the plan closely resembled the "un-

---

*The amended Section 2 provides: "No voting qualification or prerequisite to voting, or standard, practice, or procedure shall be imposed or applied by any State or political subdivision in a manner which results in a denial or abridgement of the right of any citizen of the United States to vote on account of race or color, or in contravention of the guarantees [set forth in the law]. The fact that members of a minority group have not been elected in numbers equal to the group's proportion of the population shall not, in and of itself, constitute a violation of this Section."

couth twenty-eight-sided" municipal boundary line in *Gomillion v. Light-foot* (1960), a case in which the Warren Court struck down a racial gerrymander designed to increase White political strength.[94] Justice O'Connor wrote:

> [R]eapportionment is one area in which appearances do matter ... [and a] reapportionment plan that includes in one district individuals who belong to the same race, but who are otherwise widely separated by geographical and political boundaries, and who may have little in common with one another but the color of their skin, bears an uncomfortable resemblance to political apartheid.[95]

Consequently, the Justice O'Connor–led majority concluded, strict scrutiny was required in the reapportionment context, even when the objective was to *increase minority* political strength.

With *Shaw*, the Court now has two lines of second-generation voting rights cases. The first line is a traditional *Gingles* suit in which a *minority* plaintiff challenges electoral practices designed to *decrease* minority voting strength. The second line is a *Shaw* suit in which a *White* plaintiff challenges redistricting practices designed to *increase* minority voting strength. The Rehnquist Court has looked favorably upon the latter type of suit, but not upon the former. Justice Thomas has voted with the conservative majority in every instance and has authored an opinion in each type of suit.

Holder v. Hall (1994)

Justice Thomas's concurring opinion in the *Gingles*-line case *Holder v. Hall* (1994) is one of the longest separate opinions in Supreme Court history. *Holder* involved a challenge by minority Black voters to Bleckley County, Georgia's sole commissioner form of government. The Black plaintiffs claimed that Section 2 of the Voting Rights Act and the Fourteenth and Fifteenth Amendments required Bleckley County to have a county commission of sufficient size so that the county's Black citizens would constitute a majority in a single-member district. The U.S. District Court for the Middle District of Georgia rejected both the statutory claim and the constitutional claims. The U.S. Court of Appeals for the Eleventh Circuit reversed the District Court's interpretation of the Voting Rights statute. The Eleventh Circuit held that all the *Gingles* preconditions were met and that the "totality of the circumstances" supported a finding of Section 2 liability.

Five members of the Rehnquist Court—Chief Justice Rehnquist and Justices O'Connor, Scalia, Kennedy, and Thomas—voted to reverse the Eleventh Circuit on the statutory claim and to remand for reconsideration of the constitutional claims. The Supreme Court's five most conservative members rejected the Section 2 Voting Rights Act claim on the ground that no "objective benchmark" existed by which to measure the dilutive effects of a governing authority's size. Justice Kennedy wrote the controlling opinion, in which Chief Justice Rehnquist joined in full and Justice O'Connor joined in part. Justice Kennedy acknowledged and distinguished prior holdings that deemed changes in the size of a governing authority to be subject to preclearance under Section 5. Under that section, Justice Kennedy reasoned, there was a built-in benchmark: the *existing* size of the governing authority, "retrogressions" from which must be approved in advance by the federal government. Section 2, in contrast, did not mandate a retrogression inquiry.

Justice Thomas, joined by Justice Scalia, essentially maintained that the Voting Rights Act did not cover second-generation voting rights claims *at all*.[96] "[A]s far as the Act is concerned," Justice Thomas wrote, "an 'effective' vote is merely one that has been cast and fairly counted."[97] Justice Thomas would overrule almost every Voting Rights Act case the Court had ever decided—including *Gingles*.

Justice Thomas justified his "systematic reassessment" of the Court's voting rights jurisprudence by arguing that the "gloss" the Court had placed on the text of the Voting Rights Act over the years had made challenges such as the *Holder* plaintiffs' possible.[98] Here, as in the desegregation cases chronicled in the previous section, Justice Thomas called for a return to first principles. And here, as in the desegregation cases, Justice Thomas was concerned with stereotypes. In the voting rights context the stereotype was that Blacks think—and, hence, vote—alike.

Justice Thomas prefaced a textualist analysis of the Voting Rights Act with a detailed examination of the Court's voting rights jurisprudence. His objective was to demonstrate that the Court had imposed its own "political theory" of representative government on the Act. As Justice Thomas put it, "An examination of the current state of our decisions should make obvious a simple fact that for far too long has gone unmentioned: vote dilution cases have required the federal courts to make decisions based on highly political judgments—judgments that courts are inherently ill-equipped to make."[99]

Justice Thomas identified *Allen v. State Board of Elections* (1969) as the critical case in moving the Court's interpretation of the Voting Rights Act from ballot access inquiries to voting strength inquiries. (*Allen*, as readers may recall, was the case in which the Warren Court declared that the Voting Rights Act should be given "the broadest possible scope.")[100] Justice Thomas invoked Justice John Marshall Harlan II's dissenting opinion in *Allen* and Justice Felix Frankfurter's dissenting opinion in *Baker v. Carr* (1962), the Warren Court's landmark legislative apportionment case,[101] as precursors to his concern about empowering the Court to make political theory choices about how much voting strength each racial group should have. Justice Thomas went on to say that the single-member district systems drawn with majority-minority districts to ensure minority control that were preferred by leading voting rights litigators (e.g., Lani Guinier) were simply *one* choice. There were others, including multi-member districts, which were common during the early days of the Republic.

Justice Thomas also criticized the political theory judgment the Court had made over the years that a vote was "effective" only if it resulted in controlling seats. "It is certainly possible to construct a theory of effective political participation that would accord greater importance to voters' ability to influence, rather than control, elections," he wrote.[102] Justice Thomas took his concerns about political theory one step further when he noted that once control of seats was decided to be the appropriate choice, the Court then had to make another choice: "how many" seats a particular group must be allowed to control. Justice Thomas maintained that the Court had gone the direct proportionality route, but that this, too, was a "political choice, not a result required by any principle of law."[103] Justice Thomas also suggested that the Court's existing voting rights jurisprudence did not foreclose the adoption of voting mechanisms even more controversial than proportionality, such as cumulative voting or a system using transferable votes.

Justice Thomas's exegesis on the political theory underlying the Court's voting rights jurisprudence was not meant definitively to conclude that the Court's political theory was wrong—although he plainly believed that it was—but rather to show that it *was* political theory and that the Court should leave political theory to the elected branches. Justice Thomas wrote:

We would be mighty Platonic guardians indeed if Congress had granted us the authority to determine the best form of local government for every county, city, village, and town in America. But under our constitutional system, this Court is not a centralized politburo appointed for life to dictate to the provinces the "correct" theories of democratic representation, the "best" electoral systems for securing truly "representative" government, the "fairest" proportions of minority political influence, or, as respondents would have us hold today, the "proper" sizes for local governing bodies.[104]

As troubled as Justice Thomas undeniably was by unelected judges making political theory choices, he was more troubled by the assumption underlying the political theory choices that had been made in the vote dilution context: members of racial and ethnic groups "think alike" on public policy matters.[105] This was where he employed his most evocative language—"segregating the races into political homelands," "political apartheid"—and this was where he first employed as a Supreme Court justice his often-used policy phrase, borrowed from Justice Harlan I's legendary *Plessy v. Ferguson* (1896) dissent, that ours is a "color-blind Constitution."[106] Justice Thomas also raised a practical concern: majority-minority districting systems would deepen racial divisions. He feared that under such systems White candidates in White-majority districts and Black candidates in Black-majority districts would have no incentive to appeal to citizens not of their race, or to represent them once elected.

Justice Thomas is reputed to be one of the most dedicated textualists on the Rehnquist Court. His *Holder* opinion supports this view: His preface on the political theory of the Supreme Court's Voting Rights Act jurisprudence was followed by a lengthy analysis of the statutory text. Summarily stated, Justice Thomas concluded that the size of a governing body was not a "standard, practice, or procedure" within the terms of Section 2 of the Act. "Properly understood," he wrote, "the terms 'standard, practice, or procedure' in section 2(a) refer only to practices that affect minority citizens' access to the ballot. Districting systems and electoral mechanisms that may affect the 'weight' given to a ballot duly cast and counted are simply beyond the purview of the Act."[107]

Justice Thomas began his textual analysis of the Voting Rights Act by acknowledging that "standard, practice, or procedure" was not expressly defined in the statute. He argued, however, that when these words were read in context they applied to the *act* of voting, not to the *size* or *form* of a governing authority. In other words, the Voting Rights Act was meant to cover only first-generation voting rights concerns.

Justice Thomas's overarching commitment to focusing on *individuals* rather than on *groups* in civil rights matters is readily apparent in his textual analysis of the Voting Rights Act. Here is an illustrative passage from his concurring opinion:

> Giving the terms "standard, practice, or procedure" an expansive interpretation to reach potentially dilutive practices . . . distort[s] that focus on the individual, for a vote dilution claim necessarily depends on the assertion of a group right. . . . At the heart of the claim is the contention that the members of a group collectively have been unable to exert the influence that their numbers suggest they might under an alternative system. Such a group right, however, finds no grounding in the terms of section 2(a).[108]

Justice Thomas addressed head-on an obvious impediment to his individualistic interpretation of Section 2: that the 1982 Amendments to the Voting Rights Act did not discard *Allen*'s broad reading of Section 5's "standard, practice, or procedure" language. Justice Thomas emphasized that *Allen*, decided in 1969, was a Section 5 case, not a Section 2 case. He also argued that the Court's 1980 Section 2 *Mobile v. Bolden* decision mandated a narrow reading of voting rights claims.[109]

Justice Thomas contended that the Court's Section 2 voting rights jurisprudence got off track when the *Gingles* Court pursued a "'legislative history first' method of statutory construction."[110] As a textualist, Justice Thomas is skeptical of legislative history. At a minimum, he said in *Holder*, a judge must *start* with the text. If the *Gingles* Court had done that, he argued, the Court would have found, for the reasons he articulated earlier in his concurrence, that the text was clear: vote dilution claims are not covered by Section 2. Indeed, Justice Thomas accused the *Gingles* Court of engaging in "law office history" to support the result it wanted. Consequently, Justice Thomas called for the overruling of *Gingles*.

Calling for the overruling of *Gingles* is, of course, a big step, and Justice Thomas was well aware of this fact. However, he believed that because the decision and its progeny had produced an "inherent tension" between the Court's interpretation of Section 2 and the text of the Act, and also had proved "unworkable in practice and destructive in its effects," precedent should give way.

Why has *Gingles* proved unworkable? Because, Justice Thomas maintained, it has required the judiciary to make political theory choices about what was the "best" or "fairest" voting system. Nay, more, Justice

Thomas argued that the voting system the Court has preferred over the years—proportional representation by race—was flatly prohibited by the text of the Voting Rights Act.*

Why has *Gingles* proved destructive in its effects? Because, Justice Thomas maintained, it has resulted in racial gerrymandering: carving the country into racially segregated electoral districts. Consequently, Justice Thomas dramatically concluded, the Court's "current practice should not continue. Not for another Term, not until the next case, not for another day."[111]

Justices Harry Blackmun, Stevens, Souter, and Ginsburg dissented. Their dissent took two forms. The first was a conventional dissenting opinion in which Justice Blackmun, writing for the four, argued that subtle and complex means of diluting voting strength were still prevalent, that the practice of electing a single-member county commission can be one such dilutive practice, and that a five-member commission was an appropriate benchmark on the facts presented.[112] The second form was an unconventional "separate opinion" in which Justice Stevens, writing for the four, took direct aim at Justice Thomas's concurring opinion.[113]

Justice Stevens's separate opinion criticized in the strongest possible terms Justice Thomas's reading of the Voting Rights Act. Justice Stevens thrice called Justice Thomas's reading "radical" and more than once suggested that Thomas was manipulating the record on whether Congress amended the Act with *Allen* in mind and whether the Court understood what *Allen* meant when it applied the precedent over the years. Indeed, the essence of Justice Stevens's separate opinion was a history lesson for Justice Thomas on how Congress *three times* (1970, 1975, 1982) amended the Voting Rights Act fully cognizant of the fact that the Court in *Allen* had ruled in 1969 that the Act should be given "the broadest

---

*The so-called "Dole Compromise" is codified in Section 2(b) and is an express disclaimer of any right to proportional representation. The disclaimer states: "*Provided*, That nothing in this section establishes a right to have members of a protected class elected in numbers equal to their proportion in the population." Justice Thomas identified *Johnson v. De Grandy*, 114 S.Ct. 2647 (1994), a case decided the same day as *Holder*, as a blatant example of the Court's preference for proportionality. In *De Grandy* the Court held 7 to 2 that there was no Section 2 violation where, in spite of continuing discrimination and racial bloc voting, minority voters form effective voting majorities in a number of districts roughly proportional to the minority voters' respective shares in the voting-age population. Justice Souter wrote the opinion for the Court. Justices O'Connor and Kennedy each issued concurring opinions. Justice Thomas, joined by Justice Scalia, filed a short dissent in which he incorporated his *Holder* concurrence. See ibid., 2667 (Thomas, J., dissenting).

possible scope," and that the Court had *many, many times* given the Act precisely that generous scope—including in vote dilution cases. Justice Stevens closed his opinion by asserting that it was *Justice Thomas*, not the justices Thomas criticized, who was reading his policy preferences into the Act:

> When a statute has been authoritatively, repeatedly, and consistently construed for more than a quarter century, and when Congress has reenacted and extended the statute several times with full awareness of that construction, judges have an especially clear obligation to obey settled law. Whether Justice THOMAS is correct that the Court's settled construction of the Voting Rights Act has been "a disastrous misadventure". . . should not affect the decision in this case. It is therefore inappropriate for me to comment on the portions of his opinion that are best described as an argument that the statute be repealed or amended in important respects.[114]

Bush v. Vera (1996)

The Supreme Court is as sharply divided in the *Shaw*-line cases as it is in the *Gingles*-line cases. The Court decided four majority-minority districting cases between when *Shaw* came down in the 1992 term and the end of Justice Thomas's acclimation period in the 1995 term. The combination of the Court's case-by-case approach to the *Shaw* line and the myriad of plurality, concurring, and dissenting opinions that have been issued in the cases makes it difficult to discern precisely what the Court is saying in this area. (This is a point emphasized by several of the justices.)[115] At the risk of oversimplification, the Court's *Shaw*-line decisions, including *Shaw* I, are: (1) that race-based districting is subject to strict scrutiny under the Equal Protection Clause of the Fourteenth Amendment when it results in "bizarrely-shaped" districts (*Shaw v. Reno* [1993]—*Shaw* I); (2) that a race-based district that is not bizarrely shaped still can be an unconstitutional racial gerrymander if the "predominate" motivation in redrawing the district lines was racial (*Miller v. Johnson* [1995]);[116] (3) that a plaintiff must live in the challenged district to have standing to sue (*United States v. Hayes* [1995]);[117] (4) that strict scrutiny's requirement that the districting plan be "narrowly tailored to serve a compelling state interest" means it must be *narrowly* tailored to serve a *compelling* state interest (*Shaw v. Hunt* [1996]—*Shaw* II);[118] and (5) that "careful review" of the facts is required in mixed motive cases to determine whether the districts at issue are subject to strict scrutiny (*Bush v. Vera* [1996]).[119]

Justice Thomas made clear his position on *Shaw*-line cases in *Bush v. Vera*. That case involved, above all else, the question of whether gerrymandering to preserve safe seats for incumbents is permissible when the goal was to protect the seats of minority representatives. The Supreme Court held 5 to 4 that it was not. Justice Thomas's opinion was again an opinion concurring in the judgment, joined, again, by Justice Scalia.[120]

Justice Thomas's position on *Shaw*-line cases is as unequivocal as his position on *Gingles*-line cases: The intentional creation of majority-minority districts is *always* subject to strict scrutiny. Justice Thomas relied in his *Bush v. Vera* concurrence on the Court's affirmative action decision *Adarand Constructors, Inc. v. Peña* (1995) (discussed in the next section). Justice Thomas wrote: "I am content to reaffirm our holding in *Adarand* that all racial classifications by government must be strictly scrutinized and, even in the sensitive area of state legislative redistricting, I would make no exceptions."[121] Justice Thomas maintained that the Court had already held this in its earlier *Shaw*-line cases.

Taken to its logical limit, the implication of Justice Thomas's position in the *Shaw* line of cases is that the Voting Rights Act of 1965 violates the Equal Protection Clause of the Fourteenth Amendment. This, at least, was apparently the conclusion of the dissenting justices. Justice Souter reached this conclusion without mentioning Justice Thomas by name, while Justice Stevens mentioned Justice Thomas by name without quite reaching this conclusion.

Justice Souter, joined by Justices Ginsburg and Breyer, remarked in his dissenting opinion that he was relieved to see that the plurality (Justice O'Connor, Chief Justice Rehnquist, and Justice Kennedy) was willing to "assume" for the moment that the "intentional creation of majority-minority districts is not necessarily a violation of *Shaw* I."[122] Justice Thomas was not willing to make this assumption. Justice Stevens, joined by Justices Ginsburg and Breyer, remarked in his dissenting opinion that he "doubt[s]" that any district "exists in the entire Nation" in which a majority-minority district has come to be "in spite of," not "because of," the race of its population.[123] Justice Thomas required that the majority-minority district exist "in spite of" race. Similarly, the implication of Justice Thomas's position for the future of the Voting Rights Act almost certainly explains the statement in Justice O'Connor's plurality opinion, joined by

Chief Justice Rehnquist and Justice Kennedy, that "we mean that race must be '*the predominant* factor motivating the legislature's [redistricting] decision.' . . . We thus differ from Justice THOMAS who would apparently hold that it suffices that racial considerations be *a* motivation for the drawing of a majority-minority district."[124]

Reaction to Justice Thomas's voting rights jurisprudence was fast and furious. It was also divided along partisan lines. Cleo Fields, who at the time *Holder* was decided was a liberal Democratic congressman from Louisiana, said that with his *Holder* opinion Justice Thomas had now gone "beyond the call of duty to be disassociated with the civil rights community,"[125] while Clint Bolick, a conservative lawyer and Court watcher, characterized the opinion as a "tour de force" and a "clarion call" of "enough."[126]

Edwin M. Yoder, Jr., opined in his *Washington Post* column during the summer of 1994 that "None of Thomas's disappointed critics went beyond ad hominem comments to meet his arguments [in *Holder*] head-on."[127] Lani Guinier attempted to remedy this state of affairs in a Comment in the *Harvard Law Review* devoted to the Supreme Court term in which *Holder* was decided (the 1993 term).[128]* Guinier, a law professor and Critical Race Theorist at Harvard, is perhaps this country's foremost voting rights scholar. She certainly is the most controversial. President Clinton, for one, withdrew Guinier's nomination as assistant U.S. attorney general for civil rights after the controversy over her voting rights scholarship reached a fever pitch. Guinier—labeled a "quota queen" by the most strident opponents of her nomination—has been even more outspoken since then.[129] For instance, she has had a collection of her voting rights articles published in book form under the provocative title *The Tyranny of the Majority* (1994).[130] However, it was in her *Harvard Law Review* Comment, "[E]racing Democracy: The Voting Rights Cases," where she met directly Justice Thomas's voting rights arguments.

Guinier began her Comment by stressing that the Voting Rights Act was designed to protect the voting rights of minority *groups*. She pointed out that conservative scholars such as Richard A. Epstein recognized this,

---

*The controversy sparked by Justice Thomas's call for a return to first principles is illustrated by Guinier's being one of two *Harvard Law Review* Supreme Court term case Comments devoted to criticizing opinions that Justice Thomas wrote in his first five years on the high Court. The other Comment, written by Kathleen M. Sullivan, concerned federalism. That Comment is discussed in Chapter 5.

although these same scholars maintained that the Voting Rights Act therefore constituted unconstitutional reverse discrimination.[131]*

Guinier was gravely concerned by the failure of the Court in *Holder* "to seize the opportunity to address openly the conflict between the rhetoric of colorblindness and the statutory language of group empowerment." The purpose of Guinier's Comment was to address this conflict. Her goal was to provide the "theory" necessary to reject Justice Thomas's individualistic reading of the Voting Rights Act by confronting the arguments he advanced in his "stunning" *Holder* concurrence.[132]

Readers will recall that Justice Thomas's *Holder* concurrence was in two parts. The first part was designed to show that the Court had been, but should not be, making political theory choices about the "best" form of democracy to embrace. The second part was a textualist analysis of Section 2 of the Voting Rights Act. Guinier tackled Justice Thomas's opinion in reverse order. First, she rejected his textualist conclusions by suggesting that his reading of the statutory text was devoid of necessary context. Here, Guinier offered some compelling evidence for her group-based reading of the statute. Most notable in this regard was her discussion of the Senate Report that accompanied the 1982 amendments to Section 2. The report, Guinier insisted, "contains ninety-two references to vote dilution and the representation of minority groups in its 108 pages."[133] Guinier then quoted the following language from the Senate Report:

> There is more to the right to vote than the right to mark a piece of paper and drop it in a box or the right to pull a lever in a voting booth. . . . [The] federally protected right [to vote] suffers substantial dilution . . . [when a] favored group has full voting strength . . . [and] [t]he groups not favored have their votes discounted.[134]

As impassioned as Guinier's response to Justice Thomas's textualism was, the heart of her argument concerned his handling of political theory. Guinier contended that for all of Justice Thomas's expressed concern about the Court making political theory choices, his interpretation of the Voting Rights Act itself rested on a particular political theory: "a political theory of individualized democracy."[135] The essence of this political theory, Guinier wrote, is that "political equality is satisfied by the simple

---

*As chronicled above, the logical implication of Justice Thomas's *Bush v. Vera* concurrence is that he, too, believes that the Voting Rights Act violates the Equal Protection Clause. Guinier's Comment was written before Justice Thomas's *Bush v. Vera* concurrence.

condition of universal suffrage."[136] Guinier suggested that Justice Thomas's true concern was for individuals such as himself—members of minority groups who did not share the political agenda of the minority group to which they belonged (i.e., "double minorities").[137] He couched his individualistic approach in the language of colorblindness, however: that it was "immoral" to treat minorities as members of a political interest group because that assumed that minorities "think alike."[138] In short, not only did Guinier argue that Justice Thomas's reading of the Voting Rights Act was premised *on* political theory, she argued that his was the *wrong* political theory.

Guinier called her political theory of the Voting Rights Act "a theory of interest group representation." Occasionally, she employed the terminology of Madisonian liberalism (e.g., "pluralist conception of democracy").[139] At bottom, however, she offered a communitarian-based theory of voting rights in which groups share common values and should be allowed to exercise political power commensurate with those values. Guinier wrote:

> Despite the Supreme Court's frequent emphasis on the individual in voting rights jurisprudence, the Court has also recognized that electoral rights embody "a collection of concepts," and that, as one moves from ballot access to influencing legislative policy, "voting loses its purely individual character." In other words, the right to vote should be enjoyed by individuals and by groups throughout the political process as well as at the ballot box.[140]

Consequently, Guinier strongly disagreed with Justice Thomas's individualistic reading of the Voting Rights Act as protecting nothing more than an individual's right to cast a ballot. To Guinier, "Justice Thomas's formalistic view of political participation is . . . in tension with the apparent group-based, election and post-election focus of the Voting Rights Act."[141]

Guinier also criticized Justice Thomas's argument that protecting minority groups through the Voting Rights Act was akin to preferential treatment, which he, of course, strongly opposes (see the next section). Guinier suggested that Justice Thomas was asking the wrong question. To Guinier the question was *not*, Is it wrong to treat minorities as groups rather than as collections of individuals who happen to share certain biological traits? Rather, the question was, Should minorities who happen to share certain biological traits but who also happen to share certain political interests be allowed to exercise their political power as freely and fairly as other political interest groups? And to Guinier the answer was obvious: "to ignore race treats racial minority groups differently from other groups, whose existence the political system encourages."[142]

Here, it is important to point out that Guinier was *not* saying that a minority group should be represented merely because it is a minority group. Put directly, critics such as Clint Bolick who label Guinier a "quota queen" are misrepresenting her views.[143] Indeed, Guinier could not have been more clear in her *rejection* of a quota system of representation. To Guinier, a minority group should be represented only to the extent that its members act "collectively."[144] That is to say, a minority group should be represented politically to the extent that it behaves like any other interest group in American politics.

The final component of Guinier's critique of Justice Thomas's voting rights jurisprudence was her suggestion for implementing *her* competing theory. To treat minority groups like other political interest groups in the United States, Guinier insisted, we need to adopt "innovative" electoral mechanisms such as cumulative voting and proportional representation.[145] As Justice Thomas emphasized in his *Holder* concurrence, however, proportional representation is expressly prohibited by the Voting Rights Act. The operative language of Section 2 reads: "*Provided*, That nothing in this section establishes a right to have members of a protected class elected in numbers equal to their proportion in the population." Cumulative voting—a nondistricted voting system in which each voter is given the same number of votes as open seats and in a multiseat election can aggregate those votes to reflect the intensity of her or his preferences—does not suffer from a similar disability. More fundamentally, though, the communitarian political theory that underlies Guinier's recommended remedies is inconsistent with the individualistic political theory on which the Constitution is based. It is ironic, to say the least, that Guinier forcefully invoked *legislative* history in her response to Justice Thomas's textualist argument, but ignored *constitutional* history in her response to his political theory argument, for it is constitutional history, not textualism, that Justice Thomas's voting rights jurisprudence ultimately is about. After all, it is to constitutional history that Justice Thomas turns to identify the Constitution's underlying individualistic political theory (more on this in the conclusion to this chapter).

Affirmative Action

Affirmative action is the policy of giving an edge in employment and higher education decisions to the members of groups who historically have been discriminated against (i.e., racial and ethnic minorities and women). Clarence Thomas is best known for his policy position on affirmative action: He opposes it. Chapter 1 explained, for example, how Thomas's opposition to affirmative action as a policymaker and as a "part-time political theorist" is one of the likely reasons for why he was assessed harshly during his Supreme Court confirmation process, and why he continues to be assessed harshly as a Supreme Court justice. This section explores *Justice* Thomas's views on affirmative action.

There was in the beginning, and is still today, disagreement about whether affirmative action is good *policy*.[146] There also was in the beginning, and is still today, disagreement about whether affirmative action is good *law*. The disagreement about its legality was most famously evidenced in the Supreme Court's sharply divided *Regents of the University of California v. Bakke* (1978) decision.[147]

Bakke involved a Title VI and equal protection challenge by a White male applicant to the affirmative action admissions policy of the University of California at Davis Medical School. That policy set aside a specific number of admissions slots for which only minority applicants could compete. Six separate opinions were issued by the nine Supreme Court justices who decided the case, and there were two shifting majorities. Justice Lewis Powell wrote the controlling opinion. It was, however, an opinion to which only he entirely assented. To make a long story short, Allen Bakke won his case (Justice Powell, as the swing vote, disapproved of Davis's rigid quota policy), but the Court was somewhat receptive to affirmative action itself (Justice Powell, again as the swing vote, endorsed a Harvard-style race-as-one-factor-among-many policy). Thus, as the *Wall Street Journal* reported, *Bakke* was "The Decision Everyone Won."[148]

The Supreme Court's post-*Bakke* affirmative action jurisprudence has been as muddled as *Bakke* itself. The Burger Court actually was more receptive to affirmative action programs than might have been anticipated from a careful reading of *Bakke*. Indeed, except for a series of cases in which bona fide seniority systems were involved,[149] the Burger Court tended to uphold, albeit by close votes, affirmative action programs— even those involving quotas.[150]

The Rehnquist Court has been said by some to be engaged in an "assault" upon affirmative action.[151] It is more accurate to say that the Rehnquist Court's affirmative action jurisprudence has been shaped by a struggle between the late Justice William J. Brennan Jr.'s formidable coalition-building skills *on behalf of* affirmative action and Justice O'Connor's consistent *opposition to* affirmative action. Most notable in this regard is *Metro Broadcasting, Inc. v. FCC* (1990).[152] There, Justice Brennan was able to persuade four other members of the Rehnquist Court (Justices White, Marshall, Blackmun, and Stevens) that an intermediate standard of review was appropriate for federal affirmative action programs.* The previous term found Justice O'Connor leading a 6-to-3 majority in *City of Richmond v. J. A. Croson* (1989) in striking down Richmond, Virginia's affirmative action plan pertaining to city contracts.[153] Justice O'Connor opined for both the Court in *Croson* and the dissent in *Metro Broadcasting* that strict scrutiny was the appropriate standard to apply to affirmative action programs of any kind.[154] Of course, the rigorousness of the standard of review by which the Court assesses a particular affirmative action plan matters a great deal: witness, for example, the federal plan passing constitutional muster in *Metro Broadcasting*, but the city plan being declared unconstitutional in *Croson*.

Adarand Constructors, Inc. v. Peña (1995)

Justice Thomas got an opportunity in *Adarand Constructors, Inc. v. Peña* (1995)[155] to express his views on the Brennan versus O'Connor affirmative action debate. (Justice Brennan had retired by this point.) *Adarand* overruled *Metro Broadcasting* by a 5-to-4 vote and Justice Thomas agreed with Justice O'Connor and the conservative members of the Rehnquist Court that it should. Consequently, *federal* affirmative action programs, like state and local programs, are subject to strict scrutiny review and therefore must serve a compelling governmental interest and must be narrowly tailored to further that interest.

Adarand's facts and procedural history are straightforward. At issue was a U.S. Department of Transportation affirmative action plan that provided financial incentives to prime contractors to hire subcontractors controlled by "socially and economically disadvantaged individuals" and

---

Fullilove v. Klutznick, 448 U.S. 448 (1980), was the first Supreme Court case that addressed the constitutionality of a federal affirmative action program. *Klutznick* was a plurality decision.

that used race-based assumptions to identify such individuals. Adarand Constructors was a subcontractor that competed for a subcontract to complete guardrail work on a federal highway project in Colorado. Adarand Constructors submitted the lowest bid to the prime contractor, Mountain Gravel and Construction Company, but Mountain Gravel awarded the subcontract to a minority-owned subcontractor, Gonzales Construction Company.

Adarand Constructors claimed that the subcontractor compensation program that created the financial incentives for Mountain Gravel to subcontract with Gonzales Construction violated the equal protection guarantee of the Fifth Amendment. The U.S. District Court for the District of Columbia granted summary judgment to defendant Department of Transportation, reasoning that the program was a valid remedial program under *Fullilove v. Klutznick* (1980) and *Metro Broadcasting, Inc. v. FCC* (1990). On appeal, the U.S. Court of Appeals for the Tenth Circuit affirmed. The U.S. Supreme Court granted certiorari to examine whether the lower courts were correct in applying an intermediate level of review to the federal affirmative action program at issue.

The fact that there were six opinions in the *Adarand* case speaks volumes about the controversy that continues to surround affirmative action. The controlling opinion was by Justice O'Connor. Her opinion ruled that the lower courts did not apply the appropriate standard of review and remanded the case for a determination of whether the challenged program satisfied strict scrutiny. Clearly, then, Justice O'Connor was able to achieve in *Adarand* what she had so forcefully argued for in dissent in *Metro Broadcasting*: the establishment of strict scrutiny review as the appropriate standard of review for federal *and* state and local affirmative action programs. Justice O'Connor went so far in her *Adarand* opinion as to say that this approach was consistent with what the Supreme Court had been doing in the affirmative action area all along and that the Court's 1990 *Metro Broadcasting* decision was an anomaly based on the false premise that the Constitution protected *groups* rather than *individuals*.[156]

Justice Stevens wrote the lead dissent.[157] His was a passionate defense of affirmative action. He objected to the Court's "disingenuous" treatment of the only two cases that previously had addressed *federal* affirmative action programs, *Klutznick* and *Metro Broadcasting*,[158] and to the Court's "virtually ignoring" the difference between federal and state and local affirmative action, a distinction the Court previously had spent considerable "time, effort, and paper" demarcating.[159] Perhaps even more important to Justice Stevens was the Court's failure to distinguish between government actions designed to *help* minority groups and those designed to *hurt* them. Justice Stevens wrote:

> The Court's concept of "consistency" assumes that there is no significant difference between a decision by the majority to impose a special burden on the members of a minority race and a decision by the majority to provide a benefit to certain members of that minority notwithstanding its incidental burden on some members of the majority. In my opinion that assumption is untenable. There is no moral or constitutional equivalence between a policy that is designed to perpetuate a caste system and one that seeks to eradicate racial subordination. Invidious discrimination is an engine of oppression, subjugating a disfavored group to enhance or maintain the power of the majority. Remedial race-based preferences reflect the opposite impulse: a desire to foster equality in society. No sensible conception of the Government's constitutional obligation to "govern impartially" . . . should ignore this distinction.[160]

Justice Thomas issued a relatively short concurring opinion in *Adarand*, but it was an opinion rich in meaning.[161]* He agreed with Justice O'Connor's conclusion that "strict scrutiny applies to *all* government classifications based on race." He wrote separately to make clear his position that there was no "racial paternalism" exception to the equal protection guarantee. Here, Justice Thomas also made clear his positions that the Constitution is colorblind ("under our Constitution, the government may not make distinctions based on race") and that the values the Constitution seeks to advance are those articulated in the Declaration of Independence. On this latter point he invoked the Declaration of Independence as the rule of decision. The passage that was quoted in Chapter 2 is worth quoting again:

> There can be no doubt that the paternalism that appears to lie at the heart of this [affirmative action] program is at war with the principle of inherent equality that underlies and infuses our Constitution. See Declaration of Independence ("We hold these truths to be self-evident, that all men are created equal, that they are endowed by their Creator with certain unalienable

---

*Justice Scalia filed a concurring opinion as well. He maintained that "government can never have a 'compelling interest' in discriminating on the basis of race in order to 'make up' for past racial discrimination in the opposite direction." 115 S.Ct. 2097, 2118–9 (1995) (Scalia, J., concurring in part and concurring in the judgment).

Rights, that among these are Life, Liberty, and the pursuit of Happiness.")[162]

Justice Thomas concluded his concurring opinion by reiterating his widely known philosophical view that "racial preference" programs are not only unconstitutional, but "immoral." He wrote:

> These programs not only raise grave constitutional questions, they also undermine the moral basis of the equal protection principle. Purchased at the price of immeasurable human suffering, the equal protection principle reflects our Nation's understanding that such classifications ultimately have a destructive impact on the individual and our society. . . . So-called "benign" discrimination teaches many that because of chronic and apparently immutable handicaps, minorities cannot compete with them without their patronizing indulgence. Inevitably, such programs engender attitudes of superiority or, alternatively, provoke resentment among those who believe that they have been wronged by the government's use of race. These programs stamp minorities with a badge of inferiority and may cause them to develop dependencies or to adopt an attitude that they are "entitled" to preferences.[163]

Readers will recall that Justice Stevens labeled Justice Thomas's voting rights jurisprudence "radical." Stevens labeled Thomas's affirmative action jurisprudence "extreme."[164] Most political commentators, at least those on the left, concluded likewise. Jesse Jackson, for one, was quoted as saying that Justice Thomas should "resign" after his *Adarand* concurrence.[165] Others on the left picked up on the "hypocrite" theme chronicled in Chapter 1. First and foremost, there was A. Leon Higginbotham, Jr., who said about Justice Thomas's *Adarand* concurrence: "Since by his own admission he was the beneficiary of affirmative action programs, what does his conscience say when he rejects affirmative action programs that would give to future generations the same type of opportunities he received?"[166]

The political right, by contrast, applauded Justice Thomas's *Adarand* concurrence. One Republican Senate Judiciary Committee staff member told the *Christian Science Monitor* that Justice Thomas was "saying things that conservative lawyers and theorists believe, but no one [else] on the Court has the guts to say,"[167] while Ralph A. Rossum, a Straussian political theorist, wrote in a lengthy op-ed in the *Weekly Standard* that Justices Thomas and Scalia were the first Supreme Court justices to be true to Justice Harlan I's historic *Plessy* dissent about colorblind constitutional-ism.[168]

Reaction in the legal community to Justice Thomas's *Adarand* concurrence likewise depended on the politics of the person doing the reacting. On the left, Jamin B. Raskin, a law professor at American University, organized a conference to address what he called the "hard turn to the right" the Supreme Court took in the 1994 term—the term in which *Adarand* was decided. The proceedings were published in a special symposium in the *American University Law Review* titled "Race, Law, and Justice: The Rehnquist Court and the American Dilemma."[169]

Angela Jordan Davis, chairperson of the Board of Trustees for the National Rainbow Coalition, delivered the keynote address. The substance and style of her address was vintage Critical Race Theory. Substantively, Davis argued that color did matter and that the country was a "better place" because of it.[170] Stylistically, Davis appeared to go out of her way to ridicule the conservative members of the Rehnquist Court who argued for colorblindness. Not surprisingly, Justice Thomas was the primary recipient of Davis's ire. Davis remarked:

> Justice Thomas is ashamed, embarrassed, and stigmatized by a legal remedy—a legal remedy that seeks to correct illegal, unconstitutional forms of discrimination. . . . "Remedy" does not mean "remedial," Justice Thomas. They are two different words. Remedy doesn't mean that people of color are inferior and need some kind of remedial assistance. That's not what it means. It means relief, a cure, a means to correct or redress a wrong that has been done. . . . So Justice Thomas, don't be ashamed that race was a factor in your admission to college and to Yale Law School and your appointment to the EEOC and to the federal court and to the Supreme Court—don't be ashamed.
>
> I'm not saying that you shouldn't be ashamed, because you certainly have reason to be ashamed, but not because of affirmative action.
>
> (Laughter.)[171]

Notably absent from Davis's remarks was any attempt to grapple with the political philosophy that underlay Justice Thomas's *Adarand* concurrence. In fact, the one participant who attempted to address Thomas at the level of jurisprudence—Jeffrey Rosen, legal affairs editor of the *New Republic*[172]—failed to appreciate that Thomas's originalism, at least in civil rights cases, was not the "conservative" (Rosen used the term "specific") originalism of Chief Justice Rehnquist and Justice Scalia, but rather a "liberal" originalism grounded in the natural rights political philosophy of the Declaration of Independence.* Consequently, Rosen's detailed discussion of the legislative history of the Reconstruction Amendments was misplaced, because it ignored the fact that Justice Thomas was objecting to affirmative action as a matter of political and constitutional philosophy, not legislative history.

On the right, Terry Eastland, formerly a Reagan administration official and presently the editor of *Forbes MediaCritic*, praised in *Ending Affirmative Action: The Case for Colorblind Justice* (1996) Justice Thomas's efforts on behalf of restoring what conservatives believed was the Founders' original vision of a colorblind regime.[173] Eastland's analysis of Justice Thomas's impact on the Court was far from subtle:

> *Metro Broadcasting* did not remain "good law" for very long. The majority in the case was the last one that Justice William Brennan was able to piece together before retiring. And the next year saw the retirement of Brennan's most constant voting companion, Justice Thurgood Marshall. President George Bush got the chance to fill both vacancies. The four dissenters in *Metro Broadcasting*—Justices O'Connor, Rehnquist, Scalia, and Kennedy—needed to pick up only one of the Bush appointees, David Souter and Clarence Thomas, in order to overrule the legal doctrine in *Metro Broadcasting*. Their moment arrived in 1995, as Thomas joined the dissenters to overturn *Metro Broadcasting* in the case of *Adarand Constructors v. Peña*.[174]

In short, Eastland on the right, like Davis on the left, assessed Justice Thomas's *Adarand* performance in purely partisan terms.

Northeastern Florida Chapter of the Associated General Contractors of America v. City of Jacksonville (1993)

Justice Thomas issued another important affirmative action opinion. That opinion, which came in *Northeastern Florida Chapter of the Associated General Contractors of America v. City of Jacksonville* (1993),[175] was a *majority* opinion—Justice Thomas's only majority opinion to date in a major civil rights case.

---

*As mentioned in Chapter 2, "liberal" originalism argues that the Declaration of Independence articulates the philosophical *ends* of our nation and that the Constitution embodies the *means* to effectuate those ends. "Conservative" originalism argues that the Constitution should be interpreted as the Framers themselves would have interpreted it. Scott Douglas Gerber, *To Secure These Rights: The Declaration of Independence and Constitutional Interpretation* (New York: New York University Press, 1995), introduction.

Northeastern Florida was a "standing" case. The Supreme Court's standing jurisprudence is difficult to summarize.[176] The Court itself has called its standing decisions "complicated"[177] and "not defined with complete consistency."[178] First and foremost, however, "standing to sue" is an element of the Constitution's Article III "case or controversy" requirement. "Standing to sue" means that a party bringing a particular case has a sufficient stake in an otherwise justiciable controversy to obtain judicial resolution of that controversy. Standing cases almost always are concerned with public law questions such as determinations of constitutionality and review of governmental action.

The current law of standing begins with *Association of Data Processing Service Organizations, Inc. v. Camp* (1970).[179] *Data Processing* announced a two-part test. Standing existed, the Court proclaimed, if "the plaintiff alleges that the challenged action has caused him injury in fact, economic or otherwise," and if "the interest sought to be protected by the complainant is arguably within the zone of interest to be protected or regulated by the statute or constitutional guarantee in question."[180]

The Court has issued many standing decisions since *Data Processing*. For years the Court vacillated in those decisions on how easy it should make standing to establish. According to most Court watchers, however, the Rehnquist Court has taken a consistent path—a consistent path of making standing *difficult* to establish.[181] Most notable in this regard is *Lujan v. Defenders of Wildlife* (1992),[182] in which a Justice Scalia–led majority ruled 7 to 2, with Justice Thomas among the seven, that an environmental organization lacked standing to challenge a U.S. Department of Interior regulation requiring other agencies to confer with the Secretary of Interior under the Endangered Species Act only with respect to federally funded projects in the United States and on the high seas. The Court so held because, in the majority's judgment, the environmental organization failed to show that any of its members would be directly affected by the regulation, apart from the members' special interest in the subject.

Northeastern Florida runs contrary to the Rehnquist Court's strict standing requirements. That case involved an equal protection challenge by an association of general contractors to a Jacksonville, Florida, ordinance affording preferential treatment to minority-owned businesses in the awarding of city contracts. The ordinance at issue required that 10 percent of the amount spent on city contracts be set aside each year for minority business enterprises. The association of general contractors, which was mostly nonminority, claimed that its nonminority members had been excluded from bidding on the city contracts that had been set aside. The U.S. District Court for the Middle District of Florida enjoined the enforcement of the ordinance. The U.S. Court of Appeals for the Eleventh Circuit reversed, ruling that the association lacked standing. In the Eleventh Circuit's judgment, the nonminority members of the association had not alleged that they "would have bid more success-fully on any one or more of these contracts if not for the ordi-nance."[183] Consequently, the plaintiff did not show the requisite "injury in fact."

The Supreme Court reversed in a 7-to-2 decision. The two dissenting justices, O'Connor and Blackmun, did not necessarily disagree (or agree) with the majority's analysis of the standing question, they simply believed the case was moot.[184] (Jacksonville's lawyers had asked the Court to dis-miss the case because the law originally challenged had been repealed.) Justice Thomas's relatively brief opinion for the Court turned on a char-acterization of the injury not as a failure to receive a contract, but as an "inability to compete on an equal footing" for the contract.[185] Impor-tantly, this characterization of the injury itself turned on a characteriza-tion of the Equal Protection Clause as protecting the *individual* members of *all* groups. Justice Thomas wrote:

> When the government erects a barrier that makes it more difficult for members of one group to obtain a benefit than it is for members of another group, a member of the former group seeking to challenge the bar-rier need not allege that he would have obtained the benefit but for the barrier in order to establish standing. The "injury in fact" in an equal pro-tection case of this variety is the denial of the equal treatment resulting from the imposition of the barrier, not the ultimate benefit.[186]

Bakke was the precedent on which Justice Thomas most relied. Thomas emphasized that in that landmark case Allen Bakke was allowed to challenge the University of California at Davis Medical School's affir-mative action program without showing that he would have been admit-ted without the program. To Justice Thomas, the situation in *Bakke*, wherein Bakke could not compete for the admissions places set aside for minority applicants, was "closely analogous" to the situation in *North-eastern Florida*, wherein the nonminority members of the general con-tractors' association could not compete for the portion of city contracts set aside for minority-owned businesses. Consequently, the Justice Thomas–led majority concluded, the plaintiff had standing to challenge the Jacksonville affirmative action program. The case was remanded for a determination on the merits. The lower courts have not yet made that determination.[187]

Perhaps because of the technical nature of the Court's standing jurisprudence, *Northeastern Florida* went virtually unnoticed in the popular press. The only discussion of the case that I found was by the *New York Times*'s respected Supreme Court correspondent, Linda Greenhouse.[188] Interestingly, Greenhouse did not focus on the racial aspects of the case. She emphasized that *Northeastern Florida* might mark the beginning of a more "liberal" approach to standing than the Rehnquist Court previously had adopted. Greenhouse pointed out that the numerous public interest groups who filed amicus curiae briefs in *Northeastern Florida* were arguing for this more liberal approach.

The racial aspects of *Northeastern Florida* were not lost on Girardeau A. Spann, a law professor and Critical Race Theorist who has written extensively about how, in his judgment, almost every decision the Supreme Court ever has issued in race matters has served to maintain a White supremacist regime.[189] Spann has been especially critical of the Rehnquist Court,[190] including its decision in *Northeastern Florida*.[191] He maintains that *Northeastern Florida* is "best understood as a recent addition to a long line of Supreme Court decisions that subordinate the welfare of racial minorities to the overriding interests of the [White] majority."[192]

The heart of Spann's argument in "Color-Coded Standing" was his belief that Justice Thomas manipulated the Court's standing precedents so that Whites could more easily challenge the constitutionality of affirmative action plans. Spann alleged:

As a doctrinal matter, Justice Thomas's opinion in *Northeastern Florida* ignores the invigorated standing requirements that the Supreme Court adopted during its preceding Terms. [*Lujan v. National Wildlife Federation* (1990)] holds that a plaintiff must suffer an injury that is proximate, imminent, and nonprogrammatic to establish standing. . . . In addition [*Lujan v. Defenders of Wildlife* (1992)] superimposes on an otherwise qualifying injury a rigid redressability requirement that is very difficult to satisfy when the injury is ultimately traceable to the actions of third parties. . . . The plaintiff in *Northeastern Florida* satisfied *none* of these doctrinal requirements. Moreover, the fact that the Court issued an opinion upholding the plaintiff's standing despite the rather obvious mootness of the case makes Justice Thomas's opinion seem gratuitous. Although the law of standing is quite confused, it is not so confused that one can fail to spot *Northeastern Florida* as a suspicious aberration in the Court's justiciability jurisprudence.[193]

Spann presented a detailed accounting as to why he believed that the plaintiff in *Northeastern Florida* failed to meet *every* aspect of the Court's then-existing standing requirements. That accounting was highly persuasive, but extremely technical. Suffice it to say that there was *nothing* about Justice Thomas's *Northeastern Florida* opinion with which Spann agreed. Two aspects of Spann's argument merit singling out: (1) Spann's view that if the plaintiff was White or wanted to challenge a government practice that adversely affected the interests of the White majority (e.g., affirmative action), the Court tended to grant standing to the plaintiff, but if the plaintiff was Black or wanted to challenge a practice that adversely affected the interests of Blacks, the Court tended to deny standing to the plaintiff; and (2) Spann's criticism of Justice Thomas's reliance on *Bakke*. Put succinctly, Spann insisted that Justice Thomas ignored the obvious fact that *Bakke* was decided in 1978, "prior to the Supreme Court's Scalia-inspired hardening of the [standing] doctrine in the post-1990 cases."[194] The two points are related: Spann believed that Justice Thomas relied on *Bakke* knowing that *Bakke* was inapposite because he wanted to permit Whites to challenge the merits of Jacksonville's affirmative action program.

Spann's lengthy critique of *Northeastern Florida* is one of the most tenaciously argued law review articles I have ever read. (Spann went so far as to declare that the Supreme Court itself was "engaged in 'intentional' discrimination sufficient to violate the Equal Protection Clause.")[195] Unfortunately, Spann failed to address three obvious and related points. The first point is that Justice Thomas's majority opinion was joined by several members of the Court who recently had issued powerful opinions *on behalf of* the rights of racial and ethnic minorities. It is difficult to argue, for example, that Justice Stevens is a racist. One need only recall Justice Stevens's dissenting opinions in *Holder v. Hall* (1994), a voting rights case, and *Adarand Constructors, Inc. v. Peña* (1995), an *affirmative action* case, to appreciate this fact. These opinions are among the most *pro*–minority rights opinions ever issued by a

Supreme Court justice.* The second point that Spann overlooked is that members of minority groups do not necessarily "think alike" on policy matters. Consequently, Spann's monolithic worldview is too sweeping. Indeed, Justice Thomas is *the* prototypical Black who disagrees with the so-called "conventional wisdom" of his racial class. This leads to the third, and most obvious, point Spann overlooked: Justice Thomas is himself Black. As such, it is difficult to classify *him* as a racist, as Spann appeared to do—unless, that is, Spann subscribed to the view that Justice Thomas hates himself *because* he is Black (see Chapter 1). Spann did not make the "self-hatred" point, but perhaps he believed the point was so obvious that he simply could assume it.[196]

Conclusion

Spann's provocative article about the specific area of standing provides a convenient transition to some concluding thoughts about the conflict between Justice Thomas's support for colorblind constitutionalism and Critical Race Theory's rejection of it. As this chapter has endeavored to show, central to Justice Thomas's civil rights jurisprudence is his belief that individuals should be treated as *individuals*, not as members of racial or ethnic *groups*. In fact, Justice Thomas gives Justice Scalia a run for his money for being the most "colorblind" member of the conservative Rehnquist Court: witness, for example, Thomas's apparent willingness to declare the Voting Rights Act of 1965 unconstitutional on individualistic equal protection grounds.[197] Justice Thomas's individualistic approach to civil rights explains his decisions in each of the major civil rights areas: desegregation, voting rights, and affirmative action.

Critical Race Theory, by contrast, rejects the idea that the law is, or should be, colorblind. The leading exposition of this theme is by law professor Neil Gotanda.[198] In "A Critique of 'Our Constitution Is Color-Blind,'" Gotanda argues that the Supreme Court's use of colorblind constitutionalism has worked to legitimate and perpetuate racial subordination by masking the ways in which racial power shapes American society. Of the litany of arguments Gotanda presents to support his thesis, the most powerful is his deconstruction of Justice Harlan I's dissenting

---

*Although *Northeastern Florida* was decided *before* several of Justice Stevens's pro–minority rights dissenting opinions, including *Adarand*, Spann's article condemning *Northeastern Florida* was written *after* both those opinions and his own article condemning *Adarand*.

opinion in *Plessy v. Ferguson* (1896). Of course, it is Justice Harlan's famous retort, "Our Constitution is color-blind, and neither knows nor tolerates classes among citizens,"[199] from which colorblind constitutionalism derives its name. Put directly, Gotanda maintains that Justice Harlan's evocative phrase has been wrenched out of context by conservative proponents of colorblind constitutionalism. For those who are used to reading Justice Harlan's phrase in an edited format (e.g., as precedent in later cases, in constitutional law casebooks, in monographs and articles), Gotanda provides a signal service by calling attention to the fact that the following language directly precedes Justice Harlan's oft-quoted phrase:

> The white race deems itself to be the dominant race in this country. And so it is, in prestige, in achievements, in education, in wealth and in power. So, I doubt not it will continue to be for all time, if it remains true to its great heritage and holds fast to the principles of constitutional liberty.[200]

It is this conception of Black and White as, in Gotanda's words, "neutral, apolitical descriptions, reflecting merely 'skin color' or country of ancestral origin . . . unconnected to the historical reality of Black oppression" that Gotanda equates with modern colorblind constitutionalism.[201] To his credit, Gotanda recognizes that while Justice Harlan apparently believed that a colorblind constitutional posture would maintain the status quo of White supremacy,[202] modern proponents of colorblind constitutionalism "hope that public sphere color-blindness will ultimately reduce racial divisions."[203] Justice Thomas's statements on race matters, most notably in *Adarand*, wherein he writes that "the equal protection principle reflects our Nation's understanding that such [racial] classifications have a destructive impact on the individual and our society,"[204] are consistent with Gotanda's interpretation of modern colorblind constitutionalism. Of course, Gotanda, like Critical Race Theorists generally, rejects the idea that the United States will achieve equality through colorblind views such as Justice Thomas's.[205]

Gotanda's widely cited argument *against* colorblind constitutionalism reveals how far the traditional civil rights community has fallen from grace.[206] Legal historian Andrew Kull, in his prize-winning book *The Color-Blind Constitution* (1992), documents how the civil rights community worked tirelessly, albeit unsuccessfully, for most of American history *on behalf of* colorblind constitutionalism.[207] Martin Luther King, Jr.'s "dream" that Blacks would "not be judged by the color of their skin but by the content of their character"[208] is the classic statement of the traditional civil rights view. Ironically, this is the position that many Black neoconservatives, including Justice Thomas, also support.[209*] I say "ironically" because, as this chapter and Part I make clear, Justice Thomas has been as excoriated by the traditional civil rights community as he has been by the Critical Race community.

Who has the better argument, Justice Thomas, who insists that the law should treat individuals as individuals, not as members of a group, or Critical Race Theorists, who insist that the law should treat individuals who are members of minority groups as members of minority groups? Elsewhere I have argued that individualistic colorblind constitutionalism is what the Founders intended. I even cited several of Justice Thomas's political philosophy articles for support.[210] As Thomas himself points out, however, the Founders dedicated the American regime to the *ideal* of inherent equality.[211] This does not mean we have *achieved* equality. Here, Critical Race Theorists should be commended for reminding those of us who are not minorities that, unfortunately, racism still exists in America,[212] and here Critical Race Theorists should be commended for calling attention to the fact that the traditional civil rights strategy might not be working. There is, in other words, a difference between what *is* and what *ought* to be.

At the level of regime principle—the *ought* part—Justice Thomas has the better argument. My previous research has convinced me, at any rate, that the Founders in the Declaration of Independence dedicated the United States of America to colorblind constitutionalism.[213] To reiterate, this does not mean, however, that the American regime *is* currently operating in a colorblind fashion. Indeed, Justice Thomas makes this point repeatedly in his opinions. The real question, then, is how *best* to achieve the ideal of equality: by enacting colorblind laws or by enacting color-conscious laws? Justice Thomas argues the former, Critical Race Theorists the latter. Both, I believe, are sincere, if occasionally over-aggressive, in their positions. Both, I also believe, are advancing arguments that merit

---

*A question that must be asked, then, is: Has the jurisprudence of race collapsed into itself? Obviously not, because the "self-help" ethic that underlies Justice Thomas's individualistic colorblind constitutionalism is a far cry from the recourse-to-government-assistance approach of the group rights–oriented traditional civil rights community. See John Sibley Butler, "The Return of Open Debate: School Integration, Racial Issues," *Society* 33 (March 1996): 11–8.

sober reflection. After all, what is at stake is not simply what our regime *ought* to be, but what our regime *is*. Perhaps now that the battle over Anita Hill's allegations is fading somewhat from the nation's collective consciousness and the substance of Justice Thomas's jurisprudence is beginning to receive the analysis it deserves, we can move closer to solving the problem that has always been, and is still today, the "American dilemma."

4

Civil Liberties

The Eighth Amendment is not, and should not be turned into, a National Code of Prison Regulations.
                    —Thomas, J., dissenting in *Hudson v. McMillian* (1992)

The Youngest, Cruelest Justice   —*New York Times* (1992)

"Nothing is more deeply rooted in the American political tradition than the vocabulary of rights," write Michael J. Lacey and Knud Haakonssen in their bicentennial collection on the Bill of Rights.[1] It is textbook knowledge, however, that the Constitution that was drafted in Philadelphia in 1787 did not contain a Bill of Rights, that this was a source of much controversy during the debate over whether the Constitution should be ratified, and that the Bill of Rights that was appended as a condition of ratification was a set of guarantees directed only against the power of the national government. Gradually at first,[2] but with breathtaking speed once Earl Warren became chief justice in 1953,[3] the Supreme Court made almost every guarantee in the Bill of Rights binding on the state governments as well. And it was this "nationalization" of the Bill of Rights that did more than anything else to make the Supreme Court the most powerful voice in the land in defining the rights of the American people.

Justice Thomas has not yet expressed his opinion on many of the twenty-five specific guarantees enumerated in the Bill of Rights, but he has made his views known on several of the most important.[4] Those views, like his views on civil rights chronicled in the previous chapter, have generated a great deal of controversy. This chapter explores Justice Thomas's views on civil liberties and the controversy they have sparked.*

Criminal Justice

The Bill of Rights has more guarantees pertaining to criminal justice than to any other area of the law. Of the twenty-five specific rights enumerated in the Bill of Rights, fourteen concern criminal justice. The Warren Court (1953–1969) was particularly aggressive in nationalizing these rights. Indeed, all but one of the Warren Court's ten decisions applying specific Bill of Rights guarantees to the states involved criminal justice. This fact was not lost on Richard Nixon: He based his successful 1968 presidential campaign in part on attacking the Warren Court's criminal justice decisions. More recently, the Reagan and Bush administrations pressed, albeit often unsuccessfully, for the more conservative Burger (1969–1986) and Rehnquist (1986–) Courts to overturn some of the Warren Court's major criminal justice decisions. Justice Thomas has been critical of many of these same decisions in the opinions he has issued on the Supreme Court.

Prisoners' Rights

Imprisonment as the most common form of punishment for the commission of a crime is a relatively recent phenomenon. Jails in colonial America followed the English model: they housed mainly debtors and those *accused* of crimes. Persons *convicted* of crimes were—depending on the severity of the offense—whipped, branded, carted, displayed in the stocks, banished, hanged, or burned at the stake, to mention but the most common forms of punishment. It was not until the latter half of the eighteenth century that imprisonment replaced corporal punishment in America as the principal method of penalizing convicted criminals.[5]

For much of the early history of the American penitentiary, prisoners were regarded as "slaves of the State"[6] and prison administrators were

---

*"Civil rights" are rights that the government may not deny or infringe upon because of an individual's race, gender, national origin, age, or ethnicity. Civil rights are guaranteed, most notably, by the post–Civil War Amendments (the Thirteenth, Fourteenth, and Fifteenth Amendments). "Civil liberties," in contrast, are freedoms that the government must respect, such as the freedom of speech, press, and assembly. Civil liberties are guaranteed, most notably, by the Bill of Rights.

virtually immune from judicial review. Eventually, of course, this changed. *How* it changed, how *much* it changed, and whether it *should* have changed as much as it did, are questions that have divided, and continue to divide, Supreme Court justices and the American public alike.

Like so many questions that come before the judiciary, the position that courts in general and the Supreme Court in particular have taken on prisoners' rights has varied over time. The Supreme Court's prisoners' rights jurisprudence is typically divided into three time periods: (1) the "hands-off" period (before 1964), (2) the "rights period" (1964–1978), and (3) the "deference" period (1979–present).[7]

During the first period, the so-called "hands-off" period, the Court recognized that prisoners retained some constitutional rights, but deemed it the province of the legislative and executive branches to enumerate and protect those rights. It was a rare case in which the Supreme Court—or *any* court, for that matter—intervened on behalf of prisoners.[8] Concerns about the proper role of the judiciary in the American constitutional order, about judges' lack of penological expertise, about federal-state relations, and about the potential for a flood of prison litigation are the principal explanations for why the Court was reluctant to involve itself in prisoners' rights disputes during these early years.

The Court became more receptive to claims filed by prisoners during the 1960s, just as it became more receptive to claims filed by the members of other politically powerless groups. The Warren Court's liberal politics is the most obvious explanation for this change in attitude. It is important to point out, however, that the Court's more receptive posture toward prisoners' rights lasted well after Warren Burger replaced Earl Warren in the center chair in 1969.[9] The Court's most famous statement on prisoners' rights—*Wolff v. McDonnell* (1974), in which the Court declared that "a prisoner is not wholly stripped of constitutional protections when he is in prison" and that "a mutual accommodation between institutional needs and objectives and the provisions of the Constitution" must be struck[10]—was issued by the Burger Court.

The current period in the history of the Supreme Court's prisoners' rights jurisprudence, the so-called "deference" period, was ushered in with *Bell v. Wolfish* (1979). *Wolfish* marked a turning point not simply because the Court ruled against the prisoners in question on all five of their substantive claims, but also because of the more conservative posture the Court evidenced toward prisoners' rights claims in general.

Then-Justice William Rehnquist's opinion for the Court is worth quoting at length:

> [Judges] have, in the name of the Constitution, become increasingly en-
> meshed in the minutiae of prison operations. Judges, after all, are human.
> They, no less than others in our society, have a natural tendency to believe
> that their individual solutions to often intractable problems are better and
> more workable than those of persons who are actually charged and
> trained in the running of the particular institution under examination.
> But under the Constitution, the first question to be answered is not whose
> plan is best, but in what branch of the Government is lodged the author-
> ity to initially devise the plan. This does not mean that constitutional
> rights are not to be scrupulously observed. It does mean, however, that the
> inquiry of federal courts into prison management must be limited to the
> issue of whether a particular system violates any prohibition of the Con-
> stitution. . . . The wide range of "judgement calls" that meet constitutional
> . . . requirements are confined to officials outside the Judicial Branch of
> Government.[11]

This statement, of course, sounds a great deal like a statement the Court would have made during the hands-off period, and some commentators on the liberal end of the political spectrum have argued precisely this point. One such commentator has gone so far as to call the deference that currently epitomizes the Court's prisoners' rights jurisprudence "the substitute shibboleth for 'hands-off.'"[12] As with most hyperbole, this characterization goes too far. Indeed, the discussion that follows makes plain that many members of the Rehnquist Court sometimes side with prisoners; even Justice Thomas has done so.

Moving from chronologies to categories, the Supreme Court has been asked over the years to address a host of constitutional provisions that allegedly pertain to prisoners' rights. Procedural due process, substantive due process, equal protection, freedom of religion, freedom of expression: the Court's prisoners' rights decisions run the gamut of civil rights and liberties concerns.[13] Two categories of cases merit singling out, however, both because of the frequency with which they have come before the Court and because Justice Thomas has written his major criminal justice opinions in these areas. These categories are Eighth Amendment cruel and unusual punishments claims and habeas corpus claims. I begin with the Eighth Amendment claims.

The Eighth Amendment provides that "Excessive bail shall not be required, nor excessive fines imposed, nor cruel and unusual punishments inflicted." Traditionally, the prohibition against cruel and unusual punishments has been applied to the methods of execution and to the specifics of sentences.[14] More recently—commencing in the rights period, but continuing into the deference period—the Court has extended the reach of the cruel and unusual punishments provision to deprivations suffered by a prisoner that were not part of the prisoner's official sentence. The Court has decided three types of Eighth Amendment prisoners' rights cases: (1) medical treatment cases, (2) use of force cases, and (3) conditions of confinement cases. Justice Thomas has issued one major opinion regarding the use of force and two regarding the conditions of confinement. As will be seen, Justice Thomas differs from all of his colleagues except for Justice Antonin Scalia on the threshold question of whether the Eighth Amendment applies to prisoners' claims *at all*.

Estelle v. Gamble (1976), a medical treatment case, is the landmark case on this threshold question. In that case the Court held that the Eighth Amendment *applied* to a claim filed by a prisoner for a deprivation inflicted upon him that was not part of his official sentence.[15] What the Court struggled with for a number of years after *Estelle* was the appropriate legal standard to apply to these now-cognizable prisoners' rights claims.

By the time Clarence Thomas joined the Supreme Court for the 1991 term, the justices appeared to have identified that elusive legal standard. The dispositive case was *Wilson v. Seiter* (1991). In that case the Court held that an Eighth Amendment prisoners' claim involved two components: (1) an objective component (i.e., the deprivation to which the prisoner was subjected must have been sufficiently inhumane), and (2) a subjective component (i.e., the prison official or officials who subjected the prisoner to the deprivation must have done so with a sufficiently culpable state of mind).[16] The *Wilson* decision came after the Court had earlier held in *Rhodes v. Chapman* (1981) that the *subjective* component alone was not enough,[17] and in *Whitley v. Albers* (1986) that the *objective* component alone was not enough, to establish an Eighth Amendment violation.[18]

The long-awaited legal standard articulated by the Court in *Wilson* did not last long. Just one year later, with Justice Thomas now sitting on the bench and objecting strongly, the Court held in *Hudson v. McMillian* (1992) that the subjective component can sometimes be enough to establish an Eighth Amendment prisoners' rights violation.[19]

HUDSON V. MCMILLIAN (1992)

Keith J. Hudson, an inmate at the Angola State Penitentiary in Louisiana, sued three Louisiana correctional officers in federal court. Hudson claimed that his Eighth Amendment rights were violated by a beating he received from the officers. The beating was alleged to have occurred on October 30, 1983, while the officers were escorting Hudson from his cell to another location in the prison in order to separate him from another prisoner with whom he was having an argument. Hudson alleged that one officer punched him in the mouth, eyes, chest, and stomach, while a second offer held him in place and kicked and punched him from behind. Hudson also alleged that the third officer, the supervisor of the two officers who were allegedly beating him, did nothing to stop the beating, and even went so far as to tell the other officers "not to have too much fun." Hudson sustained bruises and swelling of his face, mouth, and lips, and his teeth were loosened and his dental plate partially cracked.

The case was tried before a federal magistrate in Louisiana, who found for Hudson. Importantly, however, the magistrate also found that Hudson's injuries were "minor." The U.S. Court of Appeals for the Fifth Circuit reversed the magistrate's liability finding, but not his finding about the severity of Hudson's injuries. The Fifth Circuit ruled that a prisoner who files an Eighth Amendment excessive force claim must prove four elements: "(1) a significant injury, which (2) resulted directly and only from the use of force that was clearly excessive to the need, the excessiveness of which was (3) objectively unreasonable, and (4) the action constituted an unnecessary and wanton infliction of pain." The Fifth Circuit further held that Hudson had proved elements (2), (3), and (4), but not element (1)—the "significant injury" element.[20]

The Supreme Court granted certiorari. However, the Court stated in the writ that its review was "limited to the following question":

> Did the Fifth Circuit apply the correct legal test when determining that petitioner's claim that his Eighth Amendment rights under the Cruel and Unusual Punishment Clause were not violated as a result of a single incident of force by respondents which did not cause a significant injury?[21]

The Court in a 7-to-2 decision written by Justice Sandra Day O'Connor held that the Fifth Circuit did not apply the correct legal test; that, in other words, a prisoner need not always suffer a "significant" injury to prevail on a cruel and unusual punishments claim. Justice O'Connor spent most of her opinion for the Court revisiting the Eighth Amendment prisoners' rights precedents described above. Interestingly, she advanced a different reading of those precedents than I did, especially of *Wilson*.

According to Justice O'Connor, *Wilson* did *not* hold that to prevail on an Eighth Amendment claim a prisoner must *always* establish an objective component (i.e., that he suffered *significant* injuries). Rather, *Wilson* held, Justice O'Connor maintained, that "[w]hat is necessary to show sufficient harm for purposes of the Cruel and Unusual Punishments Clause depends on the claim at issue."[22] Quite simply, she declared, excessive force is different from other deprivations to which a prisoner might be subjected. She made this point dramatically near the end of her opinion when she addressed head-on, and rejected in no uncertain terms, Justice Thomas's position: "To deny, as the dissent does, the difference between punching a prisoner in the face and serving him unappetizing food is to ignore the 'concepts of dignity, civilized standards, humanity, and decency' that animate the Eighth Amendment."[23]

Justice Harry Blackmun filed an opinion concurring in the judgment. He objected to what he called Justice Thomas's "seriously misguided view" that an Eighth Amendment excessive force claim must be accompanied by a significant injury. According to Justice Blackmun, Justice Thomas's position might well place various kinds of "state-sponsored torture and abuse . . . entirely beyond the pale of the Constitution" because not all forms of torture and abuse leave "telltale" signs. Justice Blackmun opined that the following practices might not be redressable under Justice Thomas's interpretation of the Eighth Amendment: "lashing prisoners with leather straps, whipping them with rubber hoses, beating them with naked fists, shocking them with electric currents, asphyxiating them short of death, intentionally exposing them to undue heat or cold, or forcibly injecting them with psychosis-inducing drugs."[24]

Justice Thomas opened his dissenting opinion, in which he was joined by Justice Scalia, in a far less dramatic fashion than Justice Blackmun opened his concurring opinion. Justice Thomas reminded his colleagues that the magistrate who made the factual findings in the case emphasized that Hudson's injuries were "minor," that the Fifth Circuit did not disturb this finding, and that Hudson did not challenge it in his appeal to the Supreme Court. Consequently, Justice Thomas maintained, the "sole issue" in the case as it was presented to the Court was a "legal one": Must a prisoner who advances an Eighth Amendment cruel and unusual punishments claim establish that he suffered a "significant injury"?[25]

For Justice Thomas the Court's own Eighth Amendment prisoners' rights precedents—its *recent* precedents—made obvious the answer: A prisoner must establish that he suffered a *significant* injury. Justice Thomas devoted considerable space in his dissenting opinion to the Court's leading precedents in this area—*Estelle, Rhodes, Whitley,* and *Wilson*—and concluded that the Court had "never found a violation of the Eighth Amendment in the prison context when an inmate has failed to establish" both the objective and subjective components of his Eighth Amendment claim.[26]

Justice Thomas went beyond disagreeing with the majority's application of the Court's Eighth Amendment prisoners' rights precedents: He called those precedents into question. The most significant aspect of Justice Thomas's dissenting opinion was his plainly stated view that the Eighth Amendment did not apply *at all* in the prison context. It should be made clear here, however, that Justice Thomas did *not* say that "punching a prisoner in the face" (to borrow Justice O'Connor's phrase) was appropriate behavior or nonredressable behavior. In fact, he stressed that such behavior was "immoral," "tortious," "criminal," and possibly "remedial under other provisions of the Federal Constitution." He simply said that it was not redressable through the *Eighth Amendment* because that Amendment, until *Estelle* in 1976 ("185 years after the Eighth Amendment was adopted"),[27] only had applied to torturous punishments meted out by statutes or sentencing judges. And Justice Thomas did not merely assert this: He chronicled how the Court itself had repeatedly held this prior to *Estelle,* how leading constitutional law scholars (e.g., Joseph Story) had concluded this, and how the Framers had intended this.

One final point must be made about Justice Thomas's *Hudson* dissent: He did *not* say that the Court's *Estelle* line of cases should be overruled. Indeed, he went so far as to say in *Hudson,* as Justice Blackmun also had said, that a serious *non*-physical injury was actionable pursuant to *Estelle* if it was inflicted upon a prisoner by a prison official who manifested a sufficiently culpable state of mind. It was only later, in *Helling v. McKinney* (1993)[28] and *Farmer v. Brennan* (1994),[29] when Justice Thomas addressed the possibility of overruling *Estelle.*

HELLING V. MCKINNEY (1993) AND FARMER V. BRENNAN (1994)

Helling and *Farmer* were both conditions of confinement cases. (*Hudson* was a use of force case.) In the first of the two cases, William McKinney, a prisoner, filed a complaint in federal court that claimed that his Eighth Amendment rights were violated when he was forced to share a six-by-eight-foot cell with a prisoner who smoked five packs of cigarettes a day. McKinney alleged that this condition of his confinement posed a serious risk to his health by subjecting him to environmental tobacco smoke (ETS) and that specified officials of the Nevada State Prison in Carson City, Nevada, where he was housed, were "deliberately indifferent" to this fact.[30] McKinney further alleged that he suffered nosebleeds, headaches, chest pains, and loss of energy as a result of being exposed to ETS.

The trial judge directed a verdict that compelled exposure to ETS did not, as a matter of law, constitute cruel and unusual punishment. The trial judge also found that McKinney failed to prove deliberate indifference on the part of the prison officials in question and that he failed to establish a connection between his various ailments and his exposure to ETS. The U.S. Court of Appeals for the Ninth Circuit reversed and remanded the case to the trial judge with instructions that McKinney be allowed to attempt to prove his factual claims regarding the prison officials' state of mind and his own risk of injury. The Ninth Circuit declared that "the attitude of our society has evolved at least to a point that it violates current standards of decency to expose unwilling prisoners to ETS levels that pose an unreasonable risk of harm to their health."[31]

The Supreme Court affirmed and thereby established that an Eighth Amendment cruel and unusual punishments claim can be based on *possible future* harm to health. As in *Hudson* the vote was 7 to 2, and as in *Hudson* Justice Thomas issued a dissenting opinion in which Justice Scalia joined. Writing for the majority, Justice Byron White held that McKinney had stated a claim under the Eighth Amendment by alleging that prison officials had, with deliberate indifference, exposed him to levels of ETS that posed an unreasonable risk of serious harm to his future health. "It would be odd to deny an injunction to inmates who plainly proved an unsafe, life-threatening condition in their prison on the ground that nothing yet had happened to them," Justice White declared unequivocally when rejecting the state's position that a prisoner must allege that he was "currently suffering serious medical problems." Justice White was quite clear as well in explaining what McKinney would have to prove on remand: (1) that he was being exposed to unreasonably high levels of ETS and that society considers such exposure to be beyond contemporary standards of decency, and (2) that prison officials were deliberately indifferent to the risk of harm to his future health. Justice White also issued a mild rebuke of Justice Thomas's position: "It is undisputed that the treatment a prisoner receives in prison and the conditions under which he is confined are subject to scrutiny under the Eighth Amendment."[32]

Justice Thomas, of course, indicated in *Hudson* that he had doubts about this supposition. His dissenting opinion in *Helling* was his most detailed explanation to date of why he did.[33] Justice Thomas examined the text and history of the Eighth Amendment and called into question the majority's specific decision in *Helling* to "expand" the Eighth Amendment to a prisoner's "mere risk of injury" and its general position, since *Estelle*, that deprivations suffered by a prisoner that were not part of his official sentence could constitute "punishment" for Eighth Amendment purposes. Justice Thomas quoted five separate eighteenth-century and early nineteenth-century dictionaries for the proposition that "[a]t the time the Eighth Amendment was ratified, the word 'punishment' referred to the penalty imposed for the commission of a crime." He quoted *Black's Law Dictionary* to the effect that this "is also the primary definition of the word today."[34]

His textualist point made—that punishment "does not encompass a prisoner's injuries that bear no relation to his sentence"—Justice Thomas turned to the historical record and reached a similar, albeit slightly more equivocal, conclusion. He examined the English Declaration of Rights of 1689, Elliot's Debates on the Federal Constitution, the Annals of Congress, the respective commentaries of Joseph Story and Thomas Cooley, and the Delaware Constitution of 1792 along the way. He also reiterated a point that he made in his *Hudson* dissent: that "Judicial interpretations of the Cruel and Unusual Punishments Clause were, until quite recently, consistent" with this view.[35]

Justice Thomas concluded his *Helling* dissent with a direct assault on the Court's reasoning in *Estelle*, something he had avoided in *Hudson*. He stressed in *Helling* that the Court's "extension" of the Eighth Amendment to the prison context in *Estelle* "rested on little more than an ipse dixit."

He contended that there was "no analysis of the text of the Eighth Amendment" in that case and that the Court's discussion of history consisted of a "single sentence" that actually cut against the Court's desired result.[36] He also accused the *Estelle* Court of manipulating precedent. Justice Thomas thundered:

> although the Court purported to rely upon "our decisions interpreting" the Eighth Amendment, ibid., none of the six cases it cited, see id., at 102–103, 97 S.Ct., at 290–91, held that the Eighth Amendment applies to prison deprivations—or, for that matter, even addressed a claim that it does. All of those cases involved challenges to a sentence imposed for a criminal offense.[37]

In short, Justice Thomas concluded, *Estelle* "simply asserted" that the Eighth Amendment applied to deprivations suffered in prison.[38]

In light of his scathing attack on the *Estelle* Court's reasoning, it is perhaps surprising that Justice Thomas merely declined to "extend" *Estelle* to prisoners' claims concerning the risk of future injury, rather than call for its overruling.[39] Clearly, however, if it was not already obvious from *Hudson*, Justice Thomas manifested in *Helling* profound disagreement with *Estelle*, the Court's most significant prisoners' rights decision of the century. *Farmer v. Brennan* (1994) found Justice Thomas reiterating his concerns about *Estelle* in even more dramatic terms.

Dee Farmer was a transsexual prisoner serving a twenty-year federal sentence for credit card fraud. Farmer, who was "biologically male,"[40] had undergone estrogen therapy, received silicone breast implants, and submitted to unsuccessful testicle-removal surgery. The parties agreed that Farmer "projects feminine characteristics."[41]

The Federal Bureau of Prisons' policy was to incarcerate preoperative transsexuals with prisoners of like biological sex. As a result, Farmer was always incarcerated in all-male prisons during the course of his sentence, although he was sometimes segregated, typically for disciplinary reasons, from the general male prison population. On April 1, 1989, nine days after he was transferred from a correctional institution in Oxford, Wisconsin, to a maximum security penitentiary in Terre Haute, Indiana, Farmer was battered and forcibly raped by another male prisoner. The details of the attack were that Farmer was approached in his cell by a prisoner who demanded sex, and that when Farmer refused the prisoner punched him in the face repeatedly, pushed and kicked him, tore off his clothes, held him down on the bed, and raped him at knife point.[42]

Farmer reported the assault to prison officials and then filed a complaint in federal court in which he alleged that his Eighth Amendment rights were violated by the director and regional director of the Bureau of Prisons, the wardens of the Terre Haute penitentiary and the Oxford correctional institution, and the case manager who recommended his transfer from the correctional institution to the penitentiary. Farmer further alleged that, due to his feminine characteristics, each of these defendants knew that he would be sexually assaulted at the Terre Haute facility.

The trial court granted summary judgment for the defendants, concluding that failure to prevent inmate assaults violated the Eighth Amendment only if prison officials were "reckless in a criminal sense"—in other words, had "actual knowledge" of a potential danger—and that the defendants lacked such knowledge because Farmer never expressed any safety concerns to them. The U.S. Court of Appeals for the Seventh Circuit summarily affirmed without opinion.

The Supreme Court granted certiorari to define, for the first time, what *Estelle*'s "deliberate indifference" standard required as a matter of proof. (There was a conflict in the circuits on the question.) The Court, with Justice David Souter writing an opinion in which all the justices except Justice Thomas joined, held that a prisoner was required to prove that the prison official in question knew that the prisoner faced a substantial risk of serious harm and that the official disregarded that risk by failing to take reasonable measures to abate it.

Justice Souter's opinion for the Court was a long and intricate exposition on why this rigorous standard of proof—subjective criminal recklessness—was the appropriate standard to apply in the Eighth Amendment conditions of confinement context. Summarily stated, Justice Souter concluded that the subjective criminal recklessness standard was consistent with the Court's long-standing position that (1) the Eighth Amendment prohibited cruel and unusual "punishments," not simply cruel and unusual "conditions," and (2) an Eighth Amendment cruel and unusual punishments claim entailed a "subjective," not simply an "objective," component. Justice Souter was quick to point out, however, that though rigorous, this definition of deliberate indifference did not mean that prison officials would be free to ignore obvious risks to prisoners. "Whether a prison official had the requisite knowledge of a substantial risk is a question of fact subject to demonstration in the usual ways, including inference from circumstantial evidence, . . . and a factfinder may conclude that a prison official knew of a substantial risk from the very fact that the risk was obvious," Justice Souter wrote.[43] Because the trial court granted the defendants' motion for summary judgment without addressing Farmer's procedural allegation that the defendants were not complying with his discovery requests, the Court vacated and remanded the judgments of the lower courts and ordered that Farmer's claims be reconsidered.

Justice Blackmun issued a concurring opinion in which he made an impassioned argument that *Wilson v. Seiter* (1991) be overruled.[44] "Whether the Constitution has been violated 'should turn on the character of the punishment rather than the motivation of the individual who inflicted it,'" Justice Blackmun wrote, quoting Justice John Paul Stevens's dissenting opinion in *Estelle*.[45] In short, Justice Blackmun maintained that a prisoner's Eighth Amendment cruel and unusual punishments claim should be actionable on the basis of the objective component alone. He emphasized in his separate opinion in *Farmer*, as he had in his separate opinion in *Hudson* two terms before, the potential "horrors" of prison life in order to add weight to his call for the abandonment of the subjective component of the Court's Eighth Amendment prisoners' rights jurisprudence.[46]

Justice Thomas continued in an opinion concurring in the judgment in *Farmer* the exegesis on the Court's Eighth Amendment prisoners' rights jurisprudence that he had begun in his dissenting opinions in *Hudson* and *Helling*.[47] In *Farmer*, however, Justice Thomas wrote only for himself: Justice Scalia joined Justice Souter's opinion for the Court.[*]

Justice Thomas reiterated in *Farmer* that he believed that the text and history pertaining to the Eighth Amendment made clear that "judges or juries—but not jailers—impose 'punishment.'"[48] Consequently, he maintained that "as an original matter" he would hold that Farmer's Eighth Amendment claims failed at the threshold level. Precedent—specifically *Estelle*—was such, however, that Justice Thomas deemed it appropriate, at least on the facts before the Court in *Farmer*, simply to restate his disagreement with the *Estelle* line of cases. This said, Justice Thomas appeared even more eager in *Farmer* than he was in *Helling* to revisit *Estelle*

---

[*]There is no indication from any of the opinions in *Farmer* why Justice Scalia did not join Justice Thomas's separate opinion in the case.

in the future. He closed his concurring opinion with the following words: "I remain hopeful that in a proper case the Court will reconsider *Estelle* in light of constitutional text and history."[49]

Most of the reaction to Justice Thomas's prisoners' rights opinions was directed at his dissenting opinion in *Hudson v. McMillian* (1992), the case in which he first called into question whether the Eighth Amendment applied *at all* in the prison context. The reaction to that opinion was nastier than for any other opinion Justice Thomas issued during his acclimation period on the Supreme Court. Given the vitriolic tone of the reaction to many of his other opinions—his opinions regarding affirmative action, for example—that is saying something.

The editors of the nation's leading newspapers were particularly harsh in their criticism of Justice Thomas's *Hudson* dissent. The editors of the *New York Times*, for example, labeled Justice Thomas "the youngest, cruelest justice" in a scathing editorial about the opinion, while the editors of the *Washington Post* referred to the dissent as "mind-boggling" and the editors of the *Los Angeles Times* called it "appalling."[50]

Liberal political columnists were likewise incensed. William Raspberry, for one, devoted an entire column to dressing down Justice Thomas for his *Hudson* dissent. For reasons that will become obvious below, I quote at length from Raspberry's column:

> Clarence:
>
> I know I'm supposed to call you Justice Thomas, but I don't want to be quite that formal. I want to talk straight to a guy I thought I knew a little.
>
> You know what I want to talk about. It's that dissent of yours in the matter of *Hudson v. McMillian*. Come on, Clarence. Conservative is one thing; bizarre is another. . . .
>
> To tell you the truth, Clarence, I'm personally embarrassed. You know you weren't my choice to succeed Thurgood Marshall on the nation's highest court. You were too conservative for my taste and, more significant, I thought you lacked the requisite judicial experience. But I thought I understood your conservatism as a sort of harsh pragmatism that most of us harbor to some degree. I cautioned black America not to let your conservatism blind them to your intellectual honesty. Conservatism, I insisted, isn't the same thing as stupidity—even in a black man. And since Bush was going to name a conservative to Thurgood's seat, I said, better he should appoint a conservative who has known deprivation and unfairness and racism at firsthand.

As a matter of fact, you encouraged that view. I mean, wasn't that the whole point of your recital of your underprivileged background, of your but-for-the-grace-of-God musings about society's losers?

Look, guy, I never expected you to do a Hugo Black and become a court liberal. But I was prepared to see you put a compassionate face on conservatism. When it became clear that you would be confirmed to the court, I told my friends (your critics) that they should just watch while you surprised your right-wing supporters and confounded our enemies.

But your high-falutin' angels-on-a-pinhead opinion the other day that for prison guards to beat the hell out of a handcuffed and shackled inmate does not constitute "cruel and unusual punishment" (unless the victim winds up in intensive care) confounded only those who tried to cut you some slack....

Of course I don't expect that you will always do what strikes the rest of us as "the right thing." But why go out of your way to do the wrong?[51]

The political right had a dramatically different take on Justice Thomas's *Hudson* dissent. Terry Eastland and George F. Will, for example, each devoted columns to rebutting the sort of knee-jerk "rhetoric" (Will's word) that they felt epitomized both the political commentary from the left lambasting Justice Thomas's position and Justice O'Connor's opinion for the Court.[52]

Robert H. Bork, the most prominent conservative writing about the Court today, also defended Justice Thomas's *Hudson* dissent. Bork wrote in the *National Review* that Justice Thomas was a "bright spot" on the Court during his first term (when *Hudson* was decided) because he had "proved to be a tough-minded judge who cares about law more than popular results." Bork called Justice Thomas's dissent "admirable" and was sharply critical of those who "maligned" it. Bork wrote:

Those who find [Justice Thomas's position] cold-blooded seem to think the Constitution is the only law in this country, so that it must be available to right every wrong. There was no need to deform the concept of "cruel and unusual punishment" in this case because, as Thomas noted, Louisiana's courts are open to prisoners to sue for wrongs done by prison personnel. The process of continually extending the Constitution to do the work that other laws already accomplish trivializes the Constitution.[53]

With the exception of a myriad of law student case comments about each of the three principal Eighth Amendment prisoners' rights cases discussed in this section—*Hudson*, *Helling*, and *Farmer*[54]—the scholarly journals were remarkably silent about Justice Thomas's call for a dramatic rethinking of the Court's *Estelle* line of cases.[55] Revealingly, however, the one critique of Justice Thomas's position by a major figure in American law, that by longtime Thomas critic A. Leon Higginbotham, Jr., did little more than quote the portions of William Raspberry's op-ed that I quoted above and then declare that Justice Thomas's "views are for the 1990s . . . the moral equivalent of the views of the shameful majorities in the nineteenth century Supreme Court cases of *Dred Scott* and *Plessy*."[56] This is assertion, not analysis. There was no attempt by Higginbotham—or by any other major scholar—to grapple with the *substance* of Justice Thomas's reading of the text and history of the Eighth Amendment.

Perhaps that was because Justice Thomas was *correct* in his reading of text and history. Indeed, graduate law student Thomas K. Landry, in the most detailed attempt to date to articulate what the Eighth Amendment meant by "punishment," made plain that Justice Thomas was in fact correct as a matter of text and history to limit "punishment" to the terms of the penal statute and/or sentence at issue and to exclude from it conditions or events in prison.[57] Similarly, the only other essays that I could find that attempted to address Justice Thomas's argument on its own terms, two third-year law student case comments, also concluded that Justice Thomas's reading of the text and history surrounding the applicability of the Eighth Amendment to the prison context was correct.[58] The two leading pre–Rehnquist Court exegeses on the original intent of the Eighth Amendment, those by Raoul Berger and Anthony F. Granucci, provide additional support for Justice Thomas's position.[59]

Of course, this does *not* mean that Justice Thomas's strict interpretation of the Eighth Amendment is the best way to interpret that Amendment in the prisoners' rights context. Personally, I find Landry's position more appealing—that the Eighth Amendment applies to a prisoner's claims when, but only when, a legislature or sentencer expected or intended specific aspects of the prisoner's sentence to constitute part of the prisoner's punishment (e.g., incarcerating the prisoner in one prison rather than another)—a position that strikes a middle ground between the formalistic views of Justices Thomas and Scalia on the one hand and the more freewheeling views of the rest of the Rehnquist Court on the other.[60]

What it *does* mean, however, is that Justice Thomas has an Eighth Amendment theory that cannot be legitimately dismissed by ad hominem attacks upon his character, such as those issued by Higginbotham and the liberal members of the popular press. Particularly offensive were those "analyses" that accused Justice Thomas of "condoning" the "torture" of prisoners.[61] He did nothing of the sort. Rather, he condemned in the strongest possible terms in each of his opinions the mistreatment of prisoners. He simply argued that state law, and perhaps other provisions of the federal Constitution (e.g., the Fourteenth Amendment), were where prisoners should turn for redress. This is certainly a conservative position, but that does not mean that it is an unreasonable—let alone an "immoral"[62]—position. Indeed, what Justice Thomas's critics invariably failed to mention was that in *Hudson*, the case that generated the most vitriol, the trial court *found* that Hudson's injuries were *minor*, the Court of Appeals did not disturb this finding, and the finding was not in dispute before the Supreme Court. Justice Thomas was merely addressing in his dissent the specific question presented to the Court on certiorari: whether a prisoner's injuries must be "significant" to be cognizable under the Eighth Amendment.[63] Justice Thomas, in other words, was answering a *legal* question, not a *factual* one. Appellate judges are supposed to answer *legal* questions, not *factual* ones.

Habeas Corpus

The law-versus-fact conundrum surfaced in another of Justice Thomas's controversial criminal justice opinions. This time, the opinion concerned not the definition of criminal punishment, but the scope of the writ of habeas corpus.

The "Great Writ"[64] was so important to the Framers that they made express reference to it in the body of the original Constitution, one of only six rights to be so enumerated before the Bill of Rights was adopted.[65] Article I, Section 9, Clause 2 provides: "The Privilege of the Writ of Habeas Corpus shall not be suspended, unless when in Cases of Rebellion or Invasion the public Safety may require it."

Habeas corpus ("you have the body") is the fundamental safeguard in Anglo-American law against illegal custody of the innocent. The writ traces its origins to Section 39 of Magna Carta (1215), received Parliament's imprimatur in the Habeas Corpus Act of 1679, and was an integral part of American common law both before and after the Revolution. The Constitution protected against the suspension of the writ, and the Judiciary Act of 1789 empowered all federal courts "to grant writs of habeas corpus for the purpose of an inquiry into the cause of commitment" in a federal facility. In the 1867 Habeas Corpus Act, Congress extended the federal courts' jurisdiction to petitions by state prisoners. The 1867 Act has been amended several times, most notably in 1948, 1966, and 1996. All states have similar laws.

The Supreme Court has issued literally scores of decisions concerning habeas corpus. Almost all of them have involved a debate over the writ's history. The scope of habeas corpus at common law, the purposes of the Reconstruction Congress in enacting the 1867 Habeas Corpus Act, the meaning of the Court's own precedents—you name it and the justices have disagreed about it over the years.[66] As will now be seen, Justices Thomas and O'Connor disagreed sharply in *Wright v. West* (1992)[67] about the history of the Court's standard of review for habeas corpus petitions involving mixed questions of law and fact.[*]

WRIGHT V. WEST (1992)

Frank R. West was arrested in 1979 for allegedly stealing approximately $3,500 worth of merchandise from a vacation home in Westmoreland County, Virginia. Many of the items reported as stolen were recovered by local law enforcement officers from West's home in Gloucester County, Virginia. West testified at his jury trial that he had purchased the items at flea markets, usually from an acquaintance by the name of Ronnie Elkins. Elkins did not testify at West's trial.

Virginia law permitted an inference that a person who failed to explain, or who falsely explained, his exclusive possession of recently stolen property was guilty of theft. The jury drew this inference, and West was convicted of grand larceny and sentenced to ten years in prison. West appealed, principally on the ground that the evidence at trial—his possession of the items and his explanation about where he got them—was insufficient to support a finding of guilt beyond a reasonable doubt. In 1980 the Supreme Court of Virginia denied West's appeal.

Seven years later West filed for a writ of habeas corpus in the same court. This time he appended an affidavit in support of his petition executed by Ronnie Elkins. West's petition was summarily denied in 1988. West then filed for a writ of habeas corpus in the U.S. District Court for the Eastern District of Virginia. His petition was denied by that court, too. West appealed that ruling to the U.S. Court of Appeals for the Fourth

---

[*]A "mixed question of law and fact" is one asking "whether the rule of law applied to the established facts is or is not violated." *Pullman-Standard v. Swint*, 456 U.S. 273, 289 n. 19 (1982).

Circuit. West won that appeal in a 1991 decision in which a Fourth Circuit panel relied heavily upon an Eleventh Circuit case that also involved collateral review of a state burglary conviction that was based solely on an inference from the fact of possession.

The Commonwealth of Virginia petitioned the Fourth Circuit for a rehearing en banc before the full circuit. That petition was denied. Virginia then filed a petition for certiorari with the U.S. Supreme Court. That petition was granted. However, as it had done in *Hudson v. McMillian*, the Court itself in *Wright v. West* framed the question for the parties:

> In determining whether to grant a petition for writ of habeas corpus by a person in custody pursuant to the judgment of a state court, should a federal court give deference to the state court's application of law to the specific facts of the petitioner's case or should it review the state court's determination de novo?[68]*

The five separate opinions issued by the justices in *Wright* make it difficult (1) to realize that the decision to reverse the Fourth Circuit was unanimous and (2) to understand what the Court, as an institution, was trying to say (beyond the narrow proposition that West loses).[69] The two major opinions in the case were written by Justices Thomas and O'Connor.[70]

Justice Thomas, in what was supposed to be the first major criminal justice opinion of his Supreme Court tenure, was unable to hold together a majority on the question the Court itself had posed.[71] Chief Justice Rehnquist and Justice Scalia were willing to join Justice Thomas's opinion, but no other member of the unanimous Court was. In fact, the only statement that Justice Thomas could get all of his colleagues to agree with came near the end of his opinion: "Whatever the appropriate standard of review, we conclude that there was more than enough evidence to support West's conviction."[72] This is hardly the stuff of a landmark opinion. However, the fifteen pages preceding this unspectacular statement in which Justice Thomas answered the question presented by the Court reveal a lot about his criminal justice views, his use of precedent, the way in which his colleagues react to his opinions, and how he is viewed by those who write about the Court.

Justice Thomas maintained that federal District Court judges should employ a deferential standard of review when deciding mixed questions

*Review "de novo" means review as if no decision had been previously rendered.

of law and fact in habeas corpus petitions from state prisoners. In essence, Justice Thomas adopted the Bush administration's position that federal court judges were required to accept the findings of state court judges without further evaluation. Justice Thomas justified this deferential approach on a number of grounds, each of which, as will be seen, Justice O'Connor strongly criticized. Justice Thomas took the unusual step of including a series of lengthy footnotes in his plurality opinion in which he responded to each of Justice O'Connor's criticisms of his various arguments in support of a deferential standard of review.

Justice Thomas's first argument for a deferential standard of habeas corpus review emphasized the writ's narrow scope during the nation's early years. "For much of our history," Justice Thomas wrote, "we interpreted these bare [statutory] guidelines and their predecessors to reflect the common-law principle that a prisoner seeking a writ of habeas corpus could challenge only the jurisdiction of the court that had rendered the judgment under which he was in custody." It was only later, Justice Thomas insisted, that the writ "gradually" expanded to become what some now consider to constitute an end run around the traditional direct review appellate process.[73]

The crucial case in the Court's "modern" approach to habeas corpus review was *Brown v. Allen* (1953), because it was in that case, Justice Thomas contended, that the Court first rejected the principle that federal courts must afford absolute deference to state court findings on mixed questions of law and fact.[74] Importantly, Justice Thomas read *Brown* to permit, but not to require, de novo review. As such, Justice Thomas concluded, *Brown* did not "squarely foreclose" deferential review.[75]

His reading of *Brown* established, Justice Thomas went on to review the Court's post-*Brown* precedents, up to and including *Miller v. Fenton* (1985), the case in which the Court unequivocally held, citing *Brown*, that mixed questions were "subject to plenary federal review" on habeas.[76] Justice Thomas criticized these precedents, especially *Miller*, for reading *Brown* to *require* de novo review. "[A]n unadorned citation to *Brown* should not have been enough, at least as an original matter, to establish de novo review with respect to mixed questions," Justice Thomas wrote.[77]

Justice Thomas attributed much of the confusion in the Court's handling of mixed questions to *Jackson v. Virginia* (1979), a case in which the Court appeared schizophrenic about the deference versus de novo issue.[78] According to Justice Thomas, the *Jackson* Court called for deference in one part of its opinion, for de novo review in another part, and then concluded that, on the facts before it, both standards would lead to the same result. Justice Thomas also contended that, when the Court was not muddying the waters as it had done in *Jackson*, it "implicitly"[79] questioned in several recent cases—most notably *Teague v. Lane* (1989)[80]—the propriety of the de novo standard.

The eighteen long paragraphs that Justice Thomas devoted to explaining why the Supreme Court should require federal District Court judges to employ a deferential standard of review when deciding mixed questions of law and fact in habeas corpus petitions from state prisoners were all, of course, dicta. But that did not stop Justice O'Connor from issuing a nine-point rebuttal to Justice Thomas's "extended discussion" of the Court's habeas corpus jurisprudence.[81]

Justice O'Connor's first two rejoinders pertained to Justice Thomas's description of the Court's pre–*Brown v. Allen* (1953) habeas corpus precedents. Those precedents, she insisted, were decided before the Bill of Rights's criminal justice guarantees were made binding on the states. Consequently, they turned on the Due Process Clause of the Fourteenth Amendment, *not*, as Justice Thomas claimed, on any threshold requirements for a writ of habeas corpus. Justice O'Connor also criticized Justice Thomas for mischaracterizing Justice Lewis Powell's views in *Kuhlmann v. Wilson* (1986). She contended that Justice Powell did *not* say that prior to 1953 federal courts gave absolute deference to state court findings. Rather, he simply said that a committing court of competent jurisdiction was afforded "absolute respect," which, Justice O'Connor stated, was not the same thing as "complete deference."[82]

Justice O'Connor's next two points concerned Justice Thomas's interpretation of *Brown v. Allen*. According to Justice O'Connor, *Brown* was *not* the first case in which the Court failed to afford absolute deference to state court findings, as Justice Thomas stated. Moreover, she continued, Justice Thomas understated "the certainty with which *Brown v. Allen* rejected a deferential standard of review of issues of law."[83]

Justice O'Connor's next rejoinder was her most detailed. She argued that "Justice Thomas incorrectly states that we have never considered the standard of review to apply to mixed questions of law and fact raised on federal habeas. . . . On the contrary, we did so in the very cases cited by Justice Thomas." Justice O'Connor then went on to describe those seven cases. If that were not enough, she also string-cited twenty-one additional cases in which de novo review was applied, adding, "There have been many others."[84]

Justice O'Connor's sixth and seventh objections were that Justice Thomas "misdescribed" and "mischaracterized" two key precedents: *Jackson v. Virginia* (1979) and *Teague v. Lane* (1989). In *Jackson*, Justice O'Connor insisted, the Court "expressly rejected" the deferential standard of review that Justice Thomas advanced in his plurality opinion in the case at bar, and in *Teague*, a retroactivity case, the Court was not addressing the standard of review "at all."[85]

Next, Justice O'Connor objected to Justice Thomas's suggestion that de novo review was incompatible with the maxim that federal courts should "give great weight to the considered conclusions of a coequal state judiciary." Justice O'Connor, who is one of the Rehnquist Court's leading proponents of states' rights (see the next chapter), declared, in contrast, that federal courts "have an independent obligation to say what the law is."[86]

Finally, Justice O'Connor pointed out that Congress had considered on thirteen separate occasions since *Brown* was decided in 1953 proposals for "adopting a deferential standard of review along the lines suggested by Justice Thomas." Each proposal, she reminded her colleague, was "rejected."[87]

Perhaps because of the hypertechnical nature of the precedential distinctions and counterdistinctions at issue in *Wright v. West*, the popular press was relatively quiet about the dispute between Justices Thomas and O'Connor in that case. In fact, the only two non–law review articles about the case that I found involved Vivian Berger, a Columbia Law School professor who specializes in the criminal justice field and who works with the ACLU and the NAACP on behalf of prisoners seeking habeas corpus. In the first of the articles, Berger was quoted as saying, "We dodged the bullets but the revolver is still loaded for next term."[88] In the second article, one that Berger herself wrote for the *National Law Journal*, she explained what she meant by that statement. The title of Berger's article, "Ax Poised over Habeas," was a strong indication of what she meant: Justice Thomas was itching to put an end to the writ of habeas corpus. Her rephrasing of the question presented indicated who—Thomas or O'Connor—she thought had the better argument: Justice O'Connor. Berger rephrased the question to read:

> Should a federal district court *continue* to give de novo review to a state court's application of law to specific facts—or instead, should the rules be

changed to allow a district court to honor a state court's reasonable decision regarding these so-called mixed questions of law and fact?[89]

The italicized words "continue" and "changed" were not included in the question the Court presented. Their inclusion by Berger manifests that she did not think much of Justice Thomas's argument. The substance of her article suggests the same. Indeed, she went so far as to declare that had a majority endorsed Justice Thomas's "revisionist attack," it would have "sounded the death knell for habeas corpus."[90]

Turning to the law reviews, the major article about *Wright* was written by James S. Liebman, a colleague of Berger's at both Columbia and the NAACP. Liebman spent one hundred pages in the *Columbia Law Review* explaining why he believed Justice Thomas's approach to habeas corpus was wrong.[91] Liebman's article, "Apocalypse Next Time? The Anachronistic Attack on Habeas Corpus/Direct Review Parity," echoed Berger's "apocalyptic" vision of what Justice Thomas was trying to accomplish with his opinion in *Wright*. Liebman accused Justice Thomas of rewriting the question presented in the writ of certiorari and of submitting a "brief" in his plurality opinion so as to "destroy" the writ of habeas corpus. Liebman declared that it was "against" an "impending habeas corpus Armageddon" that his article—an earlier version of which was apparently filed as an amicus curiae brief in support of West's position—was written.[92]

Liebman attacked Justice Thomas's interpretation of the Court's habeas corpus jurisprudence in much the same way that Justice O'Connor did. Liebman, however, was even more aggressive in his criticism of Justice Thomas than Justice O'Connor was: He essentially accused Justice Thomas of *deliberately* mischaracterizing the long history of federal court de novo review of petitions for habeas corpus by state prisoners. This was how Liebman summarized Justice Thomas's argument:

De novo review of legal claims in habeas corpus? Sure, we accidentally stumbled into that rule for a few years in the mid-to-late 1980s. But we corrected our error implicitly in some decisions decided a few years later, and now we ought to correct it explicitly as well.[93]

Liebman then spent the next eighteen pages of his long and highly technical article breaking down Justice Thomas's plurality opinion and attempting to prove its analytical shortcomings. Liebman succeeded, for the most part, in demonstrating that Justice Thomas mischaracterized the Court's habeas corpus precedents. (Whether Justice Thomas *deliberately* mischaracterized them, as Liebman maintained he did, is difficult to know.) As a matter of *first principles*, however, Justice Thomas's position—that federal District Court judges must accept the findings of state supreme court judges on mixed questions of law and fact—finds considerable support.* In fact, Liebman's thesis—that habeas corpus review by federal District Court judges should be viewed as a "substitute for limited direct Supreme Court review of nationally important issues for which the Constitution permits federal court jurisdiction"[94]—is difficult to accept, given the unique role the *Supreme* Court was intended to occupy in the American constitutional system and the damage to that role federal *District* Court "surrogacy"[95] might do, and arguably has done. Indeed, opposition to then-Chief Justice Burger's proposal to create a national intermediate appellate court between the existing U.S. Court of Appeals and the U.S. Supreme Court to assist the Supreme Court in screening or deciding cases was waged—*successfully* waged—on the ground that the Supreme Court's role was different than that of any other court in the United States.[96] Surely, if a federal *appeals* court should not be performing the *Supreme* Court's responsibilities—reviewing "nationally important issues," to borrow Liebman's phrase—neither should federal *trial* courts.

As a former law clerk to an outstanding federal District Court judge (no bias here!), I in no way intend for my position on this issue to reflect adversely on federal District Court judges. Rather, it is meant as an observation about American constitutional theory. Put simply, federal District Courts are essentially *fact*-finding bodies; they should not be engaging in appellate review of the *legal* or mixed legal-factual findings of state supreme courts. The U.S. Supreme Court is charged with that responsibility. I would go so far as to say, as many opponents of Chief Justice Burger's proposal previously did say, that empowering federal District Courts with de novo review of legal or mixed legal-factual questions violates Article III's mandate that there be "one" Supreme Court. It also would be inconsistent with the compromise struck at the framing that

---

*Almost all of the many law review articles about habeas corpus contain long doctrinal summaries of what the particular author believes the precedents held. (Justices Thomas and O'Connor included case summaries in their opinions as well.) It would be pointless for me to add yet another reading of those precedents, especially when my focus is on *first principles*, rather than *case doctrine*. Readers interested in a more doctrinal approach to the Court's habeas corpus jurisprudence are directed to articles such as Liebman's.

"inferior" federal courts would not sit in judgment of their state court counterparts.

In summary, Justice Thomas would have been better served by making an argument based on first principles, which he tends to favor in any event, rather than one in which he was forced to advance a questionable reading of the Court's long history of questionable habeas corpus decisions.[97] He would have ended up in the same place: with a vision of habeas corpus that prohibits an end run around the appellate process.

Justice Scalia's Loyal Apprentice?

Clearly, Justice Thomas has a conservative view of prisoners' rights and habeas corpus, the areas of criminal justice law in which he has written the most, and in which the most has been written about him. But can any conclusions be drawn about Justice Thomas's criminal justice jurisprudence *generally*? Christopher E. Smith, a criminal justice professor at Michigan State University who has written a number of highly critical law review articles about the Rehnquist Court's criminal justice decisions,[98] has drawn a major one. In a 1995 *Drake Law Review* article comparing the criminal justice jurisprudence of Justices Thomas and Scalia, Smith concluded that Justice Thomas was a right-wing "extremist" who was a "consistent ally" of the "visionary" Justice Scalia.[99] And what the "visionary" Justice Scalia was attempting to do, with Justice Thomas firmly in tow, Smith insisted, was to "limit the definition of rights for criminal defendants and prisoners."[100]

I disagree with Smith's characterization of Justice Thomas as little more than Justice Scalia's loyal apprentice. Although Thomas *usually* voted with Scalia during his first five terms on the Supreme Court, he did not always—just as Justice Blackmun *usually* voted with Justice Stevens, but did not always (see Appendix I, Table 2). If my research about Justice Thomas has convinced me of anything, it is that he has *his own* jurisprudence.* This holds true for *all* areas of public law, including

---

*Smith admitted as much the very next year. See Christopher E. Smith, "Bent on Original Intent: Justice Thomas Is Asserting a Distinct and Cohesive Voice," *ABA Journal* 82 (October 1996): 48–52. Smith's *ABA Journal* essay is at odds with both the *Drake Law Review* article he wrote the previous year and the thesis of his (coauthored) book about Justice Scalia's jurisprudence: that Justice Scalia was the *only* "visionary justice" on the Rehnquist Court. David A. Schultz and Christopher E. Smith, *The Jurisprudential Vision of Justice Antonin Scalia* (Lanham, MD: Rowman and Littlefield, 1996), xii. Of course, most Supreme Court justices have a "jurisprudential vision." My point is simply that Justice Thomas has one, too.

criminal justice. In addition to the prisoners' rights and habeas corpus opinions discussed at length above, Justice Thomas wrote forceful opinions about jury selection and capital punishment. Both will be considered briefly here.[101]

In *Georgia v. McCollum* (1992) the Court, in a 7-to-2 decision written by Justice Blackmun, extended the *Batson v. Kentucky* (1986) prohibition against racial discrimination in jury selection to the exercise of peremptory challenges by criminal defendants.[102] Justice Thomas concurred separately, and for himself alone,[103] to make plain that his vote in *McCollum* was purely a matter of stare decisis and to express his concern about the impact decisions such as *McCollum* would have on Black criminal defendants. Justice Thomas wrote:

> I am certain that black criminal defendants will rue the day that this Court ventured down this road that inexorably will lead to the elimination of peremptory strikes. . . . Simply stated, securing representation of the defendant's race on the jury may help to overcome racial bias and provide the defendant with a better chance of having a fair trial.[104]

Without question, Justice Thomas was expressing *his own* views in *McCollum* about racial prejudice in the criminal justice system, just as he was expressing *his own* views in his civil rights opinions discussed in the previous chapter.

Justice Thomas's views about racial prejudice in the criminal justice system also were reflected in his concurring opinion in *Graham v. Collins* (1993),[105] his most extensive opinion to date about the death penalty.[106] In *Graham* the Court held 5 to 4 in an opinion by Justice White that a constitutionally invalid Texas jury instruction involved a "new" rule that was therefore not subject to retroactive application in the federal habeas corpus proceeding at issue in the case. The Court based its decision on *Teague v. Lane* (1989), which generally bars federal habeas relief that would "require the announcement of a new rule of constitutional law."[107]

Justice Thomas joined Justice White's majority opinion, but he wrote separately, and again for himself alone, to declare that *Penry v. Lynaugh* (1989) should be overruled. *Penry* held that a capital sentencing jury must be instructed that a defendant's mental retardation could be a mitigating factor in determining punishment.[108] Justice Thomas argued that *Penry* "rendered meaningless any rational standards by which a State may channel or focus the jury's discretion." Why was this a problem, and a problem so serious that a precedent as recently decided as *Penry* should be overruled? Because, Justice Thomas maintained, by expanding the discretion exercised by the capital sentencing jury *Penry* raised anew the "danger of discriminatory sentencing" and thus the potential for discrimination against minority defendants.[109] As was true of his race-conscious separate opinion in *McCollum*, Justice Thomas's race-conscious separate opinion in *Graham* demonstrated that he was more than simply Justice Scalia's loyal apprentice.[110*] Justice Thomas's major First Amendment opinions were written in a similarly independent vein.

First Amendment

The First Amendment was not first. There were two amendments submitted to the states in 1789 that, if ratified, would have preceded what has come to be known as the "First" Amendment.[111] This said, the placement of the First Amendment contributes, at least symbolically, to its importance.

The First Amendment contains four guarantees: religious freedom, free press, free speech, and freedom of assembly and petition. Justice Thomas has issued major opinions concerning the first three guarantees, the ones James Madison referred to as the "equal rights of conscience."[112] This section examines Justice Thomas's major opinions in these areas.

Religious Freedom

The colonists settled America for a variety of reasons. At the top of their list was a desire to escape religious persecution and state churches in England and on the European continent. It is perhaps surprising to note, then, that the colonists themselves were not a tolerant lot. Most of the

---

'This does not mean that Justice Thomas's views about the effects of racial prejudice on the criminal justice system are *correct*. Justice Stevens filed a separate opinion of his own in *Graham* specifically to rebut Justice Thomas's "remarkable suggestion" that *Penry* "somehow threatens what progress we have made in eliminating racial discrimination and other arbitrary sentencing considerations from the capital sentencing determination." *Graham v. Collins*, 506 U.S. 461, 500–4, 501 (Stevens, J., dissenting). See also David O. Stewart, "No Clear Standard," *ABA Journal* 79 (April 1993): 46–9 ("by citing race discrimination in opposing jury instructions that African-American capital defendants have urgently sought, Thomas has contradicted some of the presumptions in this area of the law"). Again, my point is simply that Justice Thomas has *his own* views about the law, that he is not, in other words, merely Justice Scalia's minion.

colonies had an established religion and required holders of public office to adhere to it. Catholics, Jews, atheists, and those who held no religious beliefs were typically excluded from office.

By the time the Constitution was ratified in 1789, religious toleration was becoming more widespread. Virginia, for example, had passed Thomas Jefferson's celebrated "Act for Establishing Religious Freedom" (1785). The Act, which was successfully navigated through the Virginia General Assembly by none other than James Madison, the principal framer of the First Amendment, declared "that no person shall be compelled to frequent or support any religious worship, place, or ministry whatsoever."[113] Still, a number of states continued to have established religions or to favor particular religions after the First Amendment went into effect in 1791. (The Establishment Clause of the First Amendment was not made binding on the states until 1947.)[114]

There are two provisions in the religious freedom guarantee of the First Amendment: the Establishment Clause and the Free Exercise Clause. These provide that the government "shall make no law respecting an establishment of religion, or prohibiting the free exercise thereof." As pointed out in Chapter 2, the members of the Supreme Court long have disagreed about what each of these ambiguous provisions means.[115]

Justice Thomas's major religious freedom opinion came in an Establishment Clause case, *Rosenberger v. University of Virginia* (1995).[116] Few provisions of the Bill of Rights have generated more debate than the Establishment Clause. The two leading views of the Establishment Clause are strict separationism and nonpreferentialism. The strict separationist view is epitomized by Thomas Jefferson's "wall of separation between Church and State" metaphor and was adopted by the Supreme Court in *Everson v. Board of Education* (1947), the first Establishment Clause case of the modern era.[117] The nonpreferentialist view argues against the "hostility" to religion that is alleged to be at the heart of the strict separationist view and has received increasing support in recent years as the Supreme Court has become more conservative.[118] As will now be seen, it is clear beyond cavil to which view Justice Thomas subscribes.

ROSENBERGER V. UNIVERSITY OF VIRGINIA (1995)

The University of Virginia required all students to pay a student activities fee of fourteen dollars per semester during the 1990–91 academic year. The fees were pooled into the Student Activities Fund. Any student group that qualified as a Contracted Independent Organization could submit certain of its bills to be paid out of the Fund. Per University policy, among the eligible student groups were those publishing student magazines and newspapers. Among the ineligible student groups were those participating in religious activities.

Ronald W. Rosenberger, an undergraduate student at the University during the 1990–91 academic year, applied on behalf of Wide Awake Productions for support for a magazine he helped to found, *Wide Awake: A Christian Perspective at the University of Virginia*. Wide Awake's request was denied on the basis that *Wide Awake* was a religious activity. A religious activity was defined by the University as any activity that "primarily promotes or manifests a particular belief in or about a deity or an ultimate reality."

Wide Awake sued. The students who comprised the group alleged that the University's policy of excluding religious activities from Student Activities Fund support "violated their rights to freedom of speech and press, to the free exercise of religion, and to equal protection of the law." The students lost in both the U.S. District Court for the Western District of Virginia and the U.S. Court of Appeals for the Fourth Circuit. The District Court held that the University funding guidelines at issue were reasonable attempts to avoid violating the Establishment Clause of the First Amendment. The Fourth Circuit affirmed, albeit on slightly different grounds. That court held that the University's policy amounted to content discrimination—that is, discrimination against speech because of its subject matter—but that such discrimination was warranted to avoid the unique Establishment Clause dangers inherent in direct state funding of religious activities.

The Supreme Court, in a 5-to-4 decision written by Justice Kennedy, reversed. The decision marked the first time that the Court had approved direct government funding for a religious activity. *Rosenberger* was indeed a landmark ruling. Chief Justice Rehnquist and Justices O'Connor, Scalia, and Thomas joined Justice Kennedy's opinion for the Court. Justices O'Connor and Thomas each wrote concurring opinions. Justice Souter wrote a dissenting opinion, in which he was joined by Justices Stevens, Ginsburg, and Breyer. The spirited nature of the give-and-take that occurred in the opinions, particularly between Justices Thomas and Souter, reveals the deep divisions that exist among the Rehnquist Court justices about the meaning of the Establishment Clause.

Justice Kennedy held in his opinion for the Court that the University's action in denying funds to *Wide Awake* constituted viewpoint discrimination—that is, discrimination because of the speaker's specific motivating ideology, opinion, or perspective—that was not necessary to avoid an Establishment Clause violation. Justice Kennedy recognized that "special Establishment Clause dangers exist where the government makes direct money payments to sectarian institutions," but he concluded that those special dangers were not present with respect to *Wide Awake* because the funding would have been indirect (to the printer) and not direct (to the magazine).[119]

If any area of the law is ripe for an originalist analysis, it is the Establishment Clause. Indeed, arguably the most famous originalist Supreme Court opinion issued in the modern era was then-Justice Rehnquist's dissenting opinion in *Wallace v. Jaffree* (1985). In that case the Court declared unconstitutional by a 6-to-3 vote an Alabama statute authorizing a one-minute period of silence in all public schools for "meditation or prayer."[120] According to Justice Rehnquist, the Court's holding was inconsistent with the historical record—a record that demonstrated, at least to Rehnquist, that the framers of the First Amendment held a nonpreferentialist view of the Establishment Clause.[121]

Justice Thomas paid homage in his concurring opinion in *Rosenberger* to Chief Justice Rehnquist's dissenting opinion in *Jaffree*.[122] Justice Thomas opened his concurring opinion by stating that he was writing separately to "express [his] disagreement with the historical analysis put forward by [Justice Souter's] dissent." Justice Thomas said that he was pleased to see that Justice Souter was employing originalism to answer the question before the Court, but that he was less pleased by the "misleading" nature of Justice Souter's history.[123]

The bulk of Justice Thomas's concurring opinion was devoted to discerning James Madison's church-state views, most notably as articulated in the "Memorial and Remonstrance" of 1784–85 against the proposal of Virginia's House of Delegates to provide, through assessments, for teachers of the Christian religion. In one of the great understatements of the 1994 Supreme Court term, Justice Thomas pointed out that "Legal commentators have disagreed about the historical lesson to take from the Assessment controversy." He cited a book by political scientist Robert L. Cord and a law review article by law professor Rodney K. Smith as support for the nonpreferentialist view, and a law review article by Douglas

Laycock as support for the strict separationist view. He then stated, "I find much to commend the former view."[124]

In Justice Thomas's judgment, what Madison was concerned about in his Remonstrance and in framing the Establishment Clause itself was *direct* government aid to a *favored* religion. Justice Thomas further maintained that Madison's view was widely shared at the Founding, including by Thomas Jefferson, the University of Virginia's "founder and a champion of disestablishment in Virginia." Consequently, Justice Thomas concluded,

> Though our Establishment Clause jurisprudence is in hopeless disarray, this case provides an opportunity to reaffirm one basic principle that has enjoyed an uncharacteristic degree of consensus: The Clause does not compel the exclusion of religious groups from government benefits programs that are generally available to a broad class of participants.[125]

Justice Souter divided his attention in his dissenting opinion between Justice Kennedy's reading of the Court's Establishment Clause precedents and Justice Thomas's reading of history.[126] Justice Souter's views about Justice Kennedy's efforts to distinguish precedents that Justice Souter claimed were "clearly" *against* Wide Awake's position were well captured by a pithy remark near the end of Souter's lengthy disquisition about those precedents: "The formalism of distinguishing between payment to Wide Awake so it can pay an approved bill and payment of the approved bill itself cannot be the basis of a decision of Constitutional Law."[127] Justice Souter's views about Justice Thomas's reading of history were well captured by Souter's favorable citations to scholars who advanced the strict separationist theory: Thomas J. Curry (1986), Douglas Laycock (1985–86), and Leonard W. Levy (1986). Justice Souter wrote: "In attempting to recast Madison's opposition as having principally been targeted against 'governmental preferences for particular religious faiths,' . . . , Justice Thomas wishes to wage a battle that was lost long ago."[128] Justice Souter then went on to revisit the historical record regarding the separation of church and state, much of which he had earlier discussed in his concurring opinion in *Lee v. Weisman* (1992), a case in which the Court declared unconstitutional by a 5-to-4 vote a Rhode Island public school graduation prayer.[129] Like Justice Thomas, Justice Souter paid particular attention to Madison's Remonstrance. Not surprisingly, Justice Souter had a dramatically different take on Madison's views about the separation of church and state. To Justice Thomas, Madison's views were consistent with the nonpreferentialist view of the Establishment Clause. To Justice Souter, they were consistent with the strict separationist view.

There are few issues in American life that generate more controversy and deeply felt emotion than religion. The reaction to the *Rosenberger* decision was further proof of this fact. Conservative Christians hailed *Rosenberger* as a major victory for religious freedom during an era that they claim has been epitomized by government hostility toward religion. Jay Sekulow, who heads religious broadcaster Pat Robertson's American Center for Law and Justice, said the following about the Court's decision in *Rosenberger*: "We have crossed a critical threshold in the fight for religious liberty. The message is clear: Religious speech or speakers must be treated exactly the same way as any other group. The content of that speech does not disqualify them from funding."[130]

Religious groups that favor a strict wall of separation between church and state, in contrast, were alarmed by the Court's decision. J. Brent Walker, general counsel for the Baptist Joint Committee on Public Affairs, declared: "This is a sad day for religious liberty. For the first time in our nation's history, the Supreme Court has sanctioned funding of religion with public funds. Our founders understood that, for religion to be meaningful it must be voluntary, freed from government assistance and control."[131]

With respect specifically to Justice Thomas, conservative commentators applauded his originalist concurring opinion in the case, while liberal commentators castigated it. From the right, Jeremy Rabkin wrote in the *American Spectator* that opinions such as this one revealed that Justice Thomas was now "the Court's sturdiest and often most incisive conservative voice."[132] From the left, Edd Doerr wrote in the *Humanist* that "Thomas' concurring opinion was a broad attack on the traditional understanding of church-state separation. Had Marshall not been replaced by a third rate ultraconservative, *Rosenberger* would have gone the other way."[133]

Much of the academic commentary concerning *Rosenberger* centered on the Rehnquist Court's continuing disregard of *Lemon v. Kurtzman*, the 1971 Burger Court precedent used for years to evaluate Establishment Clause cases.[134] (Under the so-called "*Lemon* test," if a law or government program is to avoid violating the Establishment Clause: (1) it must have a secular purpose, (2) its primary effect must neither advance nor inhibit religion, and (3) it must avoid excessive government entanglement with religion.) Some, however, took a less doctrinal approach. John O. McGinnis, a conservative law professor at Benjamin N. Cardozo School of Law who previously had served in the U.S. Department of Justice under presidents Reagan and Bush, wrote an essay in *Policy Review* comparing Justice Thomas's and Justice Souter's 1994 term performances.* McGinnis concluded that Justice Thomas's opinions in the 1994 term, of which *Rosenberger* was a major part, "represent the most impressive set of originalist opinions ever written by a Supreme Court justice within a single term." McGinnis was particularly impressed by Justice Thomas's ability in *Rosenberger* to "strip" the strict separationist view of the "patina of historical legitimacy Souter tried to give it." McGinnis declared that Justice Souter's dissenting opinion in the case was more about "the liberal establishment that educated him" than it was about the Framers' original intentions.[135]

From the left came two revealing essays. One was by Elliot M. Mincberg, the legal director of the People for the American Way, the public interest group that did as much as anyone to try to defeat Clarence Thomas's nomination to the Supreme Court.[136] Mincberg declared that Justice Thomas's concurring opinion "shows that he is ready to dramatically depart from existing Establishment Clause jurisprudence." He also warned that Justice Thomas's "radical reading" of history "would apparently permit direct government funding of religious institutions, including schools."[137] The left, of course, strongly opposes public funding of private religious schools.

Suzanna Sherry, a prominent liberal law professor at the University of Minnesota, was less concerned about commenting upon Justice Thomas's "radical reading" of history than she was about using *Rosenberger* to show "the indeterminacy of historical evidence" itself, and hence the futility of originalism as a method by which to interpret the Constitution. Her principal point was that since academic lawyers and political scientists disagree about what the historical record has to say about Establishment Clause questions such as that raised by *Rosenberger*, Supreme Court justices such as Clarence Thomas should stop trying to find out. Professional historians, Sherry insisted, figured this out a long time ago.[138]

*I was unable to find a law review article written about *Rosenberger* from a conservative perspective. Hence, my use of McGinnis's *Policy Review* essay.

Professional historians likely would quarrel with Sherry's characterization of what they do for a living. After all, if historians really thought that history was "indeterminate" they would call the books and articles they write fiction rather than nonfiction.* It is true that some historians caution against using history to decide Supreme Court cases,[139] but that does not mean that history has nothing to say to Supreme Court justices about the *principles* that should guide their decisionmaking. That, at least, is what the debate over original intent suggests to me.[140]

What principles are those? They are the natural rights principles of the Declaration of Independence. Justice Thomas appeared to be aware of this fact when he wrote in his concurring opinion in *Rosenberger* that "even if extreme notions of the separation of church and state can be attributed to Madison, many of them clearly stem from 'arguments reflecting the concepts of natural law, natural rights, and the social contract between government and a civil society.'"[141]

Madison was not alone in emphasizing natural rights principles in his arguments concerning the relationship between church and state. This is how Jefferson concluded the Act for Establishing Religious Freedom:

> III. And though we well know that this assembly elected by the people for the ordinary purposes of legislation only, have no power to restrain the acts of succeeding assemblies, constituted with powers equal to our own, and that therefore to declare this act to be irrevocable would be of no effect in law; yet we are free to declare, and do declare, that the rights hereby asserted are of the natural rights of mankind, and that if any act shall be hereafter passed to repeal the present, or to narrow its operation, such act will be an infringement of natural right.[142]

Clearly, though, Justice Thomas decided to forego in *Rosenberger* the liberal originalist approach of his race opinions[143]—an approach that emphasizes the *principles* to which the Founders dedicated the nation—

---

*Sherry herself has written several historical analyses of the Constitution. Her most well known is Suzanna Sherry, "The Founders' Unwritten Constitution," *University of Chicago Law Review* 54 (fall 1987): 1127–77. See also Daniel A. Farber and Suzanna Sherry, *History of the American Constitution* (St. Paul, MN: West, 1990). Sherry's argument about historical indeterminacy is also inconsistent with the thesis of her 1997 book, cowritten with Farber: that truth *is* determinate. See Daniel A. Farber and Suzanna Sherry, *Beyond All Reason: The Radical Assault on Truth in American Law* (New York: Oxford University Press, 1997). Although Sherry and Farber focus their attention in *Beyond All Reason* on "radical multiculturalists" (e.g., Critical Race Theorists, feminist legal theorists) rather than on conservative originalists, one of their most powerful arguments is that history is *not* a social construct—that, in other words, we can know what it was.

and to adopt a more traditional conservative originalist approach when deciding that the University of Virginia should not be allowed to deny funding to *Wide Awake*. A liberal originalist would have decided the case the other way. As I have suggested elsewhere, the principle at the heart of the Establishment Clause is the natural right to freedom of conscience,[144] a principle that John Locke explained well in his "Letter Concerning Toleration" (1689). Locke wrote: "I esteem it above all things necessary to distinguish exactly the business of civil government and that of religion, and to settle the just bounds that lie between the one and the other." The "commonwealth" or political community, Locke continued, is "a society of men constituted only for procuring, preserving, and advancing their own civil interests." "Civil interests" are "life, liberty, health, and indolency of body; and the possession of outward things, such as money, lands, houses, furniture and the like." The "care of souls," in contrast, is a private affair of individual conscience between a man and his God, and churches, the "outward regiment of religion," are private associations that are utterly divergent from the state.[145]

To make the point directly, the Founders may have been less dedicated to the *practice* of strict separationism than they were to the *principle* of it—a number of states, as noted earlier, had established religions or favored particular religions after the First Amendment went into effect—but that is of no consequence to a liberal originalist. Indeed, Locke himself—the natural rights theorist upon whom the Founders most relied*—sometimes took *partisan* positions that were inconsistent with the *philosophical* principles he articulated in his political philosophy: for example, he exempted atheists and Roman Catholics from toleration by the state.[146]

Freedom of the Press

I title this section "Freedom of the Press" because that was how Justice Thomas classified the case to be discussed here, *McIntyre v. Ohio Elections*

---

*Michael W. McConnell, a leading conservative law professor who specializes in religious freedom questions and who represented Wide Awake in *Rosenberger*, acknowledged in a law review article that the Founders subscribed to Locke's views on toleration. See Michael W. McConnell, "Establishment and Toleration in Edmund Burke's 'Constitution of Freedom,'" in *1995 Supreme Court Review*, ed. Dennis J. Hutchinson, David A. Strauss, and Geoffrey R. Stone (Chicago: University of Chicago Press, 1996), 393–462, 440–5. As a lawyer representing a client, however, McConnell argued that Wide Awake should be funded.

Commission (1995).[147] This is largely a procedural point, however, because the Court has not distinguished between "press" and "speech" in most areas of First Amendment law, including anonymous political writing, which is what *McIntyre* was about. Bill F. Chamberlin made the point well in a prescient 1992 essay: "The Supreme Court has not clearly differentiated the terms 'speech' and 'press' at least in part because of the practical difficulty of distinguishing which of the two protections might apply to a given circumstance. Should the pamphleteer be considered a speaker or a member of the press?"[148]

The language of the First Amendment is absolute on the protection to be afforded: The government "shall make no law . . . abridging the freedom . . . of the press."[149] However, it has been a rare member of the Supreme Court (Hugo Black is one) who has read the Free Press Clause to mean what it literally says, and the Framers almost certainly did not intend to protect *all* press speech. Indeed, one of the most famous, or better still, *in*famous, federal statutes in American history was the Sedition Act of 1798, which made it a crime to "write, print, or publish . . . any false, scandalous and malicious" statement against the government.[150] This said, we should not forget that a torrent of public outcry arose against that politically inspired attempt to silence the (opposition) press, and the law expired a scant three years after it was enacted when government power switched from Federalist to Republican hands.

If "no" law does not mean *no* law, then what does it mean? Many landmark Supreme Court cases have grappled with precisely this question. The justices, of course, often have disagreed about the answer, but the press, for the most part, has fared well in the Marble Palace. Few would dispute the statement that the press in the United States is freer than it is anywhere else in the world. The Court has played a large role in this, and the late Justice William J. Brennan, Jr., explained why the Court has done so in perhaps the most important of his many watershed opinions: his opinion for the Court in *New York Times v. Sullivan* (1964). In now-classic language, Justice Brennan wrote that the Free Press Clause registers "a profound national commitment to the principle that debate on public issues should be uninhibited, robust, and wide-open, and that it may well include vehement, caustic, and sometimes unpleasantly sharp attacks on government and public officials."[151] The Rehnquist Court's decision in *McIntyre* is consistent with this widely shared view.

MCINTYRE V. OHIO ELECTIONS COMMISSION (1995)

A referendum was placed before the voters of Westerville, Ohio, in 1988 regarding a proposed school tax levy. Margaret McIntyre opposed the tax levy. She composed, printed, and distributed a leaflet to express her opposition. The leaflet contained no personal attacks and was not even arguably libelous. McIntyre signed the leaflet "Concerned Parents and Taxpayers."

Several persons knew that McIntyre was the author of the anonymous leaflet. One such person was a Westerville school district official who supported the tax levy. The school official filed a complaint with the Ohio Elections Commission in which he charged that McIntyre had violated an Ohio statute that prohibited the distribution of anonymous campaign literature. The Elections Commission agreed and imposed a one-hundred-dollar fine. McIntyre sued, alleging that her First Amendment rights were violated. The Franklin County Court of Common Pleas agreed with her. Both the Ohio Court of Appeals and the Ohio Supreme Court did not, and the Elections Commission's decision was reinstated on the basis that the state had an interest in banning anonymous speech during election campaigns so that it would be possible to hold accountable disseminators of false statements.

The U.S. Supreme Court in a 7-to-2 decision reversed. Justice Stevens wrote the opinion for the Court, in which Justices O'Connor, Kennedy, Souter, Ginsburg, and Breyer joined. Justice Thomas concurred in the result, but not in the reasoning of Justice Stevens's opinion, and he issued a lengthy separate opinion to explain his views about why McIntyre's fine should be overturned. Justice Ginsburg issued a short concurring opinion of her own. Justice Scalia filed a lengthy dissenting opinion, in which he was joined by Chief Justice Rehnquist.

In his opinion for the Court, Justice Stevens analyzed the Ohio election law at issue in terms of free speech. He wrote for the majority that a flat ban on anonymous political speech during an election campaign such as that contained in the Ohio statute violated the First Amendment. He agreed that a state could outlaw false and defamatory speech during an election campaign, but maintained that a broad prophylactic rule such as Ohio's swept too broadly. "One would be hard pressed to think of a better example of the pitfalls of Ohio's blunderbuss approach than the facts of the case before us," Justice Stevens wrote. "The speech in which

Mrs. McIntyre engaged—handing out leaflets in the advocacy of a politically controversial viewpoint—is the essence of First Amendment expression." Justice Stevens justified the Court's decision by pointing to the "honorable tradition" of anonymous speech that has existed throughout American history, both in politics and in literature, and to the "value" that anonymous speech brings to public discourse.[152]

Justice Thomas's opinion concurring in the judgment in *McIntyre* was arguably the most explicitly originalist opinion he issued during his acclimation period on the Supreme Court.[153] He opened his opinion by declaring that he would apply a "different methodology" to the case than Justice Stevens had applied in his opinion for the Court. Justice Thomas wrote:

> Instead of asking whether "an honorable tradition" of anonymous speech has existed throughout American history or what the "value" of anonymous speech might be, we should determine whether the phrase "freedom of speech, or of the press," as originally understood, protected anonymous political leafletting.[154]

Justice Thomas then went on to quote a series of Supreme Court opinions in support of his originalist methodology, including one by Justice Brennan, who was widely regarded as the leading *opponent* of conservative originalism.[155] The irony of referring to Justice Brennan as an originalist is difficult to miss, although Justice Thomas is not alone in missing it.[156]

Methodology established, Justice Thomas turned to the historical record regarding anonymous political writing. He mentioned that there was "no record" of any discussions about anonymous political writing in the First Congress when the Bill of Rights was being drafted or in the states when it was being ratified. "Thus," he stated, "our analysis must focus on the practices and beliefs held by the Founders" about the matter. As the classic collections of pamphlets compiled by Bernard Bailyn and Paul L. Ford about, respectively, the American Revolution and the Constitution made clear, Justice Thomas maintained, there was "little doubt" that the Founders engaged in anonymous political writing.[157]

The Federalist—published under the pseudonym "Publius" and aimed at persuading the people of New York and, to a lesser degree, the other states, to ratify the Constitution—is the most obvious example of anonymous political writing by early Americans, but there are others. Justice Thomas discussed four other well-known examples: (1) the 1735 trial of

John Peter Zenger for seditious libel against the royal governor of New York, which centered around anonymous political pamphlets; (2) "Leonidas's" 1779 article in the Pennsylvania Packet attacking the members of the Continental Congress for allegedly causing inflation throughout the states and for allegedly engaging in embezzlement and fraud; (3) "Cincinnatus's" 1779 pamphlet satirizing the governor of New Jersey and the College of New Jersey; and (4) a 1784 four-part series of articles by the governor of New Jersey, written under the pseudonym of "Scipio," defending the right to publish anonymously as part of the freedom of the press.

Justice Thomas also discussed at length the ratification-era controversy over prominent Federalist newspaper editor Benjamin Russell's *refusal* to publish Anti-Federalist articles unless the author was willing to waive anonymity. Justice Thomas emphasized that Anti-Federalist writers had attacked Russell's policy, that they had done so anonymously, and that they had done so with success. To Justice Thomas, this suggested that the right to publish anonymously was included in the Founders' conception of freedom of the press. Justice Thomas wrote:

> When Federalist attempts to ban anonymity are followed by a sharp, widespread Anti-Federalist defense in the name of freedom of the press, and then by an open Federalist retreat on the issue, I must conclude that both Anti-Federalists and Federalists believed that the freedom of the press included the right to publish without revealing the author's name.[158]

Indeed, Justice Thomas continued, "only two major Federalist or Anti-Federalist pieces appear to have been signed by their true authors, and they may have had special reasons for doing so."[159]

Justice Thomas also devoted considerable space in his concurring opinion to explaining *why* the Founders thought it important to protect anonymous political writing. He concluded that it was to protect the author and to impart a message. The first reason is obvious; the second is less so. But if one recalls that the political class at the Founding was steeped in the classics to an extent that would make Newt Gingrich proud,[160] it makes sense. Historical names such as "Publius" and "Cato" meant something to the Founders, as did descriptive names such as "Common Sense" and "An American Citizen."

Justice Thomas concluded his lengthy concurring opinion by addressing a concern that Justice Scalia raised in his dissenting opinion: that the Court in *McIntyre* was overturning "a century of practice shared by almost all of the States." Justice Thomas stated that he was "loath" to join such a sweeping decision, but that the "historical evidence from the framing outweighs recent tradition."[161]

Justice Scalia devoted much of his dissenting opinion to rebutting Justice Thomas's reading of history.[162] To Justice Scalia and Chief Justice Rehnquist (who joined the former's dissenting opinion), the historical record was ambiguous about whether the Framers intended to protect anonymous political writing in the First Amendment. As such, the dissenting justices concluded, the benefit of the doubt should be given to the judgment of forty-nine states, the District of Columbia, and the national government that anonymous speech during political campaigns was too risky to permit.

Justice Scalia chastised Justice Thomas for conflating two separate issues: (1) that anonymous electioneering was used during the Founding, and (2) that the Framers considered anonymous electioneering to be a constitutional right. Justice Scalia agreed that Justice Thomas had established issue (1), but he rejected Thomas's contention that, in the absence of framing and ratification debates on the matter, issue (1) had anything to say about issue (2). Apparently, for Justice Scalia and Chief Justice Rehnquist, the Framers' intent was reflected *only* in the text of a particular provision and, if the text was unclear, in the specific legislative debates about what that provision meant to them. In the absence of such evidence, the dissenting justices maintained, the Court must consult the "long-accepted practices of the American people."[163] In *McIntyre*, then, Justice Scalia and Chief Justice Rehnquist were at once more *strict* than Justice Thomas was about what originalism was, and at the same time more willing to abandon originalism for an alternative interpretive methodology—in their case, some sort of Burkean "conventionalism" in which the meaning of a particular provision of the Constitution is defined by the consensus view of the existing political community.[164]

McIntyre was not as "spicy" a case as most of the others discussed in this book, so there was not as much reaction to it as there was to some of the others. The decision did capture the attention of two of the nation's most respected journalists, however: David S. Broder of the *Washington Post* and Linda Greenhouse of the *New York Times*. Broder focused on the adverse impact the decision likely would have on the political process. In a surprisingly caustic (for him) op-ed, he wrote: "It is presumably not the purpose of the Supreme Court to screw up the political process in this country worse than it is already. But if the learned justices had that intent, they could not be doing a better job." What concerned Broder most about *McIntyre* was the increase in character attacks that likely would result from the Court's decision to protect anonymous pamphleteering. To Broder, substantive discussions about the issues were already an anomaly in American electoral politics. *McIntyre* would just make matters worse.[165]

Whereas Broder focused on the Court's *decision* in *McIntyre*, Greenhouse focused on the various *opinions* in the case. She was especially intrigued by the contrasting views of Justices Thomas and Scalia—particularly as they pertained to the *methodology* by which the two conservative justices insisted the case be decided. Greenhouse emphasized that Justices Thomas and Scalia were both typically proponents of the sort of "historical inquiry" in which Thomas engaged in his concurring opinion, "and the two nearly always reach the same outcome in constitutional cases." "For that reason," she continued, "the difference between them today was particularly interesting."[166]

The methodological dispute between Justices Thomas and Scalia also captured the attention of scholars who commented upon the case. Surprisingly, Justice Thomas fared better with liberals than he did with conservatives in this regard. From the left, Melvin I. Urofsky, a prolific legal historian at Virginia Commonwealth University, *defended* Justice Thomas's reading of history. Urofsky wrote:

> [In *McIntyre*], two justices who often appear joined at the hip, Antonin Scalia and Clarence Thomas, disagreed. Scalia dissented, and claimed that history supported state laws prohibiting anonymous political writings. Thomas, I believe, got the better of the argument in his concurrence, in which he noted that the *Federalist Papers*, the second holiest document in the ark of the originalists, were published under a pseudonym.[167]

One should not make too much of Urofsky's defense of Justice Thomas's *McIntyre* opinion. Indeed, the thesis of the essay in which Urofsky made these remarks was the standard liberal thesis about originalism: originalist judges are result-oriented historians. In short, Urofsky "defended" Justice Thomas *not* because he *agreed* with Justice Thomas's methodology, but rather because he *disagreed* with it. Perhaps this explains Urofsky's curious claim that Justice Scalia was using originalism in his *McIntyre* dissent, when he was actually using conventionalism.

From the right came *criticism* of Justice Thomas's *McIntyre* concurring opinion—specifically from Thomas W. Merrill, a conservative law professor at Northwestern University. Merrill issued his criticism in a 1996 Federalist Society symposium on originalism. He accused Justice Thomas of being inconsistent, pointing out that Thomas appealed to history in one case, *McIntyre*, but ignored it in another case decided on the same day, *Rubin v. Coors Brewing Company* (1995).[168]

At first blush, Merrill offers a devastating criticism of Justice Thomas's jurisprudence. Upon closer inspection, however, it appears likely that Merrill's criticism of Justice Thomas's apparent methodological inconsistency was inspired by Merrill's interest in advancing *his own* conservative alternative to originalism: Burkean conventionalism. After all, what better way to suggest that *your* theory should be adopted than by raising doubts about how the preferred (conservative) alternative is applied by the leading proponent of that theory. (Merrill identified Robert Bork as the leading intellectual proponent of originalism and Justice Thomas as its leading Supreme Court proponent.) Bluntly stated, by making Justice Thomas look bad, Merrill was able to make his own alternative methodology look that much better. This red flag raised, what could explain Justice Thomas's apparent inconsistency in *Rubin*? It is that question that the final section in this chapter is designed to answer.

Freedom of Speech

Freedom of speech long has been regarded as one of the "preferred freedoms":[169] one of the freedoms that the Supreme Court deems "implicit in the concept of ordered liberty."[170] However, "commercial" speech (e.g., an advertisement promoting the sale of goods or services) has received less protection by the Court than other types of speech, most notably "political" speech (e.g., an election campaign stump speech). Alex Kozinski, a prominent conservative U.S. Court of Appeals judge, sometimes jokes, "Nobody likes commercial speech. Liberals don't like it because it's commercial. Conservatives don't like it because it's speech."[171] As will be seen, the Rehnquist Court is on the verge of changing the level of protection afforded to commercial speech, and Justice Thomas is pushing harder than any other member of the Court for that change.

A number of theories have been advanced by academics to explain why commercial speech deserves less protection than other types of speech (e.g., it is not about politics, art, or science),[172] but no one ever really has explained why the *Supreme Court* came to view commercial speech as deserving less protection—and in 1942 of *no* protection—than other speech. In fact, one of the best known articles on the subject, Alex Kozinski and Stuart Banner's "The Anti-History and Pre-History of Commercial Speech"—suggested that *Valentine v. Chrestensen* (1942) just kind of happened.[173]

Doctrinally, *Valentine* was the watershed. In that case a businessman claimed that a city ordinance that made it illegal to distribute commercial and business ads in the streets violated his right to freedom of speech. In a two-and-a-half-page opinion for a unanimous Court that amounted to little more than an assertion, Justice Owen Roberts disagreed. He wrote:

> This court has unequivocally held that streets are proper places for the exercise of the freedom of communicating information and disseminating opinion and that, though the states and municipalities may appropriately regulate the privilege in the public interest, they may not unduly burden or proscribe its employment in these public thoroughfares. We are equally clear that the Constitution imposes no such restraint on government as respects purely commercial advertising.[174]

During the 1970s, the Court changed direction a bit and began to protect commercial speech that did more than simply propose a commercial transaction. The landmark case in this regard was *Virginia State Board of Pharmacy v. Virginia Citizens Consumer Council* (1976), wherein the Court, in an 8-to-1 decision written by Justice Blackmun, declared unconstitutional a state statute that banned the advertisement of prescription drug prices.[175] The Court emphasized that information about the price of prescription drugs was vital to the public. However, the Court also emphasized that deceptive or misleading advertising, even if not false, did not serve any social interest and could be regulated. In short, the Court held that commercial speech was entitled to *some* First Amendment protection, but not as much as noncommercial speech. The Court listed in a footnote several "common-sense differences" between commercial and noncommercial speech, but these, too, were little more than assertions (e.g., that commercial speech is more verifiable than noncommercial speech).[176]

In 1980 the Court announced its much-anticipated test for determining whether government regulations impermissibly infringed upon the First Amendment right of commercial speech. The case was *Central Hudson Gas v. Public Service Commission of New York* (1980); the decision was 5 to 4; the issue was certain advertising by utilities; and the test made clear that the Court continued to believe that commercial speech deserved less protection than noncommercial speech. Under *Central Hudson* the Court must decide: (1) whether the speech concerns lawful activity and is not misleading, (2) whether the asserted governmental interest is substantial, (3) whether the regulation directly advances the governmental interest, and (4) whether less restrictive means of advancing the governmental interest exist.[177] Clearly, this test is less protective of commercial speech than traditional First Amendment analysis is of noncommercial speech. For instance, there is no requirement under traditional First Amendment analysis that the speech not be false or misleading—"there is no such thing as a false idea," as the saying goes—but there is under *Central Hudson*.

The Court spent the decade and a half between *Central Hudson* and *44 Liquormart, Inc. v. State of Rhode Island* (1996)[178]—the case in which Justice Thomas articulated his position on the First Amendment protection that should be afforded to commercial speech—applying the *Central Hudson* test to a variety of commercial speech questions. The two most important cases were *Posadas de Puerto Rico v. Tourism Company* (1986) and *Rubin v. Coors Brewing Company* (1995). *Posadas* was important because the Court, in a 5-to-4 decision written by then-Justice Rehnquist (the lone dissenter in *Virginia Pharmacy*, the prescription-drug pricing case), appeared to depart from *Central Hudson* while ostensibly adhering to it. That is to say, the Court not only upheld Puerto Rico's sweeping ban on casino advertising—a lawful activity in Puerto Rico—but also offered an alternative analysis that, if adopted in later cases, might have excluded nearly all commercial expression from First Amendment protection.[179] *Coors* was important, in contrast, because the Court, in a nearly unanimous opinion by Justice Thomas, engaged in a straightforward application of the *Central Hudson* test in striking down a federal regulation that prohibited beer labels from displaying alcohol content.[180]

Only one year later the renewed consensus about *Central Hudson* that made *Coors* so important was broken, but not in the manner in which *Posadas* suggested it might be. The case was *44 Liquormart*, arguably the most significant commercial speech case since *Virginia Pharmacy*.

44 LIQUORMART, INC. V. STATE OF RHODE ISLAND (1996)

In 1956 Rhode Island adopted two statutes that forbade sellers and the media from advertising the price of alcoholic beverages. The avowed purpose of the legislation was to promote temperance by increasing the price of alcohol. The statutes were upheld by the Rhode Island state courts in 1985.[181]

In early 1992, 44 Liquormart, a Rhode Island retail store that sold alcoholic beverages, and Peoples Super Liquor Stores, a Massachusetts retailer that wished to advertise in Rhode Island, mounted a new challenge to the statutes, this time in federal court. The U.S. District Court for the District of Rhode Island held that the advertising ban violated the retailers' free speech rights. The U.S. Court of Appeals for the First Circuit reversed. Applying *Central Hudson*, the First Circuit held that the requisite degree of fit existed between the statutes and the underlying state interest in reducing alcohol consumption. The First Circuit further held that the Twenty-First Amendment (1933), which repealed the Eighteenth Amendment's (1919) prohibition of alcohol but which also gave the states the power to regulate the use of and commerce in alcoholic beverages within their respective borders, entitled the statutes to a special presumption of validity.

The Supreme Court reversed 9 to 0. However, as is so often true in major cases during the modern era, the justices were divided in their reasoning—especially as to what test to apply. Chief Justice Rehnquist and Justices O'Connor, Souter, and Breyer maintained that *Central Hudson* provided the relevant test.[182] Justice Scalia agreed—for the moment.[183] Justices Stevens, Kennedy, and Ginsburg argued that a blanket ban on a particular type of commercial speech must be reviewed with "special care" and cannot be approved unless the speech is misleading or related to an illegal activity.[184] Justice Thomas called for the abandonment of the distinction between commercial and noncommercial speech, at least when the objective of the government regulation in question was to manipulate consumer preferences about lawful products.[185]

The two most interesting opinions were written by Justices Scalia and Thomas. Justice Scalia's concurring opinion is fairly characterized as an extension of his dissenting opinion in *McIntyre*. As he did in *McIntyre*, Justice Scalia in *44 Liquormart* called for the Court to resort to some sort of Burkean conventionalism—to appeal to "the long accepted practices of the American people"—when the Constitution's text and history provided no clear answer to the question at bar. Unlike in *McIntyre*, however, Justice Scalia in *44 Liquormart* was unable to discern what those long-accepted practices were. As a result, he grudgingly applied the *Central Hudson* test to the facts of the case, and expressed hope that those long-accepted practices would be fleshed out in a future case.[186]

Justice Thomas, in contrast, refused to apply *Central Hudson*, at least on facts like those before the Court in *44 Liquormart*: when "the government's asserted interest is to keep legal users of a product or a service ignorant in order to manipulate their choices in the marketplace." Justice Thomas quoted extensively from *Virginia Pharmacy* to make clear that he believed the Court first recognized the importance of protecting commercial speech because of the inappropriateness of "paternalism" in a "free market economy." *Central Hudson* and the Court's other post–*Virginia Pharmacy* commercial speech decisions were inconsistent with this underlying rationale, he maintained.[187]

As is his practice in civil liberties cases, Justice Thomas turned to originalism to make his affirmative case. Although his historiography was far less detailed in *44 Liquormart* than it was in the vast majority of his civil liberties opinions, he concluded that there was no "philosophical or historical basis for asserting that 'commercial' speech is of 'lower value' than 'noncommercial' speech. Indeed some historical materials suggest to the contrary." Consequently, he concluded, the Court should seriously consider dropping the distinction altogether, since the "Framers' political philosophy equated liberty and property and did not distinguish between commercial and noncommercial speech."[188]*

Most of the commentary from the liberal side of the popular press was consistent with Alex Kozinski's retort about liberals disliking commercial speech because it involves commerce. The best illustration of this was David G. Savage's *Los Angeles Times* article "First Amendment Rulings Are out of Order, Liberals Complain." In that article Savage reported how liberals were "none too happy" about the Rehnquist Court's recent free speech decisions, including those involving commercial speech. "Dismayed by these decisions, some dedicated liberals are having second thoughts about how their favorite constitutional amendment is being used," Savage wrote. Savage quoted Burt Neuborne, a New York University law professor and the former director of the American Civil Liberties Union, as "complaining," "Now it's the favorite argument for corporations and advertisers."[189]

Kozinski's retort that conservatives dislike commercial speech because it involves speech did not hold true, however. In fact, there was near eu-

---

*Justice Thomas did not say in *44 Liquormart* that the distinction between commercial and noncommercial speech should be eliminated in all cases. He limited himself to the facts before him: nonmisleading advertising about a lawful activity. However, he did appear willing to consider the "categorical" step in a future case. *44 Liquormart, Inc. v. State of Rhode Island*, 116 S.Ct. 1495, 1515–20, 1518 n. 18, 1520 (Thomas, J., concurring in part and concurring in the judgment). He also called for the overruling of *Posadas*. Justices Stevens, Kennedy, and Ginsburg did as well.

phoria about *44 Liquormart* in conservative circles. For instance, Wall Street attorney Jerome L. Wilson penned a lengthy op-ed for the American Lawyer Newspaper Group as "a toast" to *44 Liquormart*. Wilson was particularly taken with Justice Thomas's opinion in that case. He called Justice Thomas the "new champion of commercial speech" and the one member of the Court who appeared to recognize what the political branches were "up to" when they passed laws limiting commercial speech rather than restricting conduct: "covertly" attempting to change consumer behavior because they did not have the political support to do it "openly." Interestingly, Wilson closed his op-ed with a retort that was the flip-side of Kozinski's: "Again, it is worth noting that *44 Liquormart* is a 9-to-0 decision. One could suggest that this unanimity exists because, when it comes to commercial speech, the liberals on the Court believe in free speech and the conservatives believe in free markets."[190]

At this writing, *44 Liquormart* is too recent a decision (May 1996) for there to have been much discussion of it in the law reviews. From the left, Martin H. Redish, a law professor at Northwestern University who claims to have been the "first" person on record to call for First Amendment protection of commercial speech, applauded the Court's decision in general and Justice Thomas's concurring opinion in particular.[191] Why would a liberal law professor applaud a pro–commercial speech decision?[*] It is impossible to know for sure, but perhaps it has something to do with Redish's long-standing intellectual commitment to the issue. Indeed, Redish's 1971 law review article advocating First Amendment protection for commercial speech antedated the Court's *Virginia Pharmacy* decision by five years. A close reading of Redish's article about *44 Liquormart* suggests that this is the case. As Redish wrote in a stinging passage directed at those legal academics who continue to relegate commercial speech to "second class status":

> Most of these attacks [on commercial speech]—much like similar attacks against obscenity protection—may be deconstructed into little more than a result-oriented attempt to stifle advocacy of a particular ideological perspective or point of view. The First Amendment guarantee cannot be allowed to be manipulated in such a manner, if it is not to degenerate into

[*]Kathleen M. Sullivan pointed out that both conservatives and liberals were divided among themselves about whether commercial speech should be protected by the First Amendment. Kathleen M. Sullivan, "Cheap Spirits, Cigarettes, and Free Speech: The Implications of *44 Liquormart*," in *1996 Supreme Court Review*, ed. Dennis J. Hutchinson, David A. Strauss, and Geoffrey R. Stone (Chicago: University of Chicago Press, 1997), 123–61, 129–30.

nothing more than a manipulative tool of those who exercise political power.[192]

It should come as no surprise to learn, then, that Redish was particularly impressed by Justice Thomas's concurring opinion.[193] In fact, Redish offered no real criticism of Justice Thomas's analysis. The opinions of Justices Stevens, O'Connor, and Scalia did not fare nearly as well in Redish's article.

A search for reaction to *44 Liquormart* from the political right of the academic community leads back to Merrill's article calling for a conservative alternative to conservative originalism. Readers will recall that Merrill accused Justice Thomas of inconsistency for employing conservative originalism in an Establishment Clause case but not in a commercial speech case decided on the same day. Merrill failed to note, however, that Justice Thomas's opinion in the commercial speech case at issue, *Rubin v. Coors Brewing Company* (1995), was the opinion for the Court, and that he therefore had to be sensitive to making an argument to which the other members of the majority were willing to subscribe. If their votes in *44 Liquormart* tell us anything, it is that Chief Justice Rehnquist and Justices O'Connor, Souter, and Breyer would be unlikely candidates to join any commercial speech opinion that did much more than apply *Central Hudson*, which was what Justice Thomas did in his opinion for the Court in *Rubin*.

Moreover, if Merrill could have waited until after *44 Liquormart* to call Justice Thomas's commitment to conservative originalism into question, he would have had a more difficult argument to make. After all, Justice Thomas appealed to conservative originalism in his separate opinion in that case. It is probably unfair to fault Merrill for failing to predict the future. It is fair, however, to fault him for misrepresenting the original understanding of the First Amendment. Merrill wrote:

> Justice Thomas relied on precedent [when] extending the First Amendment to commercial speech [in *Rubin*], and made no attempt to explain why the original meaning of the First Amendment was not controlling. In fact, the original understanding of the First Amendment almost surely was that it did not extend to commercial advertising. See *Valentine v. Chrestensen*, 316 U.S. 52 (1942) (stating, in the Court's first confrontation with the issue, that the First Amendment is not implicated by restrictions on commercial advertising).[194]

Valentine said *nothing* about original intent. Justice Roberts's unanimous opinion for the Court in that case simply *asserted* that commercial speech* was entitled to no First Amendment protection. Justice Thomas maintained in *44 Liquormart* that conservative originalism required the opposite conclusion. Justice Stevens appeared to agree. Justice Scalia did not.[195]

A liberal originalist would find that commercial speech is entitled to the same First Amendment protection as any other form of speech, including political speech. One does not need to go as far as Charles A. Beard did[196] to appreciate that the Founders cared about property and erected the Constitution to protect it (as well as other rights). To paraphrase Learned Hand, a leading critic of protecting economic rights less vigorously than "personal" rights such as political speech: Just why commercial speech is not full-blown speech, no member of the Supreme Court has taken the time to explain.[197] Justice Thomas got it right when he observed in *44 Liquormart* that the Founders' "political philosophy equated liberty and property." To mention but two leading statements of this view, James Madison wrote in *The Federalist* No. 10 that "the first object of government" is "the protection of different and unequal faculties of acquiring property"[198] and John Adams maintained in *Discourses on Davila* that "property must be secured, or liberty cannot exist."[199] In addition, the Lockean trinity of "life, liberty, and property" is written into the Fifth and Fourteenth Amendments to the Constitution itself. Apparently, then, the subordination of commercial speech to noncommercial speech—like the subordination of economic rights to "personal" rights in general—in the hierarchy of judicial protection has been a political decision by Supreme Court justices who prefer speech about politics, art, or science to speech about commerce.

Conclusion

This chapter has addressed a variety of seemingly disparate civil liberties matters: cruel and unusual punishment, habeas corpus, the separation of

---

*Justice Roberts actually called it "advertising." The term "commercial speech" was first used by U.S. Court of Appeals Judge J. Skelly Wright in a 1971 opinion. See *Business Executives' Move for Vietnam Peace v. FCC*, 450 F.2d 642, 658 n. 38 (D.C. Cir. 1971), rev'd sub nom., *CBS, Inc. v. Democratic National Committee*, 412 U.S. 94 (1973).

church and state, anonymous political writing, and commercial speech. However, several common themes emerge as far as Justice Thomas's jurisprudence is concerned. First, the reaction to Justice Thomas's civil liberties jurisprudence was as political as was the reaction to his civil rights jurisprudence: with the possible exception of the commercial speech area, liberals criticized Justice Thomas's opinions and conservatives complimented them. Second, and related to the first, with the exception of the anonymous political writing case, Justice Thomas reached politically conservative results in the civil liberties cases in which he wrote an opinion—more conservative than even Justice Scalia. Third, and related to the second, Justice Thomas almost always wrote for himself alone in the civil liberties area, a state of affairs that calls into serious question the conventional wisdom that Justice Thomas simply signs onto Justice Scalia's opinions. Fourth, Justice Thomas frequently called for a dramatic rethinking of the particular civil liberties subject area before the Court: He did so in the final subject area considered in this chapter, commercial speech, just as he did in the first subject area considered, cruel and unusual punishment, as well as almost all of the subject areas considered in between. Fifth, finally, and perhaps most importantly, Justice Thomas was a consistent proponent of conservative originalism in civil liberties cases. In civil rights cases, in contrast, he tended to resort to the sort of liberal originalism to which I believe the Founders dedicated the nation.[200] Before I discuss the implications of this intriguing finding, it is necessary to examine the final area of public law to be discussed in this book: Justice Thomas's views about federalism.

5

Federalism

[W]here the Constitution is silent, it raises no bar to action by the
States or the people.
—Thomas, J., dissenting in *U.S. Term Limits, Inc. v. Thornton* (1995)

[Justice Thomas's dissent] makes a mockery of the entire debate
surrounding the ratification of the Constitution.
—Jack N. Rakove in the *Los Angeles Times* (1995)

The vast majority of the public law cases that the Supreme
Court has decided since 1937—the year in which the Court, under the
threat of President Franklin D. Roosevelt's infamous "court-packing"
plan, stopped striking down the New Deal—have involved the sorts of
"rights" questions discussed in the previous two chapters.[1] Prior to that
"constitutional moment,"[2] however, many, if not most, of the Court's
landmark decisions involved "powers" questions: the origins and scope of
judicial review; Congress and the development of national power; the
powers of the presidency; the modern administrative state; and the allocation of authority and responsibility between the states and the national
government.[3]

Powers questions have received renewed attention during the Rehnquist Court era (1986–),[4] especially during the years in which Justice
Thomas has served on the Court. Towering above all other powers cases
decided by the Rehnquist Court are *U.S. Term Limits, Inc. v. Thornton*
(1995)[5] and *United States v. Lopez* (1995),[6] two cases that grappled with
the most fundamental public law question of all: the nature of the federal
Union. Justice Thomas, as will be seen, issued two of his most significant
and controversial opinions in these cases.[7]

"Federalism," in the American sense of the word, relates to the allocation of power and responsibility between the national government and

the state governments. There is little doubt that the Framers made a unique contribution to political science with the *concept* of federalism they wrote into the Constitution. There is equally little doubt that many of the great political battles in American history have been couched in terms of opposing *conceptions* of federalism.* Thomas Jefferson's battle with Alexander Hamilton during the Washington administration over the proposed Bank of the United States, for example, pitted two competing conceptions of federalism against each other: The compact theory of federalism advanced by Jefferson, which posits that the national government was brought into existence by a compact among sovereign states; and the national theory of federalism advanced by Hamilton, which identifies the people of the United States, collectively, as the source of the legitimate powers of any and all governments. As political scientist Samuel H. Beer brilliantly shows in *To Make a Nation: The Rediscovery of American Federalism* (1993), these competing conceptions of federalism were also at the heart of the political battles over sectionalism, which culminated in the Civil War; over industrialism, which culminated in the Great Depression and the New Deal; and over racism, which continues to this day.[8]

The justices who have served on the Supreme Court throughout our history have also often held different conceptions of federalism, and these different conceptions have played a dispositive role in how most, if not all, questions involving the allocation of power and responsibility in American government have been decided by the Court. *McCulloch v. Maryland* (1819), to mention the most obvious example, found Chief Justice John Marshall advancing the national theory of federalism in defense of a broad reading of congressional power in general and of the national bank in particular.[9] Similarly, the Court's narrow construction of the Reconstruction-era amendments was based on a specific conception of federalism—the compact theory[10]—as was the Court's subsequent opposition to national health and safety laws at the turn of the twentieth century and to the New Deal.[11]

The relationship between conceptions of federalism and interpretations of specific national and state laws has not been lost on those

---

*A "concept" is the principle itself (e.g., federalism). A "conception" is a particular interpretation of that principle (e.g., the "national theory" of federalism). See, for example, Ronald Dworkin, "The Jurisprudence of Richard Nixon," *New York Review of Books*, 4 May 1972, 27–35.

charged with nominating justices to the Supreme Court. Presidents Franklin Roosevelt and Ronald Reagan, for example, were notorious for attempting to staff the Court with justices who shared their respective national and compact visions of American federalism.[12] As we will see, the Court—including Justice Thomas, perhaps especially Justice Thomas—is still *reacting to* President Roosevelt's national vision, and it is still *influenced by* President Reagan's compact vision.

U.S. Term Limits, Inc. v. Thornton (1995)

Term Limits was decided during the height of a national movement to put a stop to careerism in Congress. The Supreme Court in a 5-to-4 decision in the case effectively ended the movement. As important as this result was, what made *Term Limits* "one of the most important [decisions] the Court has ever issued on the structure of the Federal Government"[13] was the battle between the Justice John Paul Stevens–led majority and the Justice Clarence Thomas–led minority over the proper conception of American federalism.

At issue in the case was a referendum adopted by the voters of Arkansas on November 3, 1992, which limited U.S. representatives from Arkansas to three terms and U.S. senators to two.[14] The referendum, which became Amendment 73 to the Arkansas Constitution, was premised on the following proposition:

> The People of Arkansas find and declare that elected officials who re-
> main in office too long become pre-occupied with reelection and ignore
> their duties as representatives of the people. Entrenched incumbency has
> reduced voter participation and has led to an electoral system that is less
> free, less competitive, and less representative than the system established by
> the Founding Fathers. Therefore, the people of Arkansas, exercising their
> reserved powers, herein limit the terms of elected officials.[15]

The proposition stated the standard conservative *political* argument for terms limits.[16] As a matter of constitutional *law*, however, the Rehnquist Court had little Supreme Court precedent to go on. The precedent most closely on point was *Powell v. McCormack* (1969), a case in which the Warren Court held that *Congress* had no authority to modify or add to the qualifications for office set forth in Article I, Sections 2 and 3—the

Qualifications Clauses—of the Constitution.[17]* The Justice Stevens–led majority and the Justice Thomas–led minority disagreed sharply over whether a similar limitation of authority extended to the *states*, or, more precisely, to the *people* of the states.

The Arkansas state courts held that the provisions of the term limits amendment to the Arkansas Constitution that applied to individuals seeking reelection to Congress violated Article I of the U.S. Constitution.[18] Justice Stevens, in an opinion for the Court in which he was joined by Justices Anthony Kennedy, David Souter, Ruth Bader Ginsburg, and Stephen Breyer, agreed.

Justice Stevens opened his opinion for the Court by emphasizing the significance of *Powell* and praising the "thorough" examination of the history and meaning of the Qualifications Clauses undertaken there. In fact, a large portion of Justice Stevens's opinion was devoted to providing a "full statement" of what the Warren Court had decided in that case. The sum and substance of Justice Stevens's surprising foray into originalism was that the *Powell* Court had convincingly shown that the Constitution's age, citizenship, and residency requirements for membership in Congress were exclusive and may not be supplemented. Justice Stevens wrote: "As this elaborate summary reveals, our historical analysis in *Powell* was both detailed and persuasive. We thus conclude that, with respect to Congress, the Framers intended the Constitution to establish fixed qualifications."[19]

Justice Stevens also reviewed *Powell's* examination of "democratic principles."[20] He echoed the *Powell* Court's commitment to Alexander Hamilton's position that the "fundamental principle of our representative democracy [is] 'that the people should choose whom they please to govern them.'"[21] For Justice Stevens and the *Term Limits* majority, this meant that the states may not impose additional qualifications for service in Congress.

Justice Stevens next addressed the issues that were at the heart of Justice Thomas's dissent: the Tenth Amendment and the principle of reserved powers. The Tenth Amendment provides: "The powers not delegated to the United States by the Constitution, nor prohibited by it to the States, are reserved to the States respectively, or to the people." Justice

---

*The Qualifications Clauses specify that a member of the U.S. House of Representatives must be at least twenty-five years old, must have been a U.S. citizen for at least seven years, and must live in the state from which she or he is elected. A U.S. senator must be at least thirty years old, must have been a U.S. citizen for at least nine years, and must live in the state from which she or he is elected.

Stevens rejected Justice Thomas's argument that, because the Constitution does not expressly prohibit the states from imposing additional qualifications for congressional office, the reserved powers principle of the Tenth Amendment allows the states to add them. According to Justice Stevens, the power to add congressional qualifications was not reserved by the states through the Tenth Amendment: It did not lie within the scope of the states' "original powers." That is to say, because the power to add qualifications for service in Congress did not exist *before* the Constitution was ratified, no such power could have been reserved. Justice Stevens explained:

> In adopting [the Constitution], the Framers envisioned a uniform national system, rejecting the notion that the Nation was a collection of States, and instead creating a direct link between the National Government and the people of the United States. . . . In that National Government, representatives owe primary allegiance not to the people of a State, but to the people of the Nation.[22]

In short, Justice Stevens advanced the national theory of federalism in his opinion for the Court. In doing so, he emphasized the "revolutionary character of the government that the Framers conceived" when they decided to do more than simply amend the Articles of Confederation.[23]*

Justice Stevens ended with a flourish: He quoted the preamble of the Constitution in support of his nationalist vision of the American regime.[24] He wrote:

> In the absence of a properly passed [national] constitutional amendment, allowing individual States to craft their own qualifications for Congress would thus erode the structure envisioned by the Framers, a structure that was designed, in the words of the Preamble to our Constitution, to form a "more perfect Union."[25]**

Justice Thomas often writes long opinions in important cases. His concurring opinion in the Voting Rights Act case *Holder v. Hall* (1994),

---

*Justice Stevens invoked Chief Justice John Marshall's nationalistic opinion in *McCulloch v. Maryland* (1819) and Justice Joseph Story's nationalistic argument in *Commentaries on the Constitution of the United States* (1833) for further support of his interpretation of the character of the federal Union.

**In a footnote earlier in his opinion Justice Stevens juxtaposed the preamble of the U.S. Constitution with the preamble of the Articles of Confederation: "Compare U.S. Const., Preamble ('We the People') with The Articles of Confederation, reprinted in 2 Bailyn 926 ('we the under signed Delegates of the States')." *U.S. Term Limits, Inc. v. Thornton*, 115 S.Ct. 1842, 1863 n. 31 (1995).

for example, was extremely long.[26] His dissenting opinion in *Term Limits*, in which he was joined by Chief Justice William Rehnquist and Justices Sandra Day O'Connor and Antonin Scalia, was longer still.[27] Like most of his opinions in important cases, Justice Thomas also called in his *Term Limits* dissent for a return to "first principles."[28]

The crucial difference between Justice Thomas's dissent and Justice Stevens's opinion for the Court was that Thomas interpreted the historical materials concerning congressional qualifications from the perspective of the states and reserved powers, whereas Stevens interpreted them from the perspective of the national government and delegated powers. Nowhere was Justice Thomas's perspective—his commitment to the compact theory of federalism—more plainly stated than in the articulation of his so-called "default rule." Justice Thomas wrote:

> Nothing in the Constitution deprives the people of each State of the power to prescribe eligibility requirements for the candidates who seek to represent them in Congress. The Constitution is simply silent on this question. And where the Constitution is silent, it raises no bar to action by the States or the people.[29]

For Justice Thomas, the Tenth Amendment was where the reserved powers principle was most plainly evidenced. It also was evidenced elsewhere, including in the Preamble to the Constitution. The first footnote of Justice Thomas's dissent is worth quoting at length:

> The ringing initial words of the Constitution—"We the People of the United States"—convey something of the same idea. (In the Constitution, after all, "the United States" is consistently a plural noun. See Art. I, sec. 9, cl. 8; Art. II, sec. 1, cl. 7; Art. III, sec. 2, cl. 1; Art. III, sec. 3, cl. 1. . . .) The Preamble that the Philadelphia Convention approved before sending the Constitution to the Committee of Style is even clearer. It began: "We the people of the States of New-Hampshire, Massachusetts, Rhode-Island and Providence Plantations, Connecticut, New-York, New-Jersey, Pennsylvania, Delaware, Maryland, Virginia, North-Carolina, South-Carolina, and Georgia." . . . Scholars of style have suggested that the Committee of Style adopted the current language because it was not clear that all the States would actually ratify the Constitution.[30]

Justice Thomas's opinion was replete with similar statements about the primacy of the states, or more precisely, of the *people* of each of the states. Yet another such statement is worth singling out:

Our system of government rests on one overriding principle: all power stems from the consent of the people. To phrase the principle this way, however, is to be imprecise about something important to the notion of "reserved" powers. The ultimate source of the Constitution's authority is the consent of the people of each individual State, not the consent of the undifferentiated people of the Nation as a whole.[31]

With his commitment to the compact theory of federalism unambiguously established, Justice Thomas then went on to offer a point-by-point rebuttal of the nationalistic conclusions of Justice Stevens's opinion for the Court. First and foremost, Justice Thomas questioned what he called Justice Stevens's "enormous and untenable limitation" of the Tenth Amendment. Justice Thomas rejected Justice Stevens's conclusion that the states possessed only those powers that the Constitution affirmatively granted to them or that they had enjoyed before the Constitution was adopted. To Justice Thomas, the appropriate conclusion was different by 180 degrees: The "face" of the Tenth Amendment made this clear. In other words, wrote Justice Thomas, rephrasing his default rule, "unless the Federal Constitution affirmatively prohibits an action by the States or the people, it raises no bar to such action."[32]

Justice Thomas's reading of the Tenth Amendment led him to challenge Justice Stevens's interpretation of the Court's Tenth Amendment precedents. Most notable among these precedents was *McCulloch v. Maryland* (1819), Chief Justice Marshall's paean of praise to national power. Justice Thomas insisted that Chief Justice Marshall's opinion in that landmark case supported *his*, not Justice Stevens's, position on the reserved powers of the states. "True to the text of the Tenth Amendment ... *McCulloch* indicated that all powers as to which the Constitution does not speak (whether expressly or by necessary implication) are 'reserved' to the state level," Justice Thomas opined.[33]

Justice Thomas also had much to say about the writings of another giant of the nineteenth-century Supreme Court upon which Justice Stevens had heavily relied: Joseph Story's *Commentaries on the Constitution of the United States* (1833). However, Justice Thomas approached Justice Stevens's characterization of Justice Story's views of the nature of the Union differently than he approached Stevens's characterization of Chief Justice Marshall's views. Justice Thomas acknowledged that Justice Stevens correctly interpreted Justice Story's views, but he went on to declare that Story was wrong—wrong on the matter of original intent. Justice Thomas wrote:

> Justice Story was a brilliant and accomplished man, and one cannot casually dismiss his views. On the other hand, he was not a member of the Founding generation, and his *Commentaries on the Constitution* were written a half century after the framing. Rather than representing the original understanding of the Constitution, they represent only his own understanding. In a range of cases concerning the federal/state relation, moreover, this Court has deemed positions taken in Story's commentaries to be more nationalist than the Constitution warrants. . . . In this case too, Story's position that the only powers reserved to the States are those that the States enjoyed before the framing conflicts with both the plain language of the Tenth Amendment and the underlying theory of the Constitution.[34]

Convinced he had successfully demonstrated that "the people of Arkansas do enjoy 'reserved' powers over the selection of their representatives in Congress," Justice Thomas moved on to disagree with Justice Stevens's interpretation of the Qualifications Clauses.[35] Succinctly stated, Justice Thomas declared that *Powell v. McCormack* (1969)—the precedent on which Justice Stevens relied most—had nothing to do with the question before the Court in *Term Limits*. *Powell*, Justice Thomas contended, concerned "whether *Congress* has the power to prescribe qualifications for its own members." *Term Limits*, in contrast, was about whether "the Framers . . . deprived *the people of the States* of their reserved authority to set eligibility requirements for their own representatives."[36]

Justice Thomas supported his reading of the Qualifications Clauses with text and history. Once again he disagreed sharply with Justice Stevens's views. He maintained that as a textual matter "the fact that the Constitution specifies certain qualifications that the Framers deemed necessary to protect the competence of the National Legislature does not imply that it strips the people of the individual States of the power to protect their own interests by adding other requirements for their own representatives." Justice Thomas's interpretation of the historical evidence regarding a state's power to impose term limits on its congressional representatives was likewise unequivocal: "the historical evidence is simply inadequate to warrant the majority's conclusion that the Qualifications Clauses mean anything more than what they say."[37] And what the Qualifications Clauses "say," Justice Thomas insisted, is that *Congress* may not supplement the age, residency, and citizenship requirements of Article I.

Justice Thomas's examination of the historical record found him again reviewing the evidence marshaled by Justice Stevens. It also found him again rejecting almost every conclusion that Justice Stevens drew from that evidence. Justice Thomas maintained that the evidence surrounding the Constitutional Convention, other provisions of the Constitution relied upon by Justice Stevens (e.g., the Compensation Clauses; the Times, Places, and Manners Clause), the ratification debates, and *The Federalist Papers* did not establish the Framers' intent to keep qualifications fixed, as Justice Stevens had concluded. It only demonstrated that the Framers did not intend for *Congress* to have the power to add qualifications. Justice Thomas also insisted that state practice immediately after the Constitution went into effect regarding the addition of qualifications ran contrary to Justice Stevens's interpretation of the Qualifications Clauses. So, too, did the 1807 House debate over whether to seat Maryland's William McCreery.[38]

Justice Thomas closed his lengthy dissenting opinion by suggesting that Justice Stevens's "radical" opinion meant that no state may disqualify congressional candidates whom a court had found to be mentally incompetent, for example, or who were then in prison.[39] Similarly, Justice Thomas speculated that Justice Stevens's "radical" interpretation could empower the Court to void, pursuant to the *Qualifications Clauses,* majority-minority congressional districts "if it can be shown that nonminorities are at a significant disadvantage when they seek election in districts dominated by minority voters." Although Justice Thomas concluded by stating that the "majority's opinion may not go [this] far," he nevertheless reiterated his earlier plea to "read the Qualifications Clauses to do no more than they say."[40] According to Justice Thomas, they say *nothing* about the ability of the people of a state to impose requirements in addition to the requirements of the Constitution regarding residency, age, and American citizenship.

Such were the long and detailed arguments offered by Justice Stevens for the majority and Justice Thomas for the minority on the constitutionality of state-imposed term limits on members of the national legislature. Both opinions were occasionally redundant, and the authors of both occasionally fell victim to lawyers' tendency for overkill. But they provided fascinating reading nevertheless for those who enjoy history.

Indeed, the commentary on the *Term Limits* case suggests something of the hold the Founders still have on the "American mind," to borrow Thomas Jefferson's evocative phrase. Unfortunately, this same commentary—like the opinions themselves—was tainted by the political preferences of the respective commentators. Concisely stated, liberal commentators read history one way—the way Justice Stevens read it—and conservative commentators read it another way—the way Justice Thomas read it.

The *New York Times*, a bellwether for liberals, editorialized that Justice Thomas "spun out 88 pages of unsuccessful searching for a states'-rights principle the Founding Fathers never imagined" and that Justice Stevens correctly "found that the framers plainly intended that Federal concerns, and Federal eligibility standards, would govern the makeup of the national legislature."[41] The *Washington Post*, the nation's other major liberal newspaper, took a similar position when it editorialized that the historical record was "clear" about the fact that "when the Constitution was drafted, the Framers rejected all proposals to impose qualifications for legislative office such as property ownership and religious tests, except for three: age, citizenship, and residence."[42]

History held similar sway over commentators on the conservative end of the political spectrum. To mention but the most notable example, George F. Will, the author of a book arguing for term limits, called Justice Stevens's majority opinion "mistaken" as a matter of both history and constitutional law. Justice Thomas's dissenting opinion was correctly "Borkean" (i.e., true to the Framers' intent).[43] Will emphasized early state practices in his op-ed about the decision, and concluded that "the Framers of the Constitution, including the preeminent one, James Madison, knew that qualifications were not uniform" among the states at the framing and, consequently, they did not require them to be uniform in the Constitution.[44]

The vast majority of the other popular accounts of the *Term Limits* case were consistent with those chronicled above: liberals read history—and hence the competing opinions of Justices Thomas and Stevens—one way, and conservatives read it—and hence the opinions—another way.[45] One more popular commentary merits singling out, however, if only because it was written by Jack N. Rakove, the Pulitzer Prize–winning historian of originalism.[46]

In a lengthy essay in the *Los Angeles Times*, Rakove, a self-described "Democrat,"[47] declared, "For whatever else it accomplishes, the decision in U.S. Term Limits vs. Thornton is an ironic victory for the original meaning of the Constitution against those who insist that fidelity to the intentions of its Framers offers the most sound constitutional interpretation." Rakove went on to document historically how, in his view, "the majority got the story right" about term limits and why Justice Thomas's dissent "makes a mockery of the entire debate surrounding the ratification of the Constitution."[48]

Taken by itself, Rakove's reading of the debates surrounding the framing and ratification of the Constitution might be seen as dispositive. After all, he did win the Pulitzer Prize in history for his book about those debates. When read in context, however, Rakove's *originalist* approach to the *Term Limits* decision in his essay is at odds with the thesis of his prize-winning book: that originalism, at least conservative originalism,[49] is bankrupt as a matter of history and, hence, as a method by which to interpret the Constitution. A careful reading of Rakove's analysis of the *Term Limits* decision suggests that he, like the conservatives he criticized, was using history to justify a preconceived political preference about the nature of the Union. Indeed, Rakove's support for Justice Stevens's position rested primarily on the ground that "neither side" in the ratification debate framed the issue the way Justice Thomas did. In other words, since neither the Federalists nor the Anti-Federalists approached the controlling question in the debate over ratification (i.e., the nature of the Union) in the way Justice Thomas did in his exegesis on a much narrower question (i.e., whether the people of an individual state may impose term limits on their national representatives), the Framers must have rejected the conclusion to which Justice Thomas's exegesis leads. To make the point more directly, Rakove—a *critic* of conservative originalism—*appealed to history* to require Justice Thomas to prove a negative. No one, not even an unpopular conservative Supreme Court justice, should be required to perform such an impossible feat.

The law review commentary about *Term Limits* was likewise characterized by the political use of history—what lawyers long have referred to as "law-office history."[50] The sheer volume of that commentary speaks not only to the importance of the *Term Limits* decision itself, but also, and once again, to the hold the Founders still have on the American mind. By my count, there were over twenty law review essays about *Term Limits*. They ranged from case comments by bright young law review editors,[51] to articles by some of the biggest names in legal academe,[52] to papers and reactions to those papers in law review symposia devoted to the decision.[53]

Even lawyers who participated in the case could not resist writing articles about it,[54] and no less than the *Harvard Law Review* published a "Comment" on the case from one of the nation's leading constitutional law scholars.[55]

Two essays—one from the right, the other from the left—epitomized the reaction *Term Limits* generated among legal scholars. From the right, David N. Mayer, the author of a provocative book arguing that Thomas Jefferson's constitutional thought was best seen as libertarian,[56] declared that Justice Thomas's opinions in *Lopez* (discussed below) and *Term Limits* "reveal what is arguably his most important and permanent contribution to the Court: the rediscovery of the Tenth Amendment as the touchstone of the Constitution."[57]

What made Mayer's article important was the amount of historical evidence—page upon page about Federalists and Anti-Federalists, Jeffersonians and Hamiltonians, and Supreme Court precedent after Supreme Court precedent—he marshaled in support of his dramatic proposition. In summing up, Mayer called Justice Stevens's use of history "rather unpersuasive" and "dubious" and Justice Thomas's "correct" and "far more complete."[58] Clearly, the conservative historian Mayer had a far different take on the history surrounding the nature of the Union in general and of the constitutionality of term limits in particular than did the liberal historian Rakove.

Kathleen M. Sullivan, a liberal constitutional law scholar at Stanford, offered yet a third reading of the historical record in her Comment on the *Term Limits* decision for the *Harvard Law Review*. Her reading was that Justices Stevens and Thomas "battled" to a "draw" on the issue of whether the Framers intended to permit individual states to impose term limits on their representatives to Congress.[59]

What made Sullivan's essay important was that she did not stop there. Like her former Harvard Law School colleague Laurence H. Tribe had before her,[60] Sullivan warned of the policy implications of Justice Thomas's position, and, again like Tribe, she sounded that warning in apocalyptic terms. Sullivan argued that the Court might be "moving in . . . an antifederalist direction" and that such a shift might mean that the conservatives on the Court were poised to let the states go to extremes—to regulate commerce with interstate implications and to prohibit those who "immigrate" from one state to another from enjoying the social services of their new residence.[61]

The debate between Justice Thomas and Justice Stevens in the *Term Limits* decision, and the flood of commentary in the popular press and academic journals, brings two points to light: (1) conservative originalists seemingly have won the methodological battle over how to read the Constitution, and (2) conservative originalism is a deeply flawed methodology. With respect to the first point, when the Court's most liberal member, Justice Stevens, himself formerly one of originalism's staunchest critics,[62] employs originalism to decide one of the most important powers questions of the day—whether the people of individual states may impose term limits on their representatives to Congress—Robert H. Bork, the longtime champion of conservative originalism, can declare victory and turn his attention to substantive matters such as the decline of Western civilization (as he sees it and as he has done).[63]

As far as the deeply flawed character of conservative originalism is concerned, either everyone, including those traditionally associated with conservative originalism, is simply paying lip service to history, or history is indeterminate on many significant questions of constitutional law (such as term limits). Frankly, my reading of the opinions and commentary suggests to me that the justices and commentators were simply picking and choosing from the historical record—British practice, the Articles of Confederation, the Constitutional Convention debates, *The Federalist Papers*, the ratification debates, and early state and national practices—to find support for a preconceived policy preference. It strains credibility to believe that it was merely a coincidence that history *always* led to the policy result the particular justice or commentator favored. At a minimum, it is difficult to deny the more modest interpretive claim that history provides no clear answer to the question of whether the Framers intended to make exclusive the age, citizenship, and residency requirements enumerated in the Qualifications Clauses of the Constitution.[64]

How, then, should this important question have been decided? In my judgment, it should have been decided in the manner that a liberal originalist would have decided it: by endeavoring to ascertain whether term limits imposed by the people of an individual state upon their national representatives are consistent with the *principle* of federalism embodied in the Constitution.[65] Admittedly, this principle is complex: It is neither the reification of the national theory of federalism nor of the compact theory of federalism. Madison himself appreciated the "neither/nor" solution.* "The proposed Constitution," he wrote in *Federalist* No. 39, was neither national nor federal "but a composition of both."

> In its foundation it is federal, not national; in the sources from which the ordinary powers of government are drawn, it is partly federal and partly national; in the operations of these powers, it is national, not federal; in the extent of them, again, it is federal, not national; and, finally, in the authoritative mode of introducing amendments, it is neither wholly federal nor wholly national.[66]

The next question then becomes, Where in this complex system of American federalism do qualifications for members of Congress fall? The answer would appear to be, In "the sources from which the ordinary powers of government are drawn." After all, what the term limits debate was ultimately about was the *source* of Congress's power. Initially, the legislatures of each state selected their respective senators[67] and, consequently, the source of the Senate's power was the states.[68] The ratification of the Seventeenth Amendment in 1913 changed this, however. Now, the Senate is, as the House of Representatives always has been, "national" in the source from which its power is derived: the people of the nation as voiced in their respective electoral districts.** What this means as a matter of constitutional law is that the qualifications for office for both the Senate and the House may be set only at the national level, where the Qualifications Clauses of the Constitution speak to the matter. In summary, Justice Thomas's *Term Limits* dissent was incorrect: If the American people wish

---

*Rakove appeared to appreciate this as well—at least in his prize-winning book. He wrote: "Each passing decade taught Madison just how acute the analysis of *Federalist* 39 had been, and how hard it was to defend his original understanding of the subtleties of federalism against the simpler catechisms of national supremacy or state sovereignty." Jack N. Rakove, *Original Meanings: Politics and Ideas in the Making of the Constitution* (New York: Alfred A. Knopf, 1996), 162.

**Each state continues to have two senators, as it did before the Seventeenth Amendment was adopted. Consequently, it might be said that the Senate's power is derived from a "compound source"—the states *and* the nation—as Madison put it when describing the sources of the president's power. *The Federalist*, ed. Clinton Rossiter (New York: New American Library, 1961), No. 39, 240–6, 244. Plainly, though, one of the main objectives of the progressive reformers responsible for securing passage of the Seventeenth Amendment was to further nationalize the system at the expense of state power. Indeed, the Seventeenth Amendment is perhaps the most subtle manifestation to date of a national trend to eviscerate state power that became all but irreversible with the North's triumph in the Civil War. See, for example, Richard B. Bernstein with Jerome Agel, *Amending America: If We Love the Constitution So Much, Why Do We Keep Trying to Change It?* (New York: Random House, 1993), 122 (calling the Seventeenth Amendment "the most drastic alteration in the system of federalism since the Civil War Amendments").

to place terms limits on the members of Congress they must work through the amending process of Article V to do so.

United States v. Lopez (1995)

It is a cliché that one of the principal "vices" of the Articles of Confederation (1777, 1781) was the lack of authority Congress enjoyed under them to regulate commerce among the states.[69] Even those delegates to the federal Convention of 1787 who preferred to amend, rather than replace, the Articles recognized that something had to be done to strengthen the national government's authority over the nation's commerce. The real debate that occurred at the framing, and that has recurred throughout the course of American history, has been about the *scope* of Congress's authority under Article I, Section 8, Clause 3 of the Constitution, which empowers Congress "To regulate Commerce . . . among the several States."

Some of the Supreme Court's most important decisions have addressed precisely this question. *Gibbons v. Ogden* (1824), *United States v. E. C. Knight Company* (1895), *A. L. A. Schechter Poultry Corporation v. United States* (1935), *NLRB v. Jones and Laughlin Steel Corporation* (1937), *Wickard v. Filburn* (1942), *Katzenbach v. McClung* (1964): the list of landmark decisions interpreting the Commerce Clause, of which this is but a sample, is impressive indeed. *United States v. Lopez* (1995) must now be added to this list.

A detailed accounting of any of these landmark decisions other than *Lopez* would take me too far afield from the purpose of explicating Justice Thomas's jurisprudence. However, a conceptual road map to the decisions will make it possible to appreciate the sweep of Justice Thomas's reading of the Commerce Clause.[70]

The Supreme Court's Commerce Clause jurisprudence can be divided into three eras: (1) the first 150 years, (2) the 1937–1995 period, and (3) the *Lopez* decision and (perhaps) beyond. *Gibbons v. Ogden* (1824)[71] defined the first era. In fact, the entire history of the Court's Commerce Clause jurisprudence can be characterized as a series of reactions to the *Gibbons* decision and, for the most part, to the expansive language of Chief Justice Marshall's opinion for the Court in the case.

Gibbons involved the competing claims of two steamboat ferry operators. One operator was awarded a monopoly by the state of New York, the other was granted a federal license by Congress. The Court construed the federal license to nullify the New York grant of monopoly. More significant for present purposes, Chief Justice Marshall declared in his opinion for the Court that "Commerce, undoubtedly, is traffic, but it is something more: it is intercourse" and that Congress's power to regulate commerce "is complete in itself, may be exercised to its utmost extent, and acknowledges no limitations, other than are prescribed in the constitution." He also stated, however, that "[c]omprehensive as the word 'among' is, it may very properly be restricted to that commerce which concerns more States than one."[72] This last statement is a clear indication that, while *Gibbons* is rightly regarded as one of the most important national power cases in American history, Chief Justice Marshall was making it plain that because of our federal system a state does enjoy autonomy over intrastate commerce.[73]

The Court devoted most of its attention in Commerce Clause disputes during the remainder of the nineteenth century to a state's power to legislate on matters that affect interstate commerce but over which Congress had *not* legislated. These were the so-called "dormant" Commerce Clause cases. With the passage of the Interstate Commerce Act of 1887 (a national law designed to regulate commerce between the states, particularly as it related to the transportation of persons and property by the railroads) and the Sherman Antitrust Act of 1890 (a national law that attempted to prevent unlawful monopolies), Congress turned much of its energy to commerce matters. By then, the Court was dominated by conservative justices who favored a laissez-faire approach to the economy.[*] Consequently, the Court began sharply to restrict the scope of Congress's Commerce Clause authority by using a series of formalistic distinctions to interpret the Interstate Commerce Act, the Sherman Antitrust Act, and similar statutes (e.g., the national Child Labor Act of 1916). The Court claimed in *United States v. E. C. Knight Company* (1895), for example, that "manufacturing" was not "commerce" and in *A. L. A. Schechter Poultry Corporation v. United States* (1935) that there was a difference between a "direct" and an "indirect" effect on commerce.[74]

---

[*]Between 1889 and 1933, seven of nine presidents were Republicans who believed strongly in the advantages of a private market economy. These presidents tended to nominate justices who held similar views. See, for example, Thomas G. Walker and Lee Epstein, *The Supreme Court of the United States: An Introduction* (New York: St. Martin's Press, 1993), 18–9.

The second era of the Court's Commerce Clause jurisprudence began in 1937 with *NLRB v. Jones and Laughlin Steel Corporation*, when the Court, under increasing pressure from President Franklin Roosevelt, dropped these formalistic distinctions. *Jones and Laughlin* was one of five cases decided on April 12, 1937, that involved the constitutionality of the National Labor Relations Act, the statute commonly regarded as the most radical piece of President Roosevelt's New Deal legislation.[75] In that case the Court held 5 to 4 that Congress had the authority to regulate intrastate activities that had a "close and substantial relation" to interstate commerce.[76] In case after case after 1937 the Court was then confronted with deciding what sorts of state and local activities fell within the purview of this test and, consequently, of Congress's power to regulate.[77] *Lopez* (1995) marked only the second occasion since 1937 that the Court held that Congress had exceeded its Commerce Clause authority.* Indeed, between 1937 and 1995 the Court upheld a number of congressional Commerce Clause–based statutes aimed at addressing social (e.g., racial), and not simply *commercial,* problems.[78]

Lopez signaled that the Rehnquist Court—and especially Justice Thomas—may be ready to usher in a new era of the Court's Commerce Clause jurisprudence. It is to that landmark case that I now turn.

Alfonso Lopez, Jr., a twelfth-grade student in San Antonio, Texas, was charged under Texas law with carrying a concealed weapon on school property. The state dismissed the charges after federal authorities indicted Lopez pursuant to the 1990 Gun-Free School Zones Act. Lopez moved to dismiss the federal charges on the ground that the Act was an unconstitutional attempt by Congress to legislate control over public schools. Lopez lost in the U.S. District Court for the Western District of Texas, but prevailed in both the U.S. Court of Appeals for the Fifth Circuit and the U.S. Supreme Court.

Chief Justice Rehnquist delivered the opinion of the Court, in which he was joined by Justices O'Connor, Scalia, Kennedy, and Thomas. The chief justice emphasized "first principles" and federalism and concluded that the possession of a gun in a local school zone was not an economic activity that might, through repetition elsewhere, "substantially affect" interstate commerce. Lopez was a local student, Chief Justice Rehnquist

---

*The other occasion was *National League of Cities v. Usery* (1976). That decision was later overruled. See *National League of Cities v. Usery*, 426 U.S. 833 (1976), overruled by *Garcia v. San Antonio Metro Transit Authority*, 469 U.S. 528 (1985).

insisted, and there was no evidence that he had recently traveled outside of Texas.[79]

The core of the chief justice's opinion for the Court was an examination of the historical development of the Court's Commerce Clause jurisprudence. After revisiting *Gibbons v. Ogden* (1824), *United States v. E. C. Knight Company* (1895), *A. L. A. Schechter Poultry Corporation v. United States* (1935), *NLRB v. Jones and Laughlin Steel Corporation* (1937), *Wickard v. Filburn* (1942), and *Katzenbach v. McClung* (1964), among other cases, the chief justice declared that the Gun-Free School Zones Act had "nothing to do" with interstate commerce.[80] Rather, he argued, the Act was an attempt by Congress to exercise a nonexistent national police power over a subject—criminal law—that was primarily of state concern.* Chief Justice Rehnquist wrote:

> Even *Wickard* [in which production of a small quantity of wheat exclusively for home consumption was deemed by the Court to substantially affect interstate commerce], which is perhaps the most far reaching example of Commerce Clause authority over interstate activity, involved economic activity in a way that the possession of a gun in a school zone does not.[81]

Justice Breyer penned the lead dissent, in which he was joined by Justices Stevens, Souter, and Ginsburg.[82] He emphasized that the Court's prior Commerce Clause decisions permitted Congress to regulate local activities whose cumulative impact had a "significant effect" on interstate commerce and that it was for Congress, not the Court, to make the determination of whether a "significant effect" was likely to occur. He criticized the majority for focusing on what he considered formalistic distinctions "between 'commercial' and 'noncommercial' transactions" and for ignoring the "economic realities" of gun violence in schools. To support his position on this last point, Justice Breyer attached a lengthy appendix to his dissenting opinion in which he listed 170 reports and studies that "make clear" that Congress "could reasonably have found" that violent crime in school zones "significantly (or substantially) affects 'interstate commerce.'"[83]

Justice Thomas, in *Lopez*, issued yet another long separate opinion, but this time a concurring opinion for himself alone.[84] Once again he focused on the text and history of the constitutional provision at issue. Although

---

*The "police power" is the power of the government to place restraints on the personal freedom and property rights of persons for the public safety, health, and morals or the promotion of the public convenience and general prosperity.

he agreed with Chief Justice Rehnquist's opinion for the Court that the Commerce Clause did not grant Congress the authority to prohibit gun possession within one thousand feet of a school, he wrote "separately to observe that our case law has drifted far from the original understanding of the Commerce Clause." He objected most particularly to the fact that the "substantial effects" test, "if taken to its logical extreme," gave Congress a "police power"—a power the Constitution "quite properly" left to the individual states.[85]

Justice Thomas began his substantive case by pointing out that, at the Founding, "'commerce' consisted of selling, buying, and bartering, as well as transportation for these purposes," and that "'commerce' was used in contradistinction to productive activities such as manufacturing and agriculture." To support his position he cited a number of dictionaries from the period, the statements of both Federalists and Anti-Federalists, and other provisions in the Constitution where the term "commerce" was used. He also insisted that the New Deal and post–New Deal reading of the Commerce Clause, whereby Congress had been empowered to regulate all activities that "substantially effect" interstate commerce, rendered many of the other eighteen clauses of Article I, Section 8 "surplusage" and came close "to turning the Tenth Amendment on its head."[86]

Turning from text to history, Justice Thomas maintained that "[t]he exchanges during the ratification campaign reveal the relatively limited reach of the Commerce Clause and of federal power generally." As in his textual argument, he invoked in his historical argument a number of statements by Federalists and Anti-Federalists to support what he claimed was the original understanding of the Commerce Clause. Like the authors of the other opinions in *Lopez*, Justice Thomas offered in his opinion his own reading of the Court's Commerce Clause precedents. He concluded that "the substantial effects test is but an innovation of the 20th century,"[87] and he went so far as to endorse the reading of the Commerce Clause adopted in *United States v. E. C. Knight Company* (1895) as well as other controversial laissez-faire-era cases.

Justice Thomas closed his concurring opinion by urging the Court, "at an appropriate juncture," to "modify" its Commerce Clause jurisprudence. He was less clear, however, about whether this meant that the Court should overrule its New Deal and post–New Deal precedents. He wrote:

Although I might be willing to return to the original understanding, I recognize that many believe that it is too late in the day to undertake a fundamental reexamination of the past 60 years. Consideration of stare decisis and reliance interests may convince us that we cannot wipe the slate clean.[88]

Press and academic reaction to *Lopez* was as plentiful as it was to *Term Limits*. It was also as predictable. From the left, the *New York Times* editorialized that "the dissenters had the better case" and accused the majority, in general, of returning to the "hair-splitting, unreal distinctions between 'manufacture' and 'commerce'" of "formalistic" days gone by.[89] Jeffrey Rosen in the *New Republic* accused Justice Thomas, in particular, of both plagiarizing a 1987 law review article by a prolific conservative law professor and calling for the invalidation of large portions of the national government and the administrative state.[90]

From the right came equally predictable characterizations of the case. George F. Will, in an op-ed that closely tracked Justice Thomas's concurring opinion, praised both Chief Justice Rehnquist and Justice Thomas for "rethinking 1937" and for taking federalism seriously.[91] Douglas W. Kmiec, a former Reagan administration official who now teaches at the University of Notre Dame School of Law, wrote an essay for the *Chicago Tribune* in which he called *Lopez* "of potentially monumental significance" and "the first step in nearly 60 years toward the restoration of a constitutional order premised upon a national government of enumerated and, therefore, limited powers."[92]

Twenty law review essays about *Term Limits* is considerable. Eighty-seven about *Lopez* is mind-boggling. Four—two from the left and two from the right—should suffice to suggest that, as was true with *Term Limits*, the reaction that Justice Thomas's *Lopez* opinion received was closely linked—indeed, was inseparably tied—to the political agenda of the legal scholar in question.

From the left, Daniel A. Farber, a prominent law professor at the University of Minnesota who has long been critical of conservative originalism,[93] argued in a symposium paper in the *Michigan Law Review* that Chief Justice Rehnquist's opinion for the Court in *Lopez* and the separate opinion of Justice Thomas were merely policy pronouncements of Reaganite "New Federalism" decorated with case citations. Farber went on to say that the original understanding of the Commerce Clause was much more nationalistic than the New Federalists maintained. "To the extent that the philosophy embraced by the New Federalists . . . claims to flow from the original understanding of the Framers, it has a shaky foundation," Farber concluded.[94]

Revealingly, Farber's evidence for establishing how nationalistic the American regime was intended to be—a cover letter written by George Washington by which he submitted the proposed Constitution to the Continental Congress and to the states—suffers from the same flaws as conservative originalism itself: Why *that* document? Why *that* Framer? In short, all Farber was really able to accomplish with his paper was to provide one more piece of evidence of the shortcomings of conservative originalism as a definitive method for interpreting the Constitution.[95]

The second liberal critique of *Lopez* to be discussed here is an essay by J. Clay Smith, Jr., a law professor at Howard University. Smith, an expert on civil rights law, was concerned about the implications of *Lopez*, and especially of Justice Thomas's concurring opinion—which Smith called a "frontal attack"—for Congress's ability to protect the civil rights of Blacks. To Smith, *Lopez* was as much about laying the groundwork for a potential Court-enforced withdrawal of national supervision over state and local civil rights abuses as it was about keeping the nation's schools free from handguns. Smith wrote:

> The civil rights community and people of good will, who believe in fairness and abhor harm that could befall black people in this country, must not be misled or misdirected about the reaches of *Lopez* under the control of what appears to be a decision that invites a reexamination of federal-based power and so-called application of rules of original understanding using formalism as the Court's choice of decision making.[96]

Whether Smith's reading of the motivation of the *Lopez* Court proves true or not must await future decisions. It should be noted here, however, that simply because it might be good *public policy* for Congress to protect civil rights through the Commerce Clause does not mean that Congress has the *legal authority* under the Constitution to do so (more on this below).

While those on the left criticized the originalism at the heart of the *Lopez* decision, those on the right rejoiced in it. Raoul Berger, who was an originalist long before originalism became fashionable and who wrote a widely read book about what he believed the Framers meant by federalism,[97] was particularly taken by Justice Thomas's concurring opinion. Indeed, Berger wished that Justice Thomas had done in *Lopez* what he suggested he might do in a future case: call for the overruling of the Court's second-era Commerce Clause precedents. Berger wrote: "The precedents of 'the past 60 years' . . . are entitled to no more respect than the Court accorded those of the prior 140 years. Moreover, squatter sovereignty certainly does not run against the sovereign people; repetition does not legitimate usurpation."[98]

Richard A. Epstein, the prolific libertarian iconoclast at the University of Chicago Law School from whom Jeffrey Rosen accused Justice Thomas of plagiarizing, also wrote a law review essay that praised Justice Thomas's *Lopez* concurrence. "I have virtually nothing to say in opposition to Justice Thomas," Epstein declared, "since his views are so close to my own."[99] Epstein, like Berger, wished, however, that Justice Thomas had pursued his opinion to its logical limits. Epstein postulated that Justice Thomas would have called for the overruling of the Court's second-era Commerce Clause precedents had he been able to garner the five votes to do it.

Why did Epstein, Berger, and other conservatives want the *Lopez* Court to overrule the previous sixty years of Commerce Clause precedents? Because, wrote Epstein, until *Lopez* "just about anything" was regarded by the Court as having a "substantial relation" to interstate commerce.[100]

It is difficult to disagree with the right's reading of the scope of the national government's power under the Supreme Court's 1937–1995 Commerce Clause decisions. Justice Thomas was quite persuasive on this point when he noted that Justice Breyer could not come up with a single example in his dissenting opinion of when a particular subject area was beyond the reach of the substantial effects test.[101] This, of course, does not necessarily mean that the second-era cases were decided wrongly, it merely makes plain that Justice Thomas and the other conservatives thought they were. This said, when the Commerce Clause is read in light of the *principle* of federalism that the Framers made central to the American system of government it becomes clear, at least to me, that the conservatives were right to criticize these cases in *Lopez*—just as they were wrong to argue as they did in *Term Limits*.

To appreciate why this is so, it is necessary to recall the circumstances under which the Commerce Clause was born: The American economy was in turmoil during much of the Confederation period (1781–1789) and the key men in calling the federal Convention of 1787 (e.g., Alexander Hamilton and James Madison) were determined to rectify the situa-

tion by empowering the national government with the authority to regulate interstate commerce—a power it did not possess under the Articles of
Confederation. Although these circumstances might suggest that the national government would enjoy almost boundless authority to regulate
commerce under a constitution—under *the* Constitution—that included
a commerce clause, and Samuel Beer suggests precisely this point in con-
structing his national theory of federalism,[102] such a suggestion would
fail to tell the whole story of the circumstances under which the Commerce Clause came to be. Specifically, the national theory of federalism in
general, as advanced most systematically by Beer, and of the Commerce
Clause in particular, as advanced by the liberal members of the Supreme
Court during the second era of the Court's Commerce Clause jurisprudence (including the dissenting justices in *Lopez*), ignores the facts that
the Anti-Federalists went out of their way to object that the Constitution
should not create a government structure in which the national government was empowered to regulate "just about anything" through the
Commerce Clause[103] and that the Federalists assuaged these concerns by
insisting that it *did not*.[104] That the Constitution is neither national nor
federal, "but a composition of both," is once again in evidence.

This critique of the Supreme Court's second-era Commerce Clause jurisprudence aside, a final question that must be asked is this: Is *Lopez*
merely a flash in the pan? Is *Lopez*, in other words, the beginning *and end*
of the third era, or do the conservative members of the Rehnquist Court
intend to carry the decision forward and use it to dismantle the modern
administrative state? Justice Souter, for one, suggests that *Lopez* is not the
conservative justices' last word on the Commerce Clause. As he put it in
his dissenting opinion in the case:

> Not every epochal case has come in epochal trappings. *Jones and Laughlin*
> did not reject the direct-indirect standard in so many words; it just said the
> relation of the regulated subject matter to commerce was direct enough.
> . . . But we know what happened.[105]

Justice Thomas, at least, appears to want to carry *Lopez* forward. In an
unusually long dissent from a denial of certiorari in *Cargill, Inc. v. United
States* (1995) he argued that those provisions of the Clean Water Act that
permit the Army Corps of Engineers to assert jurisdiction over private
property based solely on the actual or potential presence of migratory
birds that cross state lines probably violate the Commerce Clause. "The

basis asserted to create jurisdiction over petitioner's land in this case seems to me to be even more far-fetched than that offered, and rejected, in *Lopez*," Justice Thomas wrote.[106] Whether he can one day convince a majority of the Court to carry *Lopez* forward remains to be seen.

Conclusion

With the possible exception of race relations, no issue goes more to the heart of the American regime than federalism. As was described at the outset of this chapter, many of the great political battles in American history have been couched in terms of competing conceptions of the proper division of power and responsibility in the political system of the United States.

With the possible exception of race relations, no issue goes more to the heart of Justice Thomas's jurisprudence than federalism. It is fair to say that Justice Thomas's two most important opinions during his acclimation period on the Supreme Court came in *Term Limits* and *Lopez*. After all, most people knew where Clarence Thomas stood on civil rights. Few knew, although many may have suspected, where he stood on the defining question of American politics: the nature of the federal Union.

This chapter has been structured around the proposition that a "value-free" analysis of American federalism is difficult to complete. Some may disagree with this proposition, but most probably will not. Even Beer admits that the national theory of federalism that is advanced in *his* history of the subject is a product of his liberal politics.[107] Clearly, the compact theory of federalism that underlies Justice Thomas's *Term Limits* and *Lopez* opinions is a product of his conservative politics. But then so are the reactions, both favorable and unfavorable, to those opinions the products of the politics of the commentators in question: conservatives loved Justice Thomas's federalism opinions; liberals hated them.

Neither the national theory of federalism advanced by liberals nor the compact theory of federalism advanced by conservatives fully captures the principle of federalism to which the Framers dedicated the nation. Nowhere, in other words, is the Framers' penchant for compromise—albeit for *necessary* compromise—better represented than in the complex division of government power and responsibility they established in the Constitution. To make the point in more immediate terms, Justice Thomas was quite *correct* in *Lopez* to criticize Justice Breyer for failing to identify even a single example of when a particular subject area might be off limits to Congress under the nationalistic reading of the Commerce Clause. But by the same token, Justice Thomas was *incorrect* to maintain, as he did in *Term Limits*, that what the Framers meant in the Constitution by "We the People" was really "We the States." If we can be certain of anything about the Constitution, we can be certain of that.

PART III

Law and Politics

6

Conclusion

[L]aw is something more than merely the preferences of the power elites writ large. The law is a distinct, independent discipline, with certain principles and modes of analysis that yield what we can discern to be correct and incorrect answers to certain problems.
　　　　—Justice Clarence Thomas, Speech to the University of
　　　　Kansas School of Law (1996)

Strict adherence to this [originalist] approach is essential if we are to fulfill our constitutionally assigned role of giving full effect to the mandate of the Framers without infusing the constitutional fabric with our own political views.
　　　　—Thomas, J., concurring in *Lewis v. Casey* (1996)

To borrow one of Justice Thomas's most memorable lines from the confirmation hearings, "I have no agenda, senator."[1] I began following Justice Thomas's career in the summer of 1991 when, as a doctoral student at the University of Virginia, I read in the newspaper that President Bush's newly announced nominee to the Supreme Court was articulating the same theory of constitutional interpretation that I was attempting to articulate in my Ph.D. dissertation. I was intrigued both by then-Judge Thomas's interest in the relationship between the Declaration of Independence and the Constitution of the United States and, after I reviewed Thomas's record, by several (though not all) of his policy positions that seemed, at least to me, to be inconsistent with the classical liberal political philosophy embodied in the Declaration. Consequently, as any budding scholar might, I wrote a law review essay about these matters: an essay that was prereleased to the Senate Judiciary Committee and to the press by the University of Virginia and the *Journal of Law and Politics* (the law review at UVA that published my essay).[2] After "enjoying" my fifteen minutes of fame, being quoted (and occasionally misquoted) in the media and by the Judiciary Committee as an "expert" on Thomas's natural law views,[3] I then returned to the solitary task of completing my dissertation.[4] However, I did not lose interest in Justice Thomas. I continued to follow his career, and I even published two more essays about him.[5]

Given the seemingly insatiable public appetite for information about Justice Thomas, I thought, as a "part-time" judicial behavioralist (to paraphrase another of Justice Thomas's memorable lines) might,[6] that the occasion of Justice Thomas's first five terms on the Supreme Court—his so-called "acclimation" or "freshman" period[7]—might warrant a book-length treatment of his jurisprudence. New York University Press, the publisher of my first book, agreed. The result is this book, which I regard as sort of a sequel to my first book, *To Secure These Rights: The Declaration of Independence and Constitutional Interpretation* (1995). This chapter endeavors to tie together into a coherent whole what the reader might have felt were two disparate parts of *First Principles*: Part I, the "Politics" part, and Part II, the "Law" part.

I will state the most obvious conclusion first: People judge *Justice* Thomas, as they judged *nominee* Thomas, in almost purely partisan terms. If my research for this book has convinced me of anything, it has convinced me of that. In fact, the commentary about Justice Thomas became so predictable that, if I knew where the author of a particular essay fell on the political spectrum (and I usually did), I could anticipate with virtual certainty what she or he was going to conclude about a particular area of Justice Thomas's jurisprudence *before* I read the essay. In some cases—for instance, the essays written by A. Leon Higginbotham, Jr.[8]—the author did not even *try* to hide the partisan nature of her or his "analysis." This is not scholarship or journalism, this is advocacy.[*]

---

[*]Although I tried to provide a balanced sampling of the commentary about Justice Thomas throughout this book, I sometimes found it difficult to find a law review essay or a press story about a particular area of Justice Thomas's jurisprudence (e.g., the Establishment Clause) that was written from a conservative perspective. My experience in this regard is consistent with the widely held belief that most academics and most journalists are liberal. See, for example, Robert H. Bork, *Slouching towards Gomorrah: Modern Liberalism and American Decline* (New York: Regan Books, 1996), chap. 5. See also Mark V. Tushnet, foreword to Jean Stefancic and Richard Delgado, *No Mercy: How Conservative Think Tanks and Foundations Changed America's Social Agenda* (Philadelphia: Temple University Press, 1996), ix-xi (stating that "[c]onservatives have correctly understood that liberals have indeed conducted their own 'culture wars' in the academy and are winning those wars").

The second most obvious conclusion, and one closely related to the first, is that Justice Thomas is *not* simply Justice Antonin Scalia's loyal apprentice—no matter how vociferously some seek to establish and maintain this myth.[9] Justice Thomas is *his own* man, with *his own* jurisprudence. Indeed, as Part II documented, Justice Thomas has written a number of provocative concurring and dissenting opinions—many of which Justice Scalia *declined* to join.[10] Careful students of the Supreme Court have become increasingly aware in recent years of the distinctions between Justice Thomas's jurisprudence and Justice Scalia's (e.g., Justice Thomas's opinions are said to be "bolder and more adventurous"),[11] but some still subscribe to the earlier view that Justice Thomas simply follows Justice Scalia.[12*]

What *is* Justice Thomas's jurisprudence? At the risk of oversimplification, it may be summarized in a brief statement: Justice Thomas is a "liberal originalist" on civil rights and a "conservative originalist" on civil liberties and federalism. That is to say, Justice Thomas appeals to the *ideal* of equality at the heart of the Declaration of Independence when he decides questions involving race, but to the Framers' *specific* intentions—as manifested in the text and historical context of the Constitution—when he decides questions involving civil liberties and federalism. Nowhere is this dichotomy better illustrated than in *Adarand Constructors, Inc. v. Peña* (1995) and *Rosenberger v. University of Virginia* (1995). In the former case, an affirmative action suit, Justice Thomas invoked the Declaration of Independence as the rule of decision. In the latter, a case involving the Establishment Clause that was decided a mere seventeen days after the former, he rejected an appeal to natural rights political philosophy and chose instead to decide the case on the basis of Borkean originalism.[13] To make the point more directly, *Justice Thomas approaches legal questions pertaining to race differently than he approaches legal questions pertaining to other matters.* The irony in this conclusion is difficult to miss. After all, EEOC *Chairman* Thomas established his reputation by arguing that Blacks should be treated the *same* as everyone else.

---

*Justice Thomas often responds in good humor to the conventional wisdom about his working relationship with Justice Scalia. For example, when asked after a 1997 speech what he thought about the rumor that Justice Scalia would resign from the Supreme Court to seek the 2000 Republican presidential nomination, Justice Thomas quipped: "Justice Scalia is leading me. I d[o]n't think he has time to be President." Clarence Thomas, Speech to the Savannah, Georgia, Bar Association, Savannah, GA, 1997, broadcast on C-SPAN.

With respect to specific legal doctrine (e.g., desegregation, prisoners' rights), this dichotomy in Justice Thomas's interpretive methodology has led him to classical liberal (i.e., Lockean) results in race cases (see Chapter 3) and to modern conservative results in almost every other type of public law case (see Chapters 4 and 5).[14] Sometimes, this has meant that he has written judicial opinions that directly contradict his confirmation hearings testimony on the legal doctrine in question. For example, *nominee* Thomas testified, "I don't have any objection or basis to object or at this point quarrel with the way that the Court has interpreted the interstate commerce clause," but *Justice* Thomas issued a dramatic concurring opinion in which he called into question the entirety of the Supreme Court's post-1937 Commerce Clause jurisprudence.[15*]

Last, but far from least, there is the undeniable fact that Justice Thomas's judicial opinions often read the same as his policy speeches and articles (both those he issued before he was nominated to the Supreme Court and those he has issued since his confirmation). This is especially apparent in civil rights, the area in which *Chairman* Thomas had the most to say as a policymaker, and the area in which *Justice* Thomas continues to say the most as a member of the Supreme Court. Indeed, Justice Thomas's judicial opinions in all three of the major areas of civil rights law—desegregation, voting rights, and affirmative action—are virtually identical to his policy statements about these matters. Recall from Chapter 2, for example, that EEOC *Chairman* Thomas criticized *Brown v. Board of Education* (1954), the Warren Court's landmark desegregation decision, for relying upon "dubious social science," rather than "reason and moral and political principles, as established in the Constitution and the Declaration of Independence,"[16] and from Chapter 3 that *Justice* Thomas became in *Missouri v. Jenkins* (1995) the first Supreme Court justice to criticize *Brown* directly—and for precisely the same reason.[17] The heart of *Justice* Thomas's concurring opinion in *Jenkins*, like the heart of *Chairman* Thomas's law review articles about segregation, is his belief

---

*The same holds true for several areas of public law in which Justice Thomas voted, but did not write an opinion. *Nominee* Thomas, for example, expressed grave concern about Justice Scalia's opinion for the Court in the free exercise of religion case *Oregon v. Smith*, 494 U.S. 872 (1990), but *Justice* Thomas in *Church of the Lukumi Babalu Aye v. City of Hialeah*, 508 U.S. 520 (1993), joined the majority opinion that endorsed *Smith*. Some have maintained that the abortion issue falls into this same category. See, for example, Joyce A. Baugh and Christopher E. Smith, "Doubting Thomas: Confirmation Veracity Meets Performance Reality," *Seattle University Law Review* 19 (spring 1996): 455–96, 465–9.

that the *Brown* Court was wrong to rely upon disputable social science evidence to declare segregation unconstitutional, and that the Court could have reached the same result by invoking the "constitutional principle" that "the Government must treat citizens as individuals, and not as members of racial, ethnic or religious groups."[18]

The congruence between *Justice* Thomas's judicial opinions and *Chairman* Thomas's policy statements continues in the voting rights area—widely regarded as the most important area of public law confronting the Supreme Court in the 1990s.[19] Recall in this regard *Chairman* Thomas's April 18, 1988, address to the Tocqueville Forum:

> The Voting Rights Act of 1965 certainly was crucial legislation. It has transformed the policies in the South. Unfortunately, many of the Court's decisions in the area of voting rights have presupposed that blacks, whites, Hispanics, and other ethnic groups will inevitably vote in blocs. Instead of looking at the right to vote as an individual right, the Court has regarded the right as protected when the individual's racial or ethnic group has sufficient clout.[20]

Compare this policy statement to *Justice* Thomas's controversial concurring opinion in *Holder v. Hall* (1994), an opinion in which he called for a dramatic rethinking of the Supreme Court's voting rights jurisprudence—including the overruling of *Thornburg v. Gingles* (1986).[21] In his *Holder* concurring opinion, Justice Thomas—who had testified during his 1991 confirmation hearings that "I absolutely support the aggressive enforcement of voting rights law and certainly support the results in those cases" (which included, by name, *Gingles*)—strongly objected to the underlying assumption of the Court's voting rights decisions: that members of racial and ethnic groups "think alike" on public policy matters.[22] Justice Thomas wrote:

> The dabbling in political theory that dilution cases have prompted, however, is hardly the worst aspect of our vote dilution jurisprudence. Far more pernicious has been the Court's willingness to accept the one underlying premise that must inform every minority vote dilution claim: the assumption that the group asserting dilution is not merely a racial or ethnic group, but a group having distinct political interests as well. Of necessity, in resolving vote dilution actions we have given credence to the view that race defines political interest. We have acted on the implicit assumption that members of racial and ethnic groups must all think alike on important matters of public policy and must have their own "minority preferred"

representatives holding seats in elected bodies if they are to be considered represented at all.[23]

Put directly, *Justice* Thomas's *judicial* opinion in *Holder v. Hall* differs from *Chairman* Thomas's *policy* speech to the Tocqueville Forum in word choice alone. The political value underlying the two is identical: a Black person should be regarded as an *individual*, not as a member of a racial *group*.

The identity between *Chairman* Thomas's *political* views and *Justice* Thomas's *legal* views is most dramatically presented in the area of civil rights with which he is most closely associated: affirmative action. In the area of affirmative action, *Chairman* Thomas's political views barely differ from *Justice* Thomas's legal views in word choice. *Chairman* Thomas wrote in a *Yale Law and Policy Review* article (1987):

> Class preferences are an affront to the rights and dignity of individuals—both those individuals who are directly disadvantaged by them, and those who are their supposed beneficiaries. I think that preferential hiring on the basis of race or gender will increase racial divisiveness, disempower women and minorities by fostering the notion that they are permanently disabled and in need of handouts, and delay the day when skin color and gender are truly the least important things about a person.[24]

Compare that policy statement with what *Justice* Thomas had to say about affirmative action in his concurring opinion in *Adarand* (1995):

> These programs not only raise grave constitutional questions, they also undermine the moral basis of the equal protection principle. Purchased at the price of immeasurable human suffering, the equal protection principle reflects our Nation's understanding that such classifications ultimately have a destructive impact on the individual and our society. . . . So-called "benign" discrimination teaches many that because of chronic and apparently immutable handicaps, minorities cannot compete with them without their patronizing indulgence. Inevitably, such programs engender attitudes of superiority or, alternatively, provoke resentment among those who believe that they have been wronged by the government's use of race. These programs stamp minorities with a badge of inferiority and may cause them to develop dependencies or to adopt an attitude that they are "entitled" to preferences.[25]

The political nature of Justice Thomas's jurisprudence is also apparent in the areas of civil liberties and federalism. Justice Thomas's position on the authoritativeness of Joseph Story's views about the Constitution is a particularly good example of this fact. Recall from Chapter 5 that Justice Thomas refused in his *Term Limits* dissent to be bound by Justice Story's views about the nature of the federal Union. Justice Thomas wrote:

> Justice Story was a brilliant and accomplished man, and one cannot casually dismiss his views. On the other hand, he was not a member of the Founding generation, and his *Commentaries on the Constitution* were written a half century after the framing. Rather than representing the original understanding of the Constitution, they represent only his own understanding. In a range of cases concerning the federal/state relation, moreover, this Court has deemed positions taken in Story's commentaries to be more nationalist than the Constitution warrants. . . . In this case too, Story's position that the only powers reserved to the States are those that the States enjoyed before the framing conflicts with both the plain language of the Tenth Amendment and the underlying theory of the Constitution.[26]

In the prisoners' rights context, in contrast, Justice Thomas relied heavily upon Justice Story's interpretation of the Eighth Amendment as explicated in said same *Commentaries on the Constitution on the United States* (1833). More specifically, Justice Thomas invoked Justice Story's *Commentaries*, among other sources, to support his conclusion that the Framers' original intent was that the Eighth Amendment did not apply to injuries that befall inmates during incarceration.[27]

Although this book is about Justice Thomas's jurisprudence, it is important to point out here that he is not alone in marrying law and politics in his Supreme Court opinions. To mention but one example, Justice John Paul Stevens, who is arguably Justice Thomas's most vocal critic on the Rehnquist Court (see Part II), is every bit as political. Indeed, it is interesting to note that in the matters just described—the nature of the federal Union and prisoners' rights—Justice Stevens invoked as authoritative Justice Story's views about the Constitution when it suited his purposes and ignored them when they did not. More specifically, Justice Stevens relied upon Justice Story's *Commentaries* in his *Term Limits* opinion,[28] but ignored them in the prisoners' rights context—and everywhere else as far as I can see.

None of this should be surprising. To state a catch phrase, "we are all realists now."[29] In other words, although Justice Thomas went to great lengths in arguably his most significant speech since joining the Supreme Court—his April 8, 1996, speech about "Judging" to the University of Kansas School of Law—to *reject* the prevailing view that law is politics,[30] my reading of his Supreme Court record leaves me unconvinced that he practices what he preaches. Justice Thomas is, in short, merely an especially fascinating example of the realist maxim that judges read their policy preferences into the law they are interpreting. Justice Felix Frankfurter, who was perhaps the only exception to this rule,[31] made this point well in a 1937 letter to President Franklin D. Roosevelt:

> People have been taught to believe that when the Supreme Court speaks it is not they [the justices] who speak but the Constitution, whereas, of course, in so many vital cases, it is *they* who speak and *not* the Constitution. And I verily believe that that is what the country needs most to understand.[32]*

~

At this writing, Justice Thomas has completed his seventh term on the Supreme Court. His "rookie years" are over, as he colorfully phrased it in a speech just prior to the commencement of his sixth term.[33] He fully intends to serve on the Court "through the next four decades."[34] It is possible that his jurisprudence will change during the coming years. After all, although it is the exception to the rule, some justices' views have changed during their time on the Court. Justice Harry Blackmun is the most famous example of this; Justice David Souter is seemingly the most recent. (Both changed from conservative to liberal.) Liberals certainly hope that Justice Thomas will change—that he will remember from where he came[35]—but most probably do not expect that he will.

Some things about Justice Thomas will almost certainly remain the same. Most notable in this regard is his continuing to be linked with Anita Hill in the minds of most Americans. This book opened with a dis-

---

*Richard A. Posner, in the article about judicial biography that greatly influenced my approach to writing about Justice Thomas, observed that "Oddly, the legal realists did not write judicial biographies. The crits [the intellectual heirs of the realists], too, have shown very little interest in the lives of judges." Posner speculated that this was because "their judicial heroes would not bear close scrutiny." Richard A. Posner, "Judicial Biography," *New York University Law Review* 70 (June 1995): 502–23, 515. Clearly, *First Principles* is written from a realist and/or critical perspective.

cussion of the controversy regarding Anita Hill and it will now close with it. The publication of Hill's *Speaking Truth to Power* (1997)[36] makes this unavoidable.[37]

By my count, Hill's is the *fifteenth* book about Clarence Thomas's 1991 Supreme Court confirmation hearings. All of the books—including Hill's—have focused on that portion of the hearings devoted to Hill's allegations that Thomas had sexually harassed her during their tenure together at the U.S. Department of Education and the EEOC.

Clarence Thomas is now enjoying a lifetime appointment on the highest court in the land. Anita Hill is now living the life of a rich and famous legal commentator. Employers, courts, and politicians now take claims of sexual harassment seriously.

It is time to move beyond Anita Hill.

I do not mean this as a criticism of Hill. If anyone has the right to author a book about the most famous confirmation hearing in American history, it is the two people whose lives it changed the most: Clarence Thomas and Anita Hill. We have now heard from Hill on the matter. I doubt we will ever hear from Justice Thomas. (Justice Thomas has let it be known on more than one occasion that he has no further comment about Hill's allegations.)

Frankly, I do not know whom to believe. Although Hill offers nothing new in her account of what transpired between her and Clarence Thomas a decade and a half ago, she at times makes a persuasive case for her position. Indeed, Hill spends considerable time in her book answering the questions raised by her doubters. On why she did not complain about Thomas's behavior prior to the fall of 1991, for example, she quite plausibly replies that the courts did not take sexual harassment claims seriously in the early 1980s and that, even if they had, she was afraid to report the incidents. "Thomas made it clear that he expected me to keep my mouth shut," Hill writes in one of the book's most chilling passages.[38]

Hill leaves other questions unanswered, however. Why, for example, would she have followed Thomas from the Department of Education to the EEOC if he had sexually harassed her? She does not say. This does not mean that there is not an answer. But Hill does not provide it. (Some experts have said that Hill's behavior in following Thomas was not unusual for someone who was a victim of sexual harassment: a kind of "harassee's syndrome.")

Unanswered substantive questions aside, *Speaking Truth to Power* suffers from a number of stylistic shortcomings. First and foremost, while Hill certainly has a lot to complain about, her book is written with a bitterness that brings to mind Robert H. Bork's confirmation hearings memoir, *The Tempting of America: The Political Seduction of the Law* (1990).[39] Bork, who was one of Hill's teachers at Yale Law School, was not well served by writing with a poison pen. Neither is Hill.

There is also the matter of Hill's narrative framework. Hill refers frequently in her book to the tremendous impact her conservative Christian upbringing has had on her life. Indeed, the book both opens and closes with poignant descriptions of the strength she received from her family and friends during her ordeal and there are so many references to prayer sprinkled throughout the remainder of the text that I sometimes felt as if I was reading Senator John C. Danforth's avowedly biblical book on the hearings, *Resurrection: The Confirmation of Clarence Thomas* (1994).[40]

For the most part, however, Hill's narrative framework is "Critical Race Feminism," an increasingly influential school of legal thought that argues that the historical experiences and contemporary realities of women of color are profoundly influenced by a legacy of racism and sexism that is neither linear nor logical.[41] Nowhere is Hill's commitment to Critical Race Feminism more apparent than in her characterization of how she felt when then-Senate Judiciary Committee Chairman Joseph R. Biden, Jr., told her after he was finished with his first round of questioning that the committee members would alternate by party during the remainder of the session. "I had not been a part of this agreement that in essence the Democrats and Republicans would take turns with me," Hill writes in one of her book's many sexual references.[42]

So why is Hill's narrative framework important? Because it suggests that if she was not captured by the "radical left" before she testified against Thomas—and she says in her book that she was not—she certainly is now. Of course, Hill has the right to associate with whomever she pleases. After all, Justice Thomas is often said to have found solace in the company of the "radical right." But knowing Hill's narrative framework might put her substantive case against Thomas in jeopardy. Why? Because the "story-telling" technique that is at the heart of Critical Race Feminism does not require an adherence to fact.

What all of this suggests to me is that we have come full circle on Thomas-Hill. Bluntly stated, Hill's book is not likely to change anybody's mind. Some people will continue to believe that she was telling the truth; others will continue to believe that he was telling the truth; and still others—including myself—will continue to be unsure.

Perhaps Hill's book will do some good, however. Perhaps now that she has written her long-anticipated account of the hearings we can move beyond what happened *then* and start paying more attention to what *Justice* Thomas is doing *now*. Those who revel in controversy will find much of interest if they do. *First Principles: The Jurisprudence of Clarence Thomas* has endeavored to take a step in this direction.

Appendices

Appendix I

Justice Thomas and the Freshman Effect Hypothesis

Judicial behavioralists long have been interested in the initial behavior of Supreme Court justices.[1] This interest is largely a result of both the Court's great power and its being susceptible to small group dynamics.[2] Analysis of the behavior of new justices is particularly relevant when the composition of the Court is rapidly and dramatically changing, as the Rehnquist Court's is. Moreover, the fact that the Rehnquist Court is divided on many major issues suggests that the vote of a new justice could be the deciding vote—perhaps the most important reason of all for assessing the impact of a new justice.[3]

Judicial behavioralists inquire into the behavior of a new member of the Court by looking for signs of the so-called "freshman" or "acclimation" effect.[4] The freshman effect hypothesis consists of three components. First, the new justice is awed and bewildered by her or his new office and responsibilities. As a result, she or he takes several years to feel confident in the performance of her or his duties. Second, the senior members of the Court, aware of the new justice's bewilderment, do not assign the new justice an equal share of the opinion writing. Third, the new justice refrains from aligning herself or himself with the Court's established voting blocs, choosing instead to explore a variety of political and jurisprudential approaches. The acclimation period typically is said to consist of the first five years of a justice's tenure on the Court.[5] Justice Thomas is on record as being in agreement with the essence of the freshman effect hypothesis.[6]

The structure of this appendix is adapted from Scott D. Gerber, "Justice Clarence Thomas: First Term, First Impressions," *Howard Law Journal* 35 (winter 1992): 115–53, 119–27. The data have been updated. I thank James Taylor for his research assistance.

Initial Bewilderment

Some of the most distinguished justices ever to sit on the Supreme Court have acknowledged initially being bewildered by their responsibilities on the Court. For example, Justice William Brennan noted, "One enters a new and wholly unfamiliar world when he joins the Supreme Court,"[7] while Justice Felix Frankfurter observed that "even Justices who have come to the Supreme Court fresh from a longish and conspicuously competent tenure on the lower federal courts do not find the demands of their new task familiar."[8] Because new justices traditionally say very little publicly about their experiences on the Court, scholars consider the initial bewilderment component of the freshman effect hypothesis to be the most difficult to measure. Thus, any conclusions that are drawn about this component are deemed tentative and speculative.[9] Contrary to Justice Frankfurter's observation, however, some scholars have found that initial bewilderment is less likely to occur for new justices with prior judicial experience.[10]

In a brief interview after his first term, Justice Thomas said that he was "a little bit anxious and apprehensive" in his early days on the Court. "There is no way to brush up on what is expected of you."[11] Justice Thomas's extensive service as chairman of the Equal Employment Opportunity Commission and his tenure, albeit brief (approximately a year and a half), on the U.S. Court of Appeals for the D.C. Circuit suggest that he was simply being modest in the interview. Indeed, as was the case with Justice Anthony Kennedy, Justice Thomas's personal modesty and humility did not necessarily translate into personal disorientation on the high Court.[12]

Opinion Writing

The opinion writing component of the freshman effect hypothesis postulates that the senior members of the Supreme Court (the chief justice if he is in the majority, the most senior associate justice in the majority if the chief justice is not), apparently believing that it takes some time for a new justice to get acclimated to the Court, will not assign a new justice a proportionate share of majority opinions. Additionally, this component assumes that any opinion assigned to a new justice is routine and relatively unimportant.

TABLE 1

Number of Opinions Authored (1991–1995 Supreme Court Terms)

	Majority Opinions	Majority Votes[a]	OAR[b]	Concurring Opinions	Dissenting Opinions[c]	Total Opinions Authored[d]
Rehnquist	56	421	12.93	8	26	90
White	29	198	14.65	6	13	48
Blackmun	28	219	12.79	26	34	88
Stevens	53	337	15.73	42	96	191
O'Connor	59	414	14.25	42	38	139
Scalia	50	407	12.29	64	42	156
Kennedy	49	448	10.94	37	18	104
Souter	48	413	11.62	32	31	111
Thomas	44	364	12.09	30	37	111
Ginsburg	26	203	12.81	22	18	66
Breyer	15	138	10.87	7	13	35
Mean	41.55	323.82	12.82	32.55	32.09	103.36
Std. Dev.	13.84	106.86	1.45	17.34	22.18	44.09

[a] The number of times a justice voted in the majority (including concurring votes).
[b] The OAR column reports percentages.
[c] Opinions are counted as dissents whether the justice dissented in part or in whole.
[d] Majority opinions + concurring opinions + dissenting opinions.

Table 1 displays the number of opinions written by each justice during the 1991–1995 Supreme Court terms, the period under review in this book. Justices Byron White, Harry Blackmun, Ruth Bader Ginsburg, and Stephen Breyer did not serve all five terms. Justice Thomas's forty-four majority opinions rank him last among the seven justices who did. With fifty-nine majority opinions, Justice Sandra Day O'Connor ranked first, and with fifty-six Chief Justice William Rehnquist ranked a close second. These numbers are misleading, however: The justices can only write majority opinions when they have voted with the majority.

This contingency can be accounted for by applying the "Opinion Assignment Ratio" (OAR). The OAR is calculated by dividing the number of times a justice was assigned the majority opinion by the number of times the justice voted with the majority, multiplied by one hundred to yield a percentage.[13]

Justice Thomas's OAR is 12.09, which places him eighth out of the eleven justices who served on the Rehnquist Court during any of the 1991–1995 terms (the OAR standardizes the percentages, so all the justices may be compared). However, given that 12.09 is only a fraction below the mean and well within one standard deviation of the mean, the opinion writing component of the freshman effect hypothesis does not apply in Justice Thomas's case—at least in terms of the proportion of majority opinions written. That is to say, the senior members of the Rehnquist Court did not appear reluctant to assign Justice Thomas the opinion for the Court. This conclusion is bolstered by the fact that the total number of opinions written by Justice Thomas, as well as his concurring opinions and dissenting opinions when separately considered, are well within one standard deviation of the Court's mean. As such, the senior members of the Rehnquist Court were likely aware that Justice Thomas is confident in his views and, therefore, that he was not apt to be intimidated by the responsibility of writing an opinion for the Court.

The second aspect of the opinion writing component of the freshman effect hypothesis is that if a new justice is assigned any majority opinions, those opinions are routine and relatively unimportant. The "importance" of opinions has been measured in a variety of ways. Elliot E. Slotnick operationally defined "important" opinions as those subsequently included in leading constitutional law casebooks,[14] while Harold J. Spaeth looked to those highlighted on the covers of the advance volumes of *Lawyers' Edition, Supreme Court Reports*.[15] However, important opinions take several years to be integrated into casebooks, and the advance volumes can be underinclusive. Therefore, for the purposes of the present analysis, an "important" opinion is one identified as a "leading case" in the widely read *Harvard Law Review* Supreme Court term-in-review issue, published each November.

According to the *Harvard Law Review*, there were 101 important decisions during Justice Thomas's first five years on the Supreme Court. Of the seven justices who served during all of these terms, Chief Justice Rehnquist, the senior member of the Court in terms of opinion assignment authority, wrote twenty-four important majority opinions, Justice Stevens, the senior associate justice among the seven justices who served all five terms, wrote twenty, Justice Kennedy wrote seventeen and one-third,[16] Justice Scalia wrote eleven, Justices O'Connor and Souter each wrote eight and one-third, and Justice Thomas wrote seven.

The fact that Justice Thomas was assigned seven important opinions for the Court is contrary to the opinion writing component of the freshman effect hypothesis. Although Justice Thomas was assigned fewer important opinions than any of the seven justices who served for all of the 1991–1995 terms, he was assigned some—and nearly as many as each of his colleagues, with the exceptions of the two most senior, Chief Justice Rehnquist and Justice Stevens, who assigned *themselves* many important opinions, and Justice Kennedy, who tended to be a swing vote in many important cases. Therefore, the senior members of the Rehnquist Court can be said to have had some confidence in Justice Thomas when it came to assigning him important opinions for the Court. Additionally, the fact that Justice Thomas wrote twelve concurring opinions and eleven dissenting opinions in the 101 important cases suggests that he was not afraid to speak out on significant issues, something which Chapters 3, 4, and 5 made clear beyond cavil. Justice Thomas's senior colleagues were almost certainly aware of his willingness to speak out when they decided to assign him seven important majority opinions.

Voting Alignment

The third and final component of the freshman effect hypothesis is that a new justice refrains from aligning herself or himself with the Court's established voting blocs, choosing instead to explore a variety of political and jurisprudential approaches. This component can be evaluated by examining the data in table 2.

Table 2 contains cell entries depicting the number of times two justices voted together. The data were derived by dividing the number of times a pair of justices voted together by the total number of cases in which they both voted. Indices of interagreement measure the strength of voting blocs. The indices are the mean of the percentages of the measured justices. By convention, an index of interagreement of .70 or greater is considered high, .60 to .69 is moderate, and .59 or less is low.[17]

TABLE 2

Voting Alignments (by Percentage Agreement) in Full Opinion Decisions
(1991–1995 Terms)

	WR	BW	HB	JPS	SDO	AS	AK	DS	CT	RBG	SB
Rehnquist	——	74.78	51.74	45.51	73.44	75.93	76.97	67.43	73.65	66.27	61.21
White	74.78	——	60.43	57.83	65.22	63.48	70.43	70.43	58.70		
Blackmun	51.74	60.43	——	73.82	57.73	41.32	55.84	64.35	40.34	66.67	
Stevens	45.51	57.83	73.82	——	56.64	43.36	57.05	64.73	39.83	73.41	69.70
O'Connor	73.44	65.22	57.73	56.64	——	65.35	70.75	70.54	62.86	67.08	72.73
Scalia	75.93	63.48	41.32	43.36	65.35	——	73.03	62.66	67.73	71.83	68.48
Kennedy	76.97	70.43	55.84	57.05	70.75	73.03	——	55.19	67.73	71.83	68.48
Souter	67.43	70.43	64.35	64.73	70.54	62.66	55.19	——	55.19	79.76	83.64
Thomas	73.65	58.70	40.34	39.83	62.86	80.08	67.63	55.19	——	36.70	51.12
Ginsburg	66.27		66.67	73.41	67.08	59.32	71.83	79.76	36.70	——	76.36
Breyer	61.21			69.70	72.73	55.15	68.48	83.64	51.12	76.36	——

NOTE: Only nonunanimous decisions are included.

At .80, the index of interagreement for Justices Thomas and Scalia—a staunch conservative[18]—is very high. (By comparison, the index of inter-agreement for the two most liberal justices, Blackmun and Stevens, is .74.) At .74, Justice Thomas also has a high level of interagreement with Chief Justice Rehnquist, another very conservative justice.[19] As a bloc, Justice Thomas, Chief Justice Rehnquist, and Justice Scalia register a high level of interagreement at .77. Justice Thomas therefore can be said to have performed contrary to the voting alignment component of the freshman effect hypothesis: he quickly joined the conservative wing of the Court. This conclusion is buttressed by noting that, as a rule, Justice Thomas voted proportionately less often with a particular justice the more liberal that justice was. Indeed, Justice Thomas was the most con-servative member of the Rehnquist Court during the 1991–1995 terms, given that he had a moderate level of interagreement in split decisions with only Justices O'Connor and Kennedy, whereas Justice Scalia had a high level of interagreement with Justice Kennedy and a moderate level with Justices White, O'Connor, Souter, and Ginsburg (more on this in Appendix II).

Conclusion

An empirical analysis of Justice Thomas's first five terms on the Supreme Court finds a jurist who quickly became assimilated into the business of the Court. Put more precisely, none of the components of the freshman effect hypothesis applied to Justice Thomas: he was not bewildered on the Court; he wrote his fair share of majority opinions, as well as some opin-ions for the Court in important cases; and he was firmly established on the Court's conservative wing.

Appendix II

Justice Thomas's Voting Behavior

Judicial behavioralists analyze many types of phenomena beyond the freshman effect hypothesis discussed in Appendix I.[1] The most meaningful such phenomenon for understanding Justice Thomas's jurisprudence is the tendency of a particular justice—in this case, Justice Thomas—to vote in a liberal versus conservative direction. The interest in this phenomenon stems from the widely shared belief among political scientists that a justice's vote in any given case is based principally upon her or his political attitudes and values.[2] In short, political scientists endeavor to quantify the central tenet of legal realism (see Chapter 6).

Table 3 provides the annual voting behavior of each member of the Rehnquist Court during the 1991–1995 terms—the terms that constitute Justice Thomas's acclimation period. It also presents the aggregate voting behavior for each justice during this period (the "total"). The data are categorized by issue area.

By convention, a justice's voting behavior is analyzed to determine whether it is "liberal" or not. Also by convention, "liberal" signifies pro-defendant votes in criminal procedure cases; pro-women or -minorities in civil rights cases; pro-individual against the government in First Amendment, due process, and privacy cases; and pro-attorney in attorney's fees and bar membership cases. In Takings Clause cases a pro-government/anti-owner vote is considered "liberal." In union cases "liberal" represents pro-union votes against both individuals and the government; and in economic cases it represents pro-government votes in challenges to government's regulatory authority and pro-competition, anti-business, pro-liability, pro-injured person, and pro-bankruptcy votes. In federalism and federal taxation cases "liberal" indicates pro-national government positions; in judicial power cases, it represents pro-judiciary positions.[3]

The data indicate that Justice Thomas was strongly conservative in every issue area during each of his first five terms on the Supreme Court. The data further indicate that Justice Thomas was typically the most conservative member of the Rehnquist Court in every issue area during each of the terms[4] and that, in the aggregate, Justice Thomas was the most conservative Rehnquist Court justice. In fact, the only aggregate category in which Justice Thomas was not the most conservative was civil rights, a category in which Justice Scalia was slightly more conservative. (Justice Thomas was nonetheless extremely conservative on civil rights.) Consequently, the empirical analyses in Appendices I and II confirm the jurisprudential analyses that form the heart of this book.

TABLE 3

Liberal Voting of the Justices (1991-1995 Terms)

Term	Civil Liberties	Criminal Procedure	Civil Rights	First Amendment	Economics
Rehnquist					
1991	32.1 (56)	23.8 (21)	50.0 (18)	37.5 (8)	50.0 (28)
1992	27.3 (55)	24.1 (29)	21.4 (14)	37.5 (8)	52.4 (21)
1993	26.1 (46)	17.4 (23)	25.0 (4)	25.0 (4)	62.5 (24)
1994	29.3 (41)	15.8 (19)	50.0 (8)	50.0 (8)	37.5 (16)
1995	34.0 (44)	24.2 (25)	28.6 (14)	80.0 (5)	54.3 (35)
Total	29.6 (243)	24.0 (117)	33.3 (69)	45.5 (33)	54.0 (124)
White					
1991	41.1 (56)	38.1 (21)	61.1 (18)	37.5 (8)	57.1 (28)
1992	40.0 (55)	37.9 (29)	35.7 (14)	37.5 (8)	61.9 (21)
Total	40.5 (111)	38.0 (50)	38.0 (32)	37.5 (16)	59.2 (49)
Blackmun					
1991	73.2 (56)	57.2 (21)	83.3 (18)	87.5 (8)	67.9 (28)
1992	78.2 (55)	72.4 (29)	78.6 (14)	87.5 (8)	52.4 (21)
1993	72.3 (47)	65.2 (23)	75.0 (24)	75.0 (24)	75.0 (24)
Total	78.0 (150)	64.4 (73)	77.3 (44)	85.0 (20)	65.8 (73)

Table 3 *(Continued)*

Term	Civil Liberties	Criminal Procedure	Civil Rights	First Amendment	Economics
	Stevens				
1991	80.4 (56)	76.2 (18)	77.8 (18)	100 (8)	53.6 (28)
1992	76.4 (55)	75.9 (29)	64.3 (14)	87.5 (8)	71.4 (21)
1993	66.0 (47)	62.5 (23)	50.0 (12)	75.0 (4)	66.7 (24)
1994	85.4 (41)	84.2 (19)	72.7 (11)	100 (8)	62.5 (16)
1995	72.3 (44)	72.0 (25)	71.4 (14)	80.0 (5)	72.1 (34)
Total	77.0 (243)	76.1 (117)	58.0 (69)	87.9 (33)	65.3 (122)
	O'Connor				
1991	57.1 (56)	52.4 (21)	61.1 (18)	87.5 (8)	42.9 (28)
1992	43.6 (55)	41.4 (29)	35.7 (14)	50.0 (8)	42.9 (21)
1993	36.2 (47)	26.1 (23)	33.3 (12)	75.0 (4)	34.8 (23)
1994	48.8 (41)	42.1 (19)	54.5 (11)	62.5 (8)	37.5 (16)
1995	52.3 (44)	44.0 (25)	50.0 (14)	100 (5)	60.5 (35)
Total	47.2 (243)	43.6 (117)	49.3 (69)	72.7 (33)	41.1 (124)
	Scalia				
1991	25.0 (56)	14.3 (21)	38.9 (18)	37.5 (8)	39.3 (28)
1992	34.5 (55)	31.0 (29)	28.6 (14)	50.0 (8)	47.6 (21)
1993	29.8 (47)	26.1 (23)	16.7 (12)	50.0 (4)	37.5 (24)
1994	29.3 (41)	26.3 (19)	27.3 (11)	37.5 (8)	43.8 (16)
1995	25.0 (44)	28.0 (25)	21.4 (14)	20.0 (5)	53.4 (35)
Total	28.8 (243)	25.6 (117)	27.5 (69)	39.4 (33)	45.2 (124)

Table 3 *(Continued)*

Term	Civil Liberties	Criminal Procedure	Civil Rights	First Amendment	Economics
Kennedy					
1991	48.2 (56)	38.1 (21)	61.1 (18)	75.0 (8)	42.9 (28)
1992	38.2 (55)	34.5 (29)	28.6 (14)	62.5 (8)	47.6 (21)
1993	44.7 (47)	43.54 (23)	33.3 (12)	50.0 (4)	45.8 (24)
1994	41.5 (41)	31.6 (19)	27.3 (11)	75.0 (8)	43.8 (16)
1995	40.9 (44)	40.0 (25)	35.7 (14)	60.0 (5)	51.3 (35)
Total	41.2 (243)	37.6 (117)	39.1 (69)	66.7 (33)	46.7 (124)
Souter					
1991	50.9 (55)	42.9 (21)	50.0 (18)	100 (8)	53.6 (28)
1992	58.2 (55)	55.2 (29)	42.9 (14)	75.0 (8)	57.1 (21)
1993	59.6 (47)	56.5 (23)	50.0 (12)	50.0 (4)	75.0 (24)
1994	73.2 (41)	57.9 (19)	81.8 (11)	87.5 (8)	43.8 (16)
1995	61.4 (44)	52.0 (25)	64.3 (14)	100 (5)	64.7 (35)
Total	54.3 (242)	53.0 (117)	56.5 (69)	84.9 (33)	60.5 (124)
Thomas					
1991	25.6 (43)	16.7 (18)	42.9 (14)	16.7 (6)	40.0 (25)
1992	30.9 (55)	24.1 (29)	35.7 (14)	37.5 (8)	42.9 (21)
1993	23.4 (47)	13.0 (23)	16.7 (12)	50.0 (4)	25.0 (24)
1994	26.8 (41)	15.8 (19)	27.3 (11)	50.0 (8)	37.5 (16)
1995	27.3 (44)	24.0 (25)	21.4 (14)	20.0 (5)	44.7 (35)
Total	25.5 (230)	20.7 (114)	29.7 (64)	35.5 (31)	39.7 (121)

Table 3 *(Continued)*

Term	Civil Liberties	Criminal Procedure	Civil Rights	First Amendment	Economics
Ginsburg					
1993	55.3 (47)	47.8 (23)	41.7 (12)	75.0 (4)	66.7 (24)
1994	68.3 (41)	52.6 (19)	63.6 (11)	100 (8)	50.0 (16)
1995	56.8 (44)	56.0 (25)	50.0 (14)	60.0 (5)	60.0 (35)
Total	56.0 (91)	49.3 (67)	51.4 (37)	88.2 (17)	60.0 (75)
Breyer					
1994	63.4 (41)	42.1 (19)	81.8 (11)	87.5 (8)	42.9 (14)
1995	65.9 (44)	56.0 (25)	71.4 (14)	100 (5)	57.1 (35)
Total	64.7 (85)	50.0 (44)	72.0 (25)	89.4 (13)	53.1 (49)

NOTE: Figures listed are the percentage of cases in which the justice took the liberal position. Figures in parentheses are the total number of cases in an issue area in which the justice participated. Readers should take care in interpreting the percentages since some of the figures on which they are based are quite small.

The issue areas are defined as follows: Civil liberties combines criminal procedure, civil rights, First Amendment, due process, privacy, and attorneys; Criminal procedure refers to the rights of persons accused of crime except for the due process rights of prisoners; Civil rights includes non–First Amendment freedom cases that pertain to classifications based on race (including Native Americans), age, indigence, voting, residence, military or handicapped status, sex, or alienage; First Amendment refers to the guarantees contained therein. Economics combines labor union activity, commercial business activity, litigation involving injured persons or things, employee actions vis-à-vis employers, zoning regulations, and governmental regulation of corruption other than that involving campaign spending.

SOURCE: Lee Epstein, Jeffrey A. Segal, Harold J. Spaeth, and Thomas G. Walker, *The Supreme Court Compendium: Data, Decisions, and Development*, 2d ed. (Washington DC: CQ Press, 1996). Data for the 1995 term were gathered by James Taylor.

Notes

NOTES TO THE INTRODUCTION

1. Samuel J. Konefsky, *The Constitutional World of Mr. Justice Felix Frank-furter* (New York: Macmillan, 1949), xi–xviii, xvi.

2. See, for example, Timothy M. Hagle, "'Freshman Effects' for Supreme Court Justices," *American Journal of Political Science* 37 (November 1993): 1142–57; Eloise C. Snyder, "The Supreme Court as a Small Group," *Social Forces* 36 (March 1958): 232–8.

3. Clarence Thomas, "Freedom: A Responsibility, Not a Right," *Ohio Northern University Law Review* 21, no. 1 (1994): 5–12, 5.

4. Clarence Thomas, Speech to the National Center for Policy Analysis, 9 September 1996, broadcast on C-SPAN, 19 October 1996.

5. See, for example, Scott D. Gerber, "The State of the Subfield: A View from the Bottom," *Law and Courts* 6 (summer 1996): 3, 27.

6. See Gordon J. McRee, *Life and Correspondence of James Iredell: One of the Associate Justices of the Supreme Court of the United States*, 2 vols. (New York: D. Appleton, 1857–58).

7. See, for example, Gary J. Aichele, *Oliver Wendell Holmes, Jr.: Soldier, Scholar, Judge* (Boston: Twayne, 1989); Liva Baker, *The Justice from Beacon Hill: The Life and Times of Oliver Wendell Holmes* (New York: HarperCollins, 1991); Catherine Drinker Bowen, *Yankee from Olympus: Justice Holmes and His Family* (Boston: Little, Brown, 1944).

8. See Charles F. Hobson, *The Great Chief Justice: John Marshall and the Rule of Law* (Lawrence: University Press of Kansas, 1996).

9. See Tinsley E. Yarbrough, *John Marshall Harlan: Great Dissenter of the Warren Court* (New York: Oxford University Press, 1992); Tinsley E. Yarbrough, *Judicial Enigma: The First Justice Harlan* (New York: Oxford University Press, 1995).

10. Richard A. Posner, "Judicial Biography," *New York University Law Review* 70 (June 1995): 502–23, 516, 523.

11. See Hadley Arkes, *The Return of George Sutherland: Restoring a Jurisprudence of Natural Rights* (Princeton: Princeton University Press, 1994); Christopher E. Smith, *Justice Antonin Scalia and the Supreme Court's Conservative Moment* (Westport, CT: Praeger, 1993). Smith's argument about Justice Scalia's irrel-

evance is largely inconsistent with the argument of his second book about the same justice. See David A. Schultz and Christopher E. Smith, *The Jurisprudential Vision of Justice Antonin Scalia* (Lanham, MD: Rowman and Littlefield, 1996).

12. See Nancy Maveety, *Justice Sandra Day O'Connor: Strategist on the Supreme Court* (Lanham, MD: Rowman and Littlefield, 1996).

13. John Henry Schlegel, "Notes toward an Intimate, Opinionated, Affectionate History of the Conference on Critical Legal Studies," *Stanford Law Review* 36 (January 1984): 391–441, 411.

14. See, for example, Sheldon Goldman and Charles M. Lamb, prologue to Sheldon Goldman and Charles M. Lamb, eds., *Judicial Conflict and Consensus: Behavioral Studies of American Appellate Courts* (Lexington: University Press of Kentucky, 1986), 1–18, 6–7.

NOTES TO CHAPTER 1

1. Thomas paid tribute during his confirmation hearings to his grandfather's influence, and he has continued to do so ever since. See, for example, Roy M. Mersky, J. Myron Jacobstein, and Bonnie L. Koneski-White, eds., *The Supreme Court of the United States: Hearings and Reports on Successful and Unsuccessful Nominations of Supreme Court Justices by the Senate Judiciary Committee, 1916–1991*, vol. 17A, Clarence Thomas (Buffalo, NY: William S. Hein and Co., 1995), 1335–8 (opening statement of Clarence Thomas); Clarence Thomas, "Victims and Heroes in the 'Benevolent State,'" Speech Delivered to the Federalist Society's Ninth Annual Lawyers Convention, Washington, DC, 22 September 1995, 1–11, 9–10 (copy in my possession). Justice Thomas's Federalist Society speech subsequently was published as Clarence Thomas, "Victims and Heroes in the 'Benevolent State,'" *Harvard Journal of Law and Public Policy* 19 (spring 1996): 671–83.

2. As quoted in Clare Cushman, "Clarence Thomas," in *The Supreme Court Justices: Illustrated Biographies, 1789–1995*, ed. Clare Cushman, 2d ed. (Washington, DC: CQ Press, 1995), 526–30, 527.

3. As quoted in ibid., 528.

4. Thomas initially was troubled by President Reagan's request that he accept a civil rights assignment. Thomas said in a 1987 speech: "I had, initially, resisted and declined taking the position of assistant secretary for civil rights simply because my career was not in civil rights and I had no intention of moving into this area. . . . I always found it curious that even though my background was in energy, taxation, and general corporate regulatory matters, that I was not seriously sought after to move into one of these areas." As quoted in ibid.

5. See, for example, Mark V. Tushnet, *Making Civil Rights Law: Thurgood Marshall and the Supreme Court, 1936–61* (New York: Oxford University Press, 1994).

6. Statement by Dr. William F. Gibson, Press Release No. 91–125, Chairman, The National Board of Directors of the NAACP on the Nomination of Judge Clarence Thomas to the U.S. Supreme Court, 31 July 1991, 1–4, 1 (copy in my possession).

7. People for the American Way Action Fund, Position Paper, "Judge Clarence Thomas: An Overall Disdain for the Rule of Law," 30 July 1991 (copy in my possession).

8. See, for example, Erwin Chemerinsky, "Clarence Thomas's Natural Law Philosophy," Analysis Prepared for the People for the American Way Action Fund, 1991 (copy in my possession); Laurence H. Tribe, "'Natural Law' and the Nominee," *New York Times*, 15 July 1991, A15.

9. See, for example, "One Woman's Story," *U.S. News and World Report*, 31 September 1991, 31 (excerpts of National Abortion Rights Action League Executive Director Kate Michelman's Senate testimony opposing Thomas's nomination).

10. Prepared Statement of Judge Clarence Thomas to the Senate Judiciary Committee, 11 October 1991, broadcast on CNN.

11. An Independent Counsel investigation into the source of the leak was unsuccessful. See *Report of Temporary Special Independent Counsel, Pursuant to Senate Resolution* (Washington, DC: U.S. Government Printing Office, 1992).

12. Dennis DeConcini, "Examining the Judicial Nomination Process: The Politics of Advice and Consent," *Arizona Law Review* 34, no.1 (1992): 1–24, 1.

13. By focusing on law reviews and books I do not mean to imply that other professional commentaries have been uninteresting or insignificant. Space constraints make choices necessary, however. It also is commonly understood that the principal outlets for professional commentary about Supreme Court justices are law reviews and books. I should note here, though, that there have been a number of impressive empirical studies about Thomas-Hill published in the social science journals. Among the most provocative is a 1993 *Public Opinion Quarterly* article by Dianne Rucinski that compared the "fast reaction" polling data and methods that influenced the Thomas confirmation vote with the "year-after" polls that reported that a majority of the American people had changed their minds and believed Anita Hill. Rucinski suggested—although she did not definitively conclude—that public opinion did *not* really change, but rather the fast reaction polling results were biased as a consequence of time pressures and questionable research techniques. See Dianne Rucinski, "Rush to Judgment? Fast Reaction Polls in the Anita Hill–Clarence Thomas Controversy," *Public Opinion Quarterly* 57 (winter 1993): 575–92. For an analysis of the social science studies, see Scott D. Gerber, "Judging Thomas: The Politics of Assessing a Supreme Court Justice," *Journal of Black Studies* 27 (November 1996): 224–59, 227–9.

14. Laurence H. Silberman, "The Clarence Thomas Confirmation: A Retrospective," *Cumberland Law Review* 23, no. 1 (1992–93): 141–55, 153. The only

other law review article even remotely supportive of Thomas's position on the Hill matter was a transparently self-serving effort by then-Senator Dennis DeConcini, the lone Democratic member of the Senate Judiciary Committee to vote for Thomas's confirmation. See DeConcini, "Examining the Judicial Nomination Process."

15. Harvey Rochman, editor's introduction to "Gender, Race, and the Politics of Supreme Court Appointments: The Import of the Anita Hill/Clarence Thomas Hearings," *Southern California Law Review* 65 (March 1992): 1279–80, 1280.

16. See Chemerinsky, "Clarence Thomas's Natural Law Philosophy."

17. Erwin Chemerinsky, "October Tragedy," *Southern California Law Review* 65 (March 1992): 1497–516, 1498.

18. Gary J. Simson, "Thomas's Supreme Unfitness—A Letter to the Senate on Advice and Consent," *Cornell Law Review* 78 (May 1993): 619–63, 619.

19. Anita Hill, *Speaking Truth to Power* (New York: Doubleday, 1997).

20. Sandra L. Ragan, ed., *The Lynching of Language: Gender, Politics, and Power in the Hill-Thomas Hearings* (Urbana: University of Illinois Press, 1996), and Paul Siegel, ed., *Outsiders Looking In: A Communication Perspective on the Hill/Thomas Hearings* (Cresskill, NJ: Hampton Press, 1996), are similar in both style and substance to two earlier collections edited by Toni Morrison and Geneva Smitherman, respectively, and will not be discussed in the text. Christopher E. Smith, *Critical Judicial Nominations: The Impact of Clarence Thomas* (Westport, CT: Praeger, 1993), and Paul Simon, *Advice and Consent: Clarence Thomas, Robert Bork and the Intriguing History of the Supreme Court's Nomination Battles* (Washington, DC: National Press Books, 1992), address the hearings in some detail, but their foci are on other matters. They, too, will not be discussed in the text. There also has been at least one doctoral dissertation about Thomas-Hill. See Tonia Kates-Stewart, "The Social Drama of the Clarence Thomas/Anita Hill Hearings," unpublished doctoral dissertation, Bowling Green State University, 1996. There have been three children's books about Justice Thomas as well, each of which discusses the highly charged Senate confirmation hearings involving Justice Thomas and Anita Hill in one way or other. See, for example, William J. Halliburton, *Clarence Thomas: Supreme Court Justice* (Hillside, NJ: Enslow Publishers, 1993).

21. Timothy M. Phelps and Helen Winternitz, *Capitol Games: Clarence Thomas, Anita Hill and the Story of a Supreme Court Nomination* (New York: Hyperion, 1992), xiv–xv. Mark V. Tushnet, a self-described "radical" law professor who teaches at Georgetown University and is one of the most prolific legal scholars in the nation, went even further. He suggested that since it was highly unlikely that Justice Thomas would be impeached, the American people should do the next best thing and not regard cases decided by the Supreme Court by a 5-to-4 vote, with Justice Thomas in the majority, as binding law. See Mark V. Tushnet, "Clarence Thomas: The Constitutional Problems," *George Washington University*

Law Review 63 (March 1995): 466–78 (review essay about *Strange Justice*). Like much of the commentary surrounding Thomas-Hill, Tushnet's remarks took on a life of their own. See, for example, Jan Crawford Greenburg, "Anti-Thomas Article: Worth a Look or Waste of Trees?" *Chicago Tribune*, 7 December 1995, 1; Gregory E. Maggs and Sheldon T. Bradshaw, "Virtual Impeachment and Book Review Conviction: Talk about *Strange Justice*," *George Washington University Law Review* 64 (April 1996): 703–13; Tony Mauro, "Should We Just Ignore Thomas?" *Legal Times*, 4 December 1995, 11.

22. Nina Totenberg, introduction to *The Complete Transcripts of the Clarence Thomas–Anita Hill Hearings: October 11, 12, 13, 1991*, ed. Anita Miller (Chicago: Academy Chicago Publishers, 1994), 5–8, 7.

23. See, for example, Larry J. Sabato, *Feeding Frenzy: How Attack Journalism Has Transformed American Politics* (New York: Free Press, 1991).

24. L. Gordon Crovitz, ed., *Clarence Thomas: Confronting the Future* (Washington, DC: Regnery Gateway, 1992).

25. Mark Cunningham, "Books in Brief—*Clarence Thomas—Confronting the Future: Selections from the Senate Confirmation Hearings and Prior Speeches*," *National Review*, 30 March 1992, 50.

26. See, for example, Ronald Dworkin, "Justice for Clarence Thomas," *New York Review of Books*, 7 November 1991, 41–5.

27. Toni Morrison, ed., *Race-ing Justice, En-Gendering Power: Essays on Anita Hill, Clarence Thomas, and the Construction of Social Reality* (New York: Pantheon Books, 1992); Robert Chrisman and Robert L. Allen, eds., *Court of Appeal: The Black Community Speaks Out on the Racial and Sexual Politics of Clarence Thomas vs. Anita Hill* (New York: Ballantine Books, 1992).

28. Ronald Dworkin, "One Year Later, the Debate Goes On," *New York Times Book Review*, 25 October 1992, 1, 33, 38–9, 33.

29. See A. Leon Higginbotham, Jr., "An Open Letter to Justice Clarence Thomas from a Federal Judicial Colleague," reprinted in *Race-ing Justice, En-Gendering Power*, 3–39. Higginbotham's letter originally was published in the *University of Pennsylvania Law Review* 140 (January 1992): 1005–28.

30. Toni Morrison, "Introduction: Friday on the Potomac," in *Race-ing Justice, En-Gendering Power*, vii–xxx, xxx. Carol M. Swain's chapter in the same book, "Double Standard, Double Blind: African American Leadership after the Thomas Debacle," echoed Morrison's view.

31. John O'Sullivan, "Believing Is Seeing," *National Review*, 15 March 1993, 60–1.

32. Robert Chrisman, introduction to *Court of Appeal*, xi–xliii, xiii.

33. Orlando Patterson, "Race, Gender, and Liberal Fallacies," in ibid., 160–4; Ronald W. Walters, "Clarence Thomas and the Meaning of Blackness," in ibid., 215–8; Maya Angelou, "I Dare to Hope," in ibid., 33–5. Patterson later recanted under pressure.

34. Geneva Smitherman, ed., *African American Women Speak Out on Anita Hill–Clarence Thomas* (Detroit: Wayne State University Press, 1995).

35. Geneva Smitherman, "Testifyin, Sermonizin, and Signifyin: Anita Hill, Clarence Thomas, and the African American Verbal Tradition," in ibid., 224–42, 239 (emphasis in original).

36. Linda F. Williams, "Anita Hill, Clarence Thomas, and the Crisis of Black Political Leadership," in ibid., 243–65, 244.

37. Anita Faye Hill and Emma Coleman Jordan, eds., *Race, Gender, and Power in America: The Legacy of the Hill-Thomas Hearings* (New York: Oxford University Press, 1995).

38. Anita Faye Hill, "Marriage and Patronage in the Empowerment and Disempowerment of African American Women," in ibid., 271–9, 273.

39. Emma Coleman Jordan, acknowledgements, in ibid.

40. Ramesh Ponnuru, "Books in Brief—*Race, Gender, and Power in America: The Legacy of the Hill-Thomas Hearings*," *National Review*, 6 November 1995, 68–9.

41. John C. Danforth, *Resurrection: The Confirmation of Clarence Thomas* (New York: Viking, 1994), 208.

42. Jeffrey Rosen, "Confirmations: Hill, Thomas, and the Dirt on Everybody," *New Republic*, 19 December 1994, 27–33, 27, 28.

43. David Brock, *The Real Anita Hill: The Untold Story* (New York: Free Press, 1993); Jane Mayer and Jill Abramson, *Strange Justice: The Selling of Clarence Thomas* (Boston: Houghton Mifflin, 1994).

44. In addition to his work on Anita Hill, Brock is well known for an exposé on President Clinton's sex life. See David Brock, "Living with the Clintons," *American Spectator*, January 1994, 18–30.

45. Brock, *The Real Anita Hill*, 108.

46. Thomas Sowell, "Clarence Thomas Vindicated," *Forbes*, 10 May 1993, 70; George F. Will, "Anita Hill's Tangled Web," *Newsweek*, 19 April 1993, 74.

47. David J. Garrow, "How Anita Hill's Charges Became Political Grist," *Newsday*, 4 May 1993, 58; Signe Wilkinson, "The Case against Anita Hill," *New York Times Book Review*, 23 May 1993, 11.

48. Jane Mayer and Jill Abramson, "The Surreal Anita Hill," *New Yorker*, 24 May 1993, 90–6.

49. Brock later retracted his claim about MacKinnon's involvement. See David Brock, *The Real Anita Hill: The Untold Story*, rev. ed. (New York: Free Press, 1994), 398.

50. "Doubting Thomas," *National Review*, 18 October 1993, 20.

51. David Brock, "Jane and Jill and Anita Hill," *American Spectator*, August 1993, 24–30.

52. Rosen, "Confirmations," 29; Tushnet, "Clarence Thomas," 466.

53. John O'Sullivan, "Soothsaying," *National Review*, 5 December 1994, 4; R.

Emmett Tyrell, Jr., "The Worst Book of the Year," *American Spectator*, March 1995, 12–4.

54. David Brock, "Strange Lies," *American Spectator*, January 1995, 30–41, 68–77, 30, 31.

55. Letter from Jane Mayer and Jill Abramson to David Brock, reprinted in *American Spectator*, March 1995, 12.

56. Letter to the editor from Merrill Orne Young, in ibid., 69 (emphasis in original).

57. Many people certainly do not like it. In one of the nastiest remarks made to date about Justice Thomas, Julianne Malveaux, a contributor to several of the essay collections about Thomas-Hill, is reported to have said: "I hope his wife feeds him lots of eggs and butter and he dies early, as many black men do, of heart disease." As quoted in Brock, "Strange Lies," 76 n. 12.

58. See Virginia Lamp Thomas, "Breaking Silence," *People*, 11 November 1991, 108–16; Marc Fisher, "The Private World of Justice Thomas," *Washington Post*, 11 September 1995, B1.

59. See, for example, Susan N. Herman, "Clarence Thomas," in *The Justices of the United States Supreme Court: Their Lives and Major Opinions, 1789–1995*, ed. Leon Friedman and Fred L. Israel, rev. ed., vol. 5 (New York: Chelsea House, 1995), 1829–58.

60. Aaron Epstein, "Justice Thomas's Less-Traveled Road to the Right," *Atlanta Journal and Constitution*, 9 July 1995, B1. See also William H. Freivogel, "Thomas Making Mark in Court Decisions: Distinctive, Conservative Judicial Voice Developing," *St. Louis Post-Dispatch*, 28 May 1995, 1A. Epstein and Freivogel, both respected Supreme Court correspondents, initially had viewed Justice Thomas as a clone of Justice Scalia. See, for example, Aaron Epstein, "Newest Justice Aligns with Scalia: Rightward Bent Evident after Four Months on Top Court," *Buffalo News*, 4 March 1992, A3; William H. Freivogel, "Thomas Proves Conservative in First Term: His Votes and Writings Reflect the Influence of Justice Scalia," *St. Louis Post-Dispatch*, 6 July 1992, 1B.

61. As quoted in Valerie Burgher, "Praying for Justice," *Village Voice*, 3 October 1995, 31.

62. As quoted in Thomas Sowell, "Few Critics Have Read His Opinions," *Atlanta Journal and Constitution*, 27 June 1995, A8.

63. See, for example, Timothy M. Hagle, "'Freshman Effects' for Supreme Court Justices," *American Journal of Political Science* 37 (November 1993): 1142–57; Eloise C. Snyder, "The Supreme Court as a Small Group," *Social Forces* 36 (March 1958): 232–8. I have more to say in Appendix I about the so-called "freshman effect" hypothesis.

64. David G. Savage, "Thomas Shows Signs of Being a Hard-liner," *Los Angeles Times*, 18 January 1992, A21; L. Gordon Crovitz, "Justice Thomas's Opinions: No Wonder They Wanted to Stop Him," *Wall Street Journal*, 29 January 1992, A13;

Ruth Marcus, "Early Returns Show Justice Thomas as Advertised: Conservative," *Washington Post*, 1 March 1992, A6; Linda Greenhouse, "Judicious Activism: Justice Thomas Hits the Ground Running," *New York Times*, 1 March 1992, E1; Marshall Ingerwerson, "Clear Tendency to the Right for Thomas," *Christian Science Monitor*, 3 March 1992, 1.

65. Scott D. Gerber, "Justice Clarence Thomas: First Term, First Impressions," *Howard Law Journal* 35 (winter 1992): 115–53, 153.

66. Christopher E. Smith and Scott Patrick Johnson, "The First-Term Performance of Justice Clarence Thomas," *Judicature* 76 (December 1992–January 1993): 172–8, 178.

67. Smith has changed how he approaches writing about Justice Thomas: He is now among Justice Thomas's most partisan critics. See, for example, Joyce A. Baugh and Christopher E. Smith, "Doubting Thomas: Confirmation Veracity Meets Performance Reality," *Seattle University Law Review* 19 (spring 1996): 455–96.

68. Donald P. Judges, "Confirmation as Consciousness-raising: Lessons for the Supreme Court from the Clarence Thomas Confirmation Hearings," *St. John's Journal of Legal Commentary* 7 (fall 1991): 147–77, 177 (emphasis in original).

69. Rodney K. Smith, "Justice Clarence Thomas: Doubt, Disappointment, Dismay, and Diminishing Hope," *St. John's Journal of Legal Commentary* 7 (fall 1991): 277–93, 277.

70. As quoted in David Margolick, "When a Critical Article on Justice Thomas Is Found Too Robust for Comfort," *New York Times*, 11 September 1992, B8.

71. Ronald Suresh Roberts, *Clarence Thomas and the Tough Love Crowd: Counterfeit Heroes and Unhappy Truths* (New York: New York University Press, 1995), 158.

72. Julian Abele Cook, Jr., "Thurgood Marshall and Clarence Thomas: A Glance at Their Philosophies," *Michigan Bar Journal* (March 1994): 298–302, 302.

73. A. Leon Higginbotham, Jr., "Justice Thomas in Retrospect," *Hastings Law Journal* 45 (August 1994): 1405–33, 1426.

74. Ibid., 1427.

75. Jeffrey Toobin, "The Burden of Clarence Thomas," *New Yorker*, 27 September 1993, 38–51.

76. "Doubting Thomas," 20.

77. Lincoln Caplan, "The Accidental Jurist," *Playboy*, January 1995, 140–2, 182–4; Jack E. White, "Uncle Tom Justice," *Time*, 26 June 1995, 36.

78. Rosen, "Confirmations," 52. In a subsequent article, Rosen wrote that Justice Thomas is "less bitter" after several years on the Court than he initially was. Jeffrey Rosen, "Moving On," *New Yorker*, 29 April–6 May, 1996, 67–73.

79. George E. Curry, "Editor's Note: We Were Too Kind," *Emerge*, November 1996, n.p.

80. See, for example, Michael Paul Williams, "Thomas Foes Must Find Way around Him," *Richmond Times Dispatch*, 17 February 1997, B1 (discussing the reaction). Conservatives, of course, condemned the issue. See, for example, Armstrong Williams, "Politics of Race Wrong Regardless of Perpetrator's Color," *Idaho Statesman*, 21 November 1996, n.p.

81. *The Federalist*, ed. Clinton Rossiter (New York: New American Library, 1961), No. 78, 464–72, 465.

82. See generally David M. O'Brien, *Storm Center: The Supreme Court in American Politics*, 4th ed. (New York: W. W. Norton, 1996).

83. See, for example, Henry J. Abraham, *Justices and Presidents: A Political History of Appointments to the Supreme Court*, 3d ed. (New York: Oxford University Press, 1992), 293–4; Randall W. Bland, *Private Pressure on Public Law: The Legal Career of Justice Thurgood Marshall, 1934–1991*, rev. ed. (Lanham, MD: University Press of America, 1993), 151–5; Carl T. Rowan, *Dream Makers, Dream Breakers: The World of Justice Thurgood Marshall* (Boston: Little, Brown, 1993), 296–306.

84. Higginbotham, "Justice Clarence Thomas in Retrospect," 1413.

85. Clarence Thomas, Speech Delivered at Walter F. George School of Law, Mercer University, 1 May 1993, 1–7, 6 (copy in my possession). See also Clarence Thomas, Speech to the National Bar Association, Memphis, TN, 29 July 1998, broadcast on C-SPAN.

86. Prepared Statement of Clarence Thomas, in *The Complete Transcripts of the Clarence Thomas–Anita Hill Hearings*, 13–18, 17.

87. Higginbotham, "An Open Letter to Justice Clarence Thomas," 13.

88. As quoted in "NAACP Chief Urges End to Thomas Bashing," *Chicago Tribune*, 15 February 1997, 12.

89. See, for example, "NAACP Leader Criticized for Call to End Thomas 'Fixation,'" *Pantagraph*, 15 February 1997, A3; Samuel F. Yette, "Mfume's NAACP: Some Question His Leadership," *Philadelphia Tribune*, 28 February 1997, 2A. See also Neil A. Lewis, "Invitation to Justice Thomas Creates Furor," *New York Times*, 29 May 1998, A13. But see Editorial, "Justice Thomas Speaks," *Washington Post*, 31 July 1998, A24.

NOTES TO CHAPTER 2

1. In Roy M. Mersky, J. Myron Jacobstein, and Bonnie L. Koneski-White, eds., *The Supreme Court of the United States: Hearings and Reports on Successful and Unsuccessful Nominations of Supreme Court Justices by the Senate Judiciary Committee, 1916–1991*, vol. 17A, Clarence Thomas (Buffalo, NY: William S. Hein and Co., 1995), 1230. It has been said that "[w]e are in the midst of a natural law revival"—a revival for which Clarence Thomas is largely responsible. Randy E. Barnett, "Getting Normative: The Role of Natural Rights in Constitutional Adjudica-

tion," *Constitutional Commentary* 12 (spring 1995): 93–122, 93. See, for example, Symposium on Natural Law, *Southern California Interdisciplinary Law Journal* 4 (summer 1995); Symposium on Natural Law and the Constitution, *Benchmark* 5 (winter 1995); Symposium on Natural Law, *Michigan Law Review* 90 (August 1992); Symposium on Natural Law, *University of Cincinnati Law Review* 61 (summer 1992). See also Scott Douglas Gerber, *To Secure These Rights: The Declaration of Independence and Constitutional Interpretation* (New York: New York University Press, 1995); Stephen B. Presser, *Recapturing the Constitution: Race, Religion, and Abortion Reconsidered* (Washington, DC: Regnery, 1994).

2. See, for example, Leo Strauss, *Natural Right and History* (Chicago: University of Chicago Press, 1953).

3. Clarence Thomas, Speech to the Savannah, Georgia, Bar Association, Savannah, Georgia, 1997, broadcast on C-SPAN.

4. Michael J. Gerhardt and Thomas D. Rowe, Jr., *Constitutional Theory: Arguments and Perspectives* (Charlottesville, VA: Michie, 1993), vii.

5. See generally Robert H. Bork, *The Tempting of America: The Political Seduction of the Law* (New York: Free Press, 1990).

6. Clarence Thomas, "Toward a 'Plain Reading' of the Constitution—The Declaration of Independence in Constitutional Interpretation," *Howard Law Journal* 30 (fall 1987): 983–95, 995.

7. Mersky, Jacobstein, and Koneski-White, eds., *Hearings*, 1396. See also 1340.

8. Ibid., 1431.

9. See, for example, ibid., 1362, 1495.

10. For leading examples of so-called "Critical Theory" scholarship, see Kimberlè Crenshaw, Neil Gotanda, Gary Peller, and Kendall Thomas, eds., *Critical Race Theory: The Key Writings That Formed the Movement* (New York: New Press, 1995); Catherine A. MacKinnon, *Toward a Feminist Theory of the State* (Cambridge, MA: Harvard University Press, 1989); Mark V. Tushnet, *Red, White, and Blue: A Critical Analysis of Constitutional Law* (Cambridge, MA: Harvard University Press, 1988).

11. Clarence Thomas, "Judging," *University of Kansas Law Review* 45 (November 1996): 1–8, 4 (emphasis in original). See also Clarence Thomas, "Speech: Cordell Hull Speakers Forum," *Cumberland Law Review* 25, no. 3 (1994–95): 611–21 (criticizing law professors for teaching law students that the law is nothing but politics).

12. Mersky, Jacobstein, and Koneski-White, eds., *Hearings*, 1363. See also 1399.

13. Ibid., 1711. See also 1460, 1469, 1710.

14. Thomas, "Toward a 'Plain Reading' of the Constitution."

15. See, for example, Mersky, Jacobstein, and Koneski-White, eds., *Hearings*, 1464 (remarks of Senator Howell Heflin [D-AL]).

16. Laurence H. Tribe, "'Natural Law' and the Nominee," *New York Times*, 15

July 1991, A15. See also Erwin Chemerinsky, "Clarence Thomas's Natural Law Philosophy," Analysis Prepared for the People for the American Way Action Fund, 1991 (copy in my possession). See generally *Lochner v. New York*, 198 U.S. 45 (1905); *Bradwell v. Illinois*, 83 U.S. 130 (1872); *Roe v. Wade*, 410 U.S. 113 (1973).

17. "Court Nominee Defends His Views on Theory of 'Natural Law' Rights," *Washington Post*, 9 September 1991, A6. See generally Gerber, *To Secure These Rights*; Presser, *Recapturing the Constitution*. Thomas did have his defenders. Prominent conservative law professor Michael W. McConnell, for one, wrote an op-ed criticizing the attacks—most notably by Tribe—on Thomas's natural law views. See Michael W. McConnell, "Trashing Natural Law," *New York Times*, 16 August 1991, A23.

18. See, for example, Clarence Thomas, "The Higher Law Background of the Privileges or Immunities Clause of the Fourteenth Amendment," *Harvard Journal of Law and Public Policy* 12 (winter 1989): 63–8. See generally Scott D. Gerber, "The Jurisprudence of Clarence Thomas," *Journal of Law and Politics* 8 (fall 1991): 107–41.

19. Mersky, Jacobstein, and Koneski-White, eds., *Hearings*, 1500, 1502.

20. Ibid., 1504–5. See also 1407, 1466, 1467, 1497, 1498, 1531.

21. 115 S.Ct. 2097, 2119 (1995) (Thomas, J., concurring in part and concurring in the judgment).

22. Mersky, Jacobstein, and Koneski-White, eds., *Hearings*, 1479. See also 1659, 1690 (remarks of Senator Howard M. Metzenbaum [D-OH]). See generally Scott D. Gerber and Keeok Park, "The Quixotic Search for Consensus on the U.S. Supreme Court: A Cross-Judicial Empirical Analysis of the Rehnquist Court Justices," *American Political Science Review* 91 (June 1997): 390–408.

23. Joseph R. Biden, Jr., "Law and Natural Law: Questions for Judge Thomas," *Washington Post*, 8 September 1991, C1, C4.

24. Thomas's criticism of Oliver Wendell Holmes, Jr., who ridiculed the use of natural law in judicial decisionmaking, is further evidence of Thomas's belief that natural law has a role to play in adjudication. See Clarence Thomas, "How to Talk about Civil Rights: Keep It Principled and Positive," Speech to the Pacific Research Institute's Civil Rights Task Force, 4 August 1988, Washington, DC, as quoted in Mersky, Jacobstein, and Koneski-White, eds., *Hearings*, 1700. See generally *Southern Pacific Co. v. Jensen*, 244 U.S. 205, 218–23, 222 (1917) (Holmes, J., dissenting) (characterizing natural law as a "brooding omnipresence in the sky").

25. Robert H. Bork, "Natural Law and the Constitution," *First Things*, March 1992, 16–20, 16.

26. "Straussians," as the late Leo Strauss's students are typically called, are an eclectic—and often internally feuding—bunch. There is one infallible rule of thumb about them, however. In the acknowledgments they attach to their works, or in their footnotes, they all identify Strauss or one or more of his students as their teacher(s) or most profound influence(s). See Scott D. Gerber, review of

Richard G. Stevens, *The American Constitution and Its Provenance* (1997), *Perspectives on Political Science* 27 (summer 1998): 189. Jaffa, among the most prominent of Strauss's students, is best known for his book *Crisis of the House Divided: An Interpretation of the Issues in the Lincoln-Douglas Debates* (Garden City, NY: Doubleday, 1959). Lincoln's argument about the significance of the Declaration of Independence for the American regime is at the heart of that book. Jaffa's personal views about the relationship between the Declaration and the Constitution are conveniently collected in Harry V. Jaffa, *Original Intent and the Framers of the Constitution: A Disputed Question* (Washington, DC: Regnery Gateway, 1994).

27. Ken Masugi, "Justice Affirmed," *On Principle* 2 (winter 1994): 3, 5–6, 3.

28. Ken Masugi, "Natural Right and Oversight: The Use and Abuse of 'Natural Law' in the Clarence Thomas Hearings," *Political Communication* 9 (October–December 1992): 231–50, 232–3.

29. Mersky, Jacobstein, and Koneski-White, eds., *Hearings*, 1396. See also 1342.

30. See Catherine Pierce Wells, "Clarence Thomas: The Invisible Man," *Southern California Law Review* 67 (November 1993): 117–48, 143–5.

31. Clarence Thomas, "Why Black Americans Should Look to Conservative Policies," Heritage Lectures, 18 June 1987, 1–9, 9 (copy in my possession). This speech was regarded by conservatives to be so important that it was reprinted in *Policy Review* to mark the occasion of Thomas's confirmation to the Supreme Court. See Clarence Thomas, "No Room at the Inn: The Loneliness of the Black Conservative," *Policy Review*, fall 1991, 72–8.

32. Only Senators Metzenbaum and David Pryor (D-AR) voted against Thomas's confirmation to the U.S. Court of Appeals. 101 *Congressional Record* S2,013–30 (1990). Pryor, who was not on the Judiciary Committee, objected to the way in which Thomas handled age discrimination cases—allegedly letting the statute of limitations on many such cases expire—while he was chairman of the EEOC. Ibid., S2,028.

33. Mersky, Jacobstein, and Koneski-White, eds., *Hearings*, 1659.

34. 487 U.S. 654 (1988). See generally Clarence Thomas, "Keynote Address Celebrating the Formation of the Pacific Research Institute's Civil Rights Task Force," 4 August 1988, as quoted in Mersky, Jacobstein, and Koneski-White, eds., *Hearings*, 1346.

35. Mersky, Jacobstein, and Koneski-White, eds., *Hearings*, 1516.

36. Richard A. Posner is a notable exception to this view. He maintains that judges cannot, and should not, defer to the Framers' intent. See, for example, Richard A. Posner, "What Am I? A Potted Plant?" *New Republic*, 28 September 1987, 23–5. See also Presser, *Recapturing the Constitution*.

37. Clarence Thomas, "Notes on Original Intent," undated, as quoted in Mersky, Jacobstein, and Koneski-White, eds., *Hearings*, 1347–8, 1352.

38. Clarence Thomas, Speech before the Pacific Research Institute, 10 August 1987, San Francisco, CA, reprinted in ibid., 1378–95, 1392. See also Clarence Thomas, "A Second Emancipation Proclamation," review of Clint Bolick, *Changing Course: Civil Rights at the Crossroads* (1988), *Policy Review*, summer 1988, 84–5.

39. See generally Gerber, *To Secure These Rights*.

40. Mersky, Jacobstein, and Koneski-White, eds., *Hearings*, 1467. See also 1396, 1712.

41. Clarence Thomas, "Civility and Public Discourse," Speech to the New England School of Law, 21 November 1996, 1–6, 3 (copy in my possession). This speech was subsequently published as Clarence Thomas, "Civility and Public Discourse," *New England Law Review* 31 (winter 1997): 515–21. See also Clarence Thomas, "A Return to Civility," *Tulsa Law Journal* 33 (fall 1997): 7–12, 9; Clarence Thomas, Speech, University of Mississippi School of Law, 19 October 1995, 1–9, 2 (copy in my possession). The Mississippi speech was subsequently published as Clarence Thomas, "The James McClure Memorial Lecture in Law," *Mississippi Law Journal* 65 (spring 1996): 463–75.

42. Academicians who criticized Thomas during the confirmation process for not offering a systematic account of his jurisprudence failed to mention this fact. See, for example, Mersky, Jacobstein, and Koneski-White, eds., *Hearings*, 2083 (testimony of former law school Dean Erwin N. Griswold).

43. Ibid., 1420.

44. Ibid., 1356. See generally Thomas, "Why Black Americans Should Look to Conservative Policies."

45. Thomas, "Toward a 'Plain Reading' of the Constitution," 994.

46. Ibid., 992. See also Clarence Thomas, "Colorblindness," *Wall Street Journal*, 20 February 1987, 21.

47. Thomas, "Why Black Americans Should Look to Conservative Policies," 9.

48. Thomas, "The Higher Law Background of the Privileges or Immunities Clause," 68; Thomas, "Toward a 'Plain Reading' of the Constitution," 990–2. See generally *Brown v. Board of Education*, 347 U.S. 483 (1954).

49. 391 U.S. 430 (1968).

50. Clarence Thomas, "Civil Rights as a Principle versus Civil Rights as an Interest," in *Assessing the Reagan Years*, ed. David Boaz (Washington, DC: Cato Institute, 1988), 391–402, 393.

51. Ibid.

52. Ibid., 392 (emphasis in original).

53. Ibid. See Clarence Thomas, Speech to the National Bar Association, Memphis, TN, 29 July 1998, broadcast of C-SPAN.

54. Clarence Thomas, "The Modern Civil Rights Movement: Can a Regime of Individual Rights and the Rule of Law Survive?" Tocqueville Forum, Winston-Salem, NC, 18 April 1988, 1–26, 17 (copy in my possession). Note the emphasis on individual rights in the title to the speech.

55. Mersky, Jacobstein, and Koneski-White, eds., *Hearings*, 1674. "Those cases" included *Thornburg v. Gingles*, 478 U.S. 30 (1986), which is discussed at length in the next chapter.

56. Mersky, Jacobstein, and Koneski-White, eds., *Hearings*, 1652–3.

57. See, for example, Clarence Thomas, "Affirmative Action Goals and Timetables: Too Tough? Not Tough Enough!" *Yale Law and Policy Review* 5 (spring–summer 1987): 402–11; Thomas, "Civil Rights as a Principle versus Civil Rights as an Interest."

58. Thomas, "Affirmative Action Goals and Timetables," 403 n. 3.

59. Mersky, Jacobstein, and Koneski-White, eds., *Hearings*, 1529.

60. Ibid., 1591.

61. Ibid.

62. See, for example, Clarence Thomas, "Civility in the Era of the New Intolerance," Speech Delivered at Walter F. George School of Law, Mercer University, 1 May 1993, 1–7, 6 (copy in my possession). Thomas, Speech to National Bar Association.

63. See, for example, Clarence Thomas, "The Equal Employment Opportunity Commission: Reflections on a New Philosophy," *Stetson Law Review* 15 (fall 1985): 29–36, 35; Thomas, "Why Black Americans Should Look to Conservative Policies," 9.

64. Clarence Thomas, "Visionary's Blurred View of Equality," review of William Julius Wilson, *The Truly Disadvantaged: The Inner City, the Underclass, and Public Policy* (1987), *Washington Times*, 19 October 1987, E8.

65. See, for example, Clarence Thomas, "The Other Side of Freedom," Speech Delivered at the Claremont Institute, 20 November 1993 (copy in my possession). See also Clarence Thomas, "Victims and Heroes in the 'Benevolent State,'" Speech to the Federalist Society's Ninth Annual Lawyers Convention, Washington, DC, 22 September 1995 (copy in my possession). The latter speech was subsequently published as Clarence Thomas, "Victims and Heroes in the 'Benevolent State,'" *Harvard Journal of Law and Public Policy* 19 (spring 1996): 71–83. Thomas also emphasized self-help during his confirmation hearings. See, for example, Mersky, Jacobstein, and Koneski-White, eds., *Hearings*, 1608.

66. See, for example, Glenn C. Loury, *One by One from the Inside Out: Essays and Reviews on Race and Responsibility in America* (New York: Free Press, 1995), 65–6; Jeffrey Rosen, "Moving On," *New Yorker*, 29 April–6 May, 1996, 67–73.

67. Clarence Thomas, Address for Pacific Research Institute, San Francisco, CA, 10 August 1987, 1–13, 3–4 (copy in my possession).

68. See Mersky, Jacobstein, and Koneski-White, eds., *Hearings*, 1339–44. See generally Richard A. Epstein, *Takings: Private Property and the Power of Eminent Domain* (Cambridge, MA: Harvard University Press, 1985); Stephen Macedo, *Liberal Virtues: Citizenship, Virtue, and Community in Liberal Constitutionalism* (New York: Oxford University Press, 1990).

69. Thomas, Address for Pacific Research Institute, 6, 11.

70. Clarence Thomas, ABA Address, Luncheon Meeting of the Business Law Section, 11 August 1987, 1–18, 9 (emphasis in original) (copy in my possession).

71. Tribe, "'Natural Law' and the Nominee," A15.

72. Mersky, Jacobstein, and Koneski-White, eds., *Hearings*, 1401. See also 1653–5.

73. See ibid., 1624, 1654–6.

74. Ibid., 1600. See also 1468.

75. See, for example, Clarence Thomas, Speech Delivered at Ohio Northern University, 7 April 1994, 1–7, 6 (copy in my possession); Thomas, "The Other Side of Freedom," 2, 3–4. The Ohio Northern speech subsequently was published as Clarence Thomas, "Freedom: A Responsibility, Not a Right," *Ohio Northern University Law Review* 21, no.1 (1994): 5–12.

76. See *West Coast Hotel v. Parrish*, 300 U.S. 379 (1937) (upholding a state minimum wage law); *National Labor Relations Board v. Jones and Laughlin Steel Corporation*, 301 U.S. 1 (1937) (upholding the National Labor Relations Act).

77. White House Working Group on the Family, "The Family: Preserving America's Future" (Washington, DC, 1986), 12.

78. Thomas, "The Higher Law Background of the Privileges or Immunities Clause," 63 n. 2.

79. Clarence Thomas, "How Republicans Can Win Blacks," *Chicago Defender*, 21 February 1987.

80. Thomas, "Why Black Americans Should Look to Conservative Policies," 8.

81. Lewis Lehrman, "The Declaration of Independence and the Right to Life: One Leads Unmistakably from the Other," *American Spectator*, April 1987, 21–3.

82. Mersky, Jacobstein, and Koneski-White, eds., *Hearings*, 2948–9 (emphasis in original).

83. Ibid., 1264. Senator Kennedy fired a similar shot across the bow before the commencement of Robert Bork's confirmation hearings. See *Congressional Record*, 133d Cong., 1st sess., 1987, S9188-S89 [daily ed., July 1].

84. I have argued elsewhere that neither the pro-life view nor the pro-choice view is necessarily consistent with the political philosophy of the Declaration of Independence. See Gerber, *To Secure These Rights*, 182–3.

85. See, for example, Mersky, Jacobstein, and Koneski-White, eds., *Hearings*, 1449–52.

86. See *Planned Parenthood of Southeastern Pennsylvania v. Casey*, 505 U.S. 833 (1992). The "essential holding" of *Roe* survived by a 5-to-4 vote. Justice Thomas joined the dissenting opinions of Chief Justice Rehnquist and Justice Scalia calling for *Roe*'s reversal.

87. Thomas, Speech to the Savannah, Georgia, Bar Association.

88. 381 U.S. 479 (1965).

89. Ibid., 484. Justice Douglas referenced the First, Third, Fourth, Fifth, and Ninth Amendments.

90. See ibid., 507–27 (Black, J., dissenting), 527–31 (Stewart, J., dissenting).

91. Bork, *The Tempting of America*, 99.

92. Mersky, Jacobstein, and Koneski-White, eds., *Hearings*, 1355. See also 1358.

93. See, for example, David M. O'Brien, *Privacy, Law, and Public Policy* (New York: Praeger, 1979). See also *Griswold*, 381 U.S. at 486–99, 488 (Goldberg, J., concurring).

94. Mersky, Jacobstein, and Koneski-White, eds., *Hearings*, 1612. See also 1455, 1602.

95. See, for example, Lawyers' Committee for Civil Rights Under Law, 17 September 1991, reprinted in ibid., 1948–2079, 2020–1; "Endangered Liberties: What Judge Clarence Thomas's Record Portends for Women," A Report by the Women's Legal Defense Fund, 30 July 1991, reprinted in ibid., 2231–8, 2299–301.

96. See Bork, *The Tempting of America*, 183–5.

97. Thomas, "Civil Rights as a Principle versus Civil Rights as an Interest," 398.

98. Ibid., 399.

99. Bork, *The Tempting of America*, 185.

100. Thomas, "Civil Rights as a Principle versus Civil Rights as an Interest," 398.

101. See, for example, Henry J. Abraham and Barbara A. Perry, *Freedom and the Court: Civil Rights and Liberties in the United States*, 7th ed. (New York: Oxford University Press, 1998), chap. 6.

102. Symposium, "Black America under the Reagan Administration," *Policy Review*, fall 1985, 27–41, 38.

103. Mersky, Jacobstein, and Koneski-White, eds., *Hearings*, 1484. See also 1493.

104. See *Lemon v. Kurtzman*, 403 U.S. 602 (1971); Thomas Jefferson, Address to the Danbury Baptist Association, 1 January 1802, in *The Writings of Thomas Jefferson*, ed. Andrew A. Lipscomb and Albert E. Bergh, vol. 16 (Washington, DC: Thomas Jefferson Memorial Association, 1904–5), 281.

105. As quoted in "Justice Thomas Recalls Benchmarks of Spiritual Life in Liberty Speech," *Daily Press*, 12 May 1996, B3.

106. As quoted in National Report, *Jet*, 11 September 1995, 8.

107. Mersky, Jacobstein, and Koneski-White, eds., *Hearings*, 1627. See also 1364. See generally *Oregon v. Smith*, 494 U.S. 872 (1990).

108. 374 U.S. 398 (1963).

109. Mersky, Jacobstein, and Koneski-White, eds., *Hearings*, 1627. See also 1626.

110. Ibid., 1488.

111. Ibid., 1562. See generally *Miranda v. Arizona*, 384 U.S. 436 (1966).

112. Mersky, Jacobstein, and Koneski-White, eds., *Hearings*, 1361. See generally *Payne v. Tennessee*, 501 U.S. 808 (1991).

113. Mersky, Jacobstein, and Koneski-White, eds., *Hearings*, 1651.

114. Ibid., 1652.

115. Clarence Thomas, Speech Delivered to the Federalist Society and the Manhattan Institute, 16 May 1994, 1–7, 1 (copy in my possession).

116. Ibid., 2.

117. John Locke, *The Second Treatise of Government*, ed. Thomas Peardon (New York: Macmillan, 1952), secs. 3, 6.

118. Thomas, Speech Delivered to the Federalist Society and the Manhattan Institute, 6–7.

119. See, for example, Mersky, Jacobstein, and Koneski-White, eds., *Hearings*, 1252, 1263.

120. In addition to the subjects discussed in this chapter, Thomas's concern for protecting individual rights to their fullest extent was expressed in testimony supporting the incorporation doctrine (which makes most of the specific guarantees of the Bill of Rights binding on the states) and opposing Chief Justice Rehnquist's opinion in *Payne v. Tennessee* (1991) (which held that precedent is less controlling in individual rights cases than it is in commercial cases). See ibid., 1592, 1475.

121. My reading of Thomas's natural law views contrasts sharply with the reading advanced by conservative scholars Terry Eastland, Matthew J. Franck, and Ken Masugi. Eastland, Franck, and Masugi maintain that Thomas subscribed in his writings, speeches, and confirmation hearings testimony to the legal positivistic position that natural law has no role to play in judicial decisionmaking. See Terry Eastland, "Clarence Thomas: The Anti-Holmesian Legal Positivist," *Benchmark* 5 (winter 1993): 71–93; Matthew J. Franck, *Against the Imperial Judiciary: The Supreme Court vs. the Sovereignty of the People* (Lawrence: University Press of Kansas, 1996), 15–9; Masugi, "Natural Right and Oversight," 248 n. 45. Masugi's position on this question is particularly intriguing. After all, he claims to have been the person who introduced Thomas to natural rights political philosophy. See Masugi, "Justice Affirmed," 3. Thomas's statements—and actions (see his concurring opinion in *Adarand*)—endorsing the use of natural law in constitutional interpretation suggest that he was not—and is not—simply reading a script prepared by others. The charge that Thomas does not have *his own* ideas is, of course, most often invoked with respect to his working relationship with Justice Scalia.

122. See Gerber, "The Jurisprudence of Clarence Thomas."

123. See, for example, Thomas, "Civility and Public Discourse."

124. See, for example, Bernard Bailyn, *The Ideological Origins of the American Revolution* (Cambridge, MA: Harvard University Press, 1967); J. G. A. Pocock,

The Machiavellian Moment: Florentine Political Thought and the Atlantic Republican Tradition (Cambridge, MA: Harvard University Press, 1975); Gordon S. Wood, *The Creation of the American Republic, 1776–1787* (Chapel Hill: University of North Carolina Press, 1969). See generally Scott D. Gerber, "Whatever Happened to the Declaration of Independence? A Commentary on the Republican Revisionism in the Political Thought of the American Revolution," *Polity* 26 (winter 1993): 207–31.

125. See, for example, Seymour Martin Lipset, "Affirmative Action and the American Creed," reprinted in *American Government: Readings and Cases*, ed. Karen O'Connor (Boston: Allyn and Bacon, 1995), 152–7.

126. See generally Gerber, *To Secure These Rights*.

127. Michael J. Lacey and Knud Haakonssen, eds., *A Culture of Rights: The Bill of Rights in Philosophy, Politics, and Law—1791 and 1991* (New York: Cambridge University Press, 1991).

128. See Gerber, "The Jurisprudence of Clarence Thomas."

129. Michael Cominsky, "Can the Senate Examine the Constitutional Philosophies of Supreme Court Nominees?" *PS: Political Science and Politics* 26 (September 1993): 495–500, 496–97.

NOTES TO CHAPTER 3

1. Gunnar Myrdal, *An American Dilemma: The Negro Problem and Modern Democracy* (New York: Harper and Row, 1944).

2. Slavery was recognized in three places in the original Constitution, though the words "slavery" and "slaves" were never used. For purposes of taxation and representation in the House of Representatives, Article 1, Section 2, counted "three fifths of all other [non-free] Persons." Article 1, Section 9, permitted the "Migration or Importation of such [non-free] Persons" until at least 1808, and Article 4, Section 2 required, on demand of the owner, the return of fugitive slaves.

3. See generally John Hope Franklin and Alfred A. Moss, Jr., *From Slavery to Freedom: A History of Negro Americans*, 7th ed. (New York: McGraw-Hill, 1994).

4. Abraham L. Davis and Barbara Luck Graham, *The Supreme Court, Race, and Civil Rights* (Thousand Oaks, CA: Sage, 1995), xx.

5. Criminal justice and other civil liberties matters with racial components are addressed in the next chapter. This chapter focuses on desegregation, voting rights, and affirmative action because Justice Thomas views these areas as presenting a unique set of questions: questions that go to the heart of colorblind constitutionalism.

6. Cornel West, foreword to Kimberlè Crenshaw, Neil Gotanda, Gary Peller, and Kendall Thomas, eds., *Critical Race Theory: The Key Writings That Formed the Movement* (New York: New Press, 1995), xi.

7. This story is well told in the introduction to Crenshaw et al., eds., *Critical Race Theory*, xiii–xxxii.

8. See generally Derrick A. Bell, Jr., *Race, Racism, and American Law*, 3d ed. (Boston: Little, Brown, 1992).

9. Crenshaw et al., introduction to *Critical Race Theory*, xix.

10. See Crenshaw et al., eds., *Critical Race Theory*; Richard Delgado, ed., *Critical Race Theory: The Cutting Edge* (Philadelphia: Temple University Press, 1995). Critical Race Theorists are extending their influence beyond the walls of the legal academy. See, for example, Anita Hill, *Speaking Truth to Power* (New York: Doubleday, 1997); Charles R. Lawrence III and Mari J. Matsuda, *We Won't Go Back: Making the Case for Affirmative Action* (Boston: Houghton Mifflin, 1997).

11. Crenshaw et al., introduction to *Critical Race Theory*, xxvii–xxviii.

12. Ibid., xxxi.

13. Every new school of legal thought is inevitably criticized by others in the legal academy. Critical Race Theory is no exception. See, for example, Daniel A. Farber and Suzanna Sherry, *Beyond All Reason: The Radical Assault on Truth in American Law* (New York: Oxford University Press, 1997).

14. 347 U.S. 483 (1954). See generally Symposium, *"Brown v. Board of Education* after Forty Years: Confronting the Promise," *William and Mary Law Review* 36 (January 1995).

15. 349 U.S. 294 (1955).

16. See generally Richard Delgado and Jean Stefancic, "The Social Construction of *Brown v. Board of Education*: Law Reform and the Reconstruction Paradox," *William and Mary Law Review* 36 (January 1995): 547–70.

17. Richard Kluger, *Simple Justice: The History of Brown v. Board of Education and Black America's Struggle for Equality* (New York: Alfred A. Knopf, 1976); Juan Williams, *Eyes on the Prize: America's Civil Rights Years, 1954–1965* (New York: Viking, 1987).

18. Gerald N. Rosenberg, *The Hollow Hope: Can Courts Bring About Social Change?* (Chicago: University of Chicago Press, 1991); Michael J. Klarman, *"Brown,* Racial Change and the Civil Rights Movement," *Virginia Law Review* 80 (February 1994): 7–150.

19. Derrick A. Bell, Jr., *And We Are Not Saved: The Elusive Quest for Racial Justice* (New York: Basic Books, 1987).

20. *Cooper v. Aaron*, 358 U.S. 1 (1958).

21. *Swann v. Charlotte-Mecklenburg Board of Education*, 402 U.S. 1 (1971).

22. 495 U.S. 33 (1990).

23. 498 U.S. 237 (1991).

24. 503 U.S. 467 (1992).

25. 112 S.Ct. 2727 (1992).

26. Ibid., 2732.

27. Ibid., 2738.

28. 391 U.S. 430 (1968).

29. 478 U.S. 385 (1986).

30. 112 S.Ct. at 2743–4 (O'Connor, J., concurring).

31. Ibid., 2746–53 (Scalia J., concurring in the judgment in part and dissenting in part).

32. Ibid., 2744–6 (Thomas, J., concurring).

33. See, for example, Glenn C. Loury, *One by One from the Inside Out: Essays and Reviews on Race and Responsibility in America* (New York: Free Press, 1995), 65–6; Jeffrey Rosen, "Moving On," *New Yorker*, 29 April–6 May, 1996, 67–73.

34. 112 S.Ct. at 2744 (Thomas, J., concurring).

35. Ibid., 2746.

36. Ibid. (emphasis in original).

37. As quoted in Ruth Marcus, "Court Sees Broad Duty to Erase College Bias," *Washington Post*, 27 June 1992, A1.

38. As quoted in Linda Greenhouse, "Court, 8–1, Faults Mississippi on College Bias in College System," *New York Times*, 27 June 1992, A1.

39. See, for example, Mary Jordan, "In Mississippi, an Integration Uproar," *Washington Post*, 17 November 1992, A1. This concern was evident during the course of the litigation. For instance, there was considerable tension between the Bush administration and the Black plaintiffs over how strongly to make the case that the future of the historically Black institutions had to be assured as part of any remedy. President Bush himself intervened and instructed Solicitor General Starr to ask for increased funding. Greenhouse, "Court, 8–1, Faults Mississippi on Bias in College System."

40. See William Raspberry, "Keepers of a Culture Endangered by Ruling on Mississippi's State Schools," *Houston Chronicle*, 1 July 1992, 11. See also William Raspberry, "Forty Years Later, a Different Kind of Segregation Case," *Washington Post*, 16 May 1994, A19.

41. See, for example, Editorial, "The Mississippi College Case," *Washington Post*, 28 June 1992, C6.

42. See, for example, Frank Adams, Jr., "Why *Brown v. Board of Education* Can Save Historically Black Colleges and Universities," *Alabama Law Review* 47 (winter 1996): 481–511; Chaka M. Patterson, "Desegregation as a Two-Way Street: The Aftermath of *United States v. Fordice*," *Cleveland State Law Review* 42 (summer 1994): 377–433.

43. See Alex M. Johnson, Jr., "Bid Whist, Tonk, and *United States v. Fordice*: Why Integrationism Fails African-Americans Again," *California Law Review* 81 (December 1993): 1401–70.

44. Ibid., 1402. Bell offered a related, albeit more veiled, critique of *Brown* in his path-breaking article, Derrick A. Bell, Jr., "Serving Two Masters: Integration Ideals and Client Interests in School Desegregation Litigation," *Yale Law Journal* 85 (March 1976): 470–516.

45. Johnson, "Why Integration Fails," 1409.

46. Ibid., 1401.

47. Ibid., 1468.

48. The Southern Education Conference sponsored a meeting in November 1994 with the purpose of finding ways to save historically Black colleges and universities. U.S. Secretary of Education Richard Riley was among those in attendance.

49. *Ayers v. Fordice*, 879 F.Supp. 1419 (N.D. Miss. 1995), affirmed without opinion, 1396 U.S. App. LEXIS 28,450 (5th Cir. September 25, 1996).

50. 115 S.Ct. 2038 (1995).

51. A detailed account of the litigation is available in Alison Morantz, "Money and Choice in Kansas City: Major Investments with Modest Returns," in *Dismantling Desegregation: The Quiet Reversal of Brown v. Board of Education*, ed. Gary Orfield and Susan E. Eaton (New York: New Press, 1996), 241–63.

52. 495 U.S. 33 (1990). *Jenkins* has been in litigation for so long and has taken so many twists and turns that commentators disagree on how to number the cases. Compare Richard A. Epstein, "The Remote Cause of Affirmative Action, or School Desegregation in Kansas City, Missouri," *California Law Review* 84 (July 1996): 1101–20 (numbering the 1990 case "II" and the 1995 case "III"), with John R. Munich and Norman E. Siegal, "One Vehicle's Baggage: *Missouri v. Jenkins*, a New Chapter in School Desegregation," *Saint Louis University Public Law Review* 15 (fall 1995): 23–40 (numbering the 1990 case "I" and the 1995 case "II"). Like Epstein, I employ the Court's numbering. *Jenkins* I, 491 U.S. 274 (1989), addressed the question of whether lawyers' fees could be recovered in a school desegregation case.

53. See Raina Brubaker, Case Note, "*Missouri v. Jenkins*: Widening the Mistakes of *Milliken v. Bradley*," *Case Western Reserve Law Review* 46 (winter 1996): 579–601; Carter M. Stewart and S. Felicita Torres, Case Note, "Limiting Federal Court Power to Impose School Desegregation Remedies," *Harvard Civil Rights-Civil Liberties Law Review* 31 (winter 1996): 241–56.

54. 115 S.Ct. at 2056–61 (O'Connor, J., concurring).

55. Ibid., 2073–91 (Souter, J., dissenting). Justice Ginsburg also issued a separate dissent. She stressed that seven years of remedies for two hundred years of injuries did not constitute a sufficient remedial period. Ibid., 2091 (Ginsburg, J., dissenting).

56. Both *Dowell* and *Pitts* made plain that the Rehnquist Court believes that the goal of *Brown* was desegregation, not integration. In *Dowell* the Court held in a 5-to-3 decision written by Chief Justice Rehnquist that formerly segregated school districts may be released from court-ordered busing once they have taken all "practicable" steps to eliminate segregation. In *Pitts* the Court held 8 to 0 that when segregation is a product not of state action but of private choice (e.g., voluntary demographic housing selection), there is no constitutional violation. See *Dowell*, 498 U.S. at 237; *Pitts*, 503 U.S. at 467.

57. Justice Souter maintained in dissent that the majority's decision effectively overruled *Hills v. Gautreaux*, 425 U.S. 284 (1976), a unanimous decision that allowed a district remedy to extend beyond the offending area. Both Chief Justice Rehnquist for the majority and Justice O'Connor in concurrence denied this.

58. 115 S.Ct. at 2061–73 (Thomas, J., concurring).

59. Ibid., 2063.

60. Ibid., 2061. See also ibid., 2065–6 ("Under this theory, segregation injures blacks because blacks, when left on their own, cannot achieve. To my way of thinking, that conclusion is the result of a jurisprudence based upon a theory of black inferiority.").

61. Ibid., 2065.

62. Ibid., 2064.

63. Justice Thomas is not alone in this view. See, for example, Donald L. Horowitz, *The Courts and Social Policy* (Washington, DC: Brookings Institution, 1977).

64. 115 S.Ct. at 2065 (Thomas, J., concurring).

65. Ibid., 2066.

66. Ibid.

67. Ibid., 2067.

68. Ibid.

69. Ibid., 2070–1.

70. See, for example, Juan Williams, "The Court's Other Bombshell: Schools, Not Voting Rights, Was Likely the Key Racial Ruling," *Washington Post*, 2 July 1995, C1.

71. David J. Garrow, "The Nation: Gavel Rousers; On Race, It's Thomas v. an Old Ideal," *New York Times*, 2 July 1995, sec. 4, p. 1; William H. Freivogel, "School Desegregation Comes to a Crossroads," *St. Louis Post-Dispatch*, 18 June 1995, 1B.

72. Gary Orfield and Susan E. Eaton, eds., *Dismantling Desegregation: The Quiet Reversal of Brown v. Board of Education* (New York: New Press, 1996).

73. Elaine R. Jones, foreword to ibid., ix.

74. See "Leading Decisions on Desegregation, 1896–1995," in ibid., xxi–xxiii.

75. Gary Orfield, "Turning Back to Segregation," in ibid., 1–22.

76. Ibid., 6.

77. Gary Orfield, "*Plessy* Parallels: Back to Traditional Assumptions," in ibid., 23–51.

78. Ibid., 34.

79. Ibid., 36.

80. The NAACP recently has been rethinking its approach to desegregation. Several prominent members of the nation's leading civil rights organization are now endorsing a position similar to Justice Thomas's. They, too, appear to believe that Black progress might be better achieved by nurturing Black youth within the

Black community. See, for example, "NAACP Rethinks School Integration," *St. Louis Post-Dispatch*, 24 June 1997, 5A.

81. Earl Warren, *The Memoirs of Earl Warren* (Garden City, NY: Doubleday, 1977), 306–10.

82. 114 S.Ct. 2581 (1994).

83. See generally Bernard Grofman, Lisa Handley, and Richard G. Niemi, *Minority Representation and the Quest for Voting Equality* (New York: Cambridge University Press, 1992), chap. 1; Robert B. McKay, "Racial Discrimination in the Electoral Process," reprinted in *Race, Law and American History, 1700–1990: African Americans and the Right to Vote*, ed. Paul Finkelman (New York: Garland, 1992), 342–58.

84. For data on Black registration and the denial of voting rights to Blacks, see, for example, the 1959 report and the 1961 voting study of the U.S. Commission on Civil Rights, subsequent annual reports, and those by the U.S. Bureau of Census.

85. Grofman, Handley, and Niemi, *Minority Representation*, 16.

86. 383 U.S. 301 (1966).

87. 393 U.S. 544, 566 (1969).

88. See *Louisiana v. United States*, 380 U.S. 145 (1965); *Katzenbach v. Morgan*, 384 U.S. 641 (1966); *North Carolina v. United States*, 395 U.S. 641 (1969).

89. 446 U.S. 55 (1980).

90. 478 U.S. 30 (1986).

91. See, for example, Grofman, Handley, and Niemi, *Minority Representation*, 1.

92. 113 S.Ct. 2816 (1993).

93. Justice Thomas also joined the conservative majority in another important voting rights case, *Presley v. Etowah County Commission*, 502 U.S. 491 (1992). *Presley* was a "third-generation" voting rights case because what was at issue was the right of minorities to *govern*, not simply to *vote* (first-generation cases) or to *elect* candidates of their choosing (second-generation cases). Justice Kennedy wrote for a 6-to-3 majority and signaled that the Rehnquist Court was not sympathetic to third-generation lawsuits. Justice Kennedy's opinion narrowly construed the Warren Court's landmark *Allen v. State Board of Elections* (1969) decision, reasoning that *Allen* and its progeny held that Section 5 preclearance was required only when a direct relation to voting and the election process was at stake. Since the changes at issue in *Presley* related to changes in decisionmaking authority (i.e., certain responsibilities were removed from the political offices to which the minorities in question were elected), the Justice Kennedy–led majority held that the minority plaintiffs failed to state a Section 5 claim.

94. 364 U.S. 339 (1960).

95. 113 S.Ct. at 2827.

96. 114 S.Ct at 2591–619 (Thomas, J., concurring in the judgment).

97. Ibid., 2605.

98. Ibid., 2591.

99. Ibid., 2592.

100. 393 U.S. at 567.

101. 369 U.S. 186 (1962). Justice Frankfurter argued in his dissenting opinion that the apportionment of state legislatures was a "political question" that the federal courts should abstain from addressing.

102. 114 S.Ct. at 2595–6 (Thomas, J., concurring in the judgment).

103. Ibid., 2597.

104. Ibid., 2602.

105. Ibid., 2597.

106. Ibid., 2598. See generally *Plessy v. Ferguson*, 163 U.S. 537, 552–64, 559 (1896) (Harlan, J., dissenting).

107. 114 S.Ct. at 2603 (Thomas, J., concurring in the judgment).

108. Ibid., 2605.

109. Justice Thomas called into question *Allen's* broad reading of the "standard, practice, or procedure" language of Section 5, but stated that he would postpone until another day whether to conclude that that case and its progeny should be overruled. Ibid., 2611 n. 27.

110. Ibid., 2612.

111. Ibid., 2618.

112. Ibid., 2619–24 (Blackmun, J., dissenting). Justice Ginsburg issued a short dissenting opinion of her own in which, in addition to stating her agreement with the arguments advanced by Justices Blackmun and Stevens, she emphasized the special responsibility the judiciary has under the Voting Rights Act to reconcile Congress's often competing concerns. Ibid., 2624–5 (Ginsburg, J., dissenting).

113. Ibid., 2625–30 (Stevens, J.).

114. Ibid., 2629–30. Justice O'Connor filed a concurring opinion in which she agreed with Justice Stevens's argument about the importance of stare decisis. Her disagreement with Justice Thomas's call for overruling the Court's Section 2 vote dilution precedents was, however, far less aggressive than Justice Stevens's. Justice O'Connor agreed with Justice Kennedy's conclusion in his plurality opinion that there was not an objective alternative benchmark in Section 2 cases, hence her vote to dismiss the vote dilution claim against Bleckley County officials. Ibid., 2588–91 (O'Connor, J., concurring in part and concurring in the judgment).

115. Justices Souter, Ginsburg, and Breyer would overrule *Shaw* for this reason. See *Bush v. Vera*, 116 S.Ct. 1941, 1997–2013 (1996) (Souter, J., dissenting).

116. 115 S.Ct. 2475 (1995).

117. 115 S.Ct. 2431 (1995).

118. 116 S.Ct. 1894 (1996).

119. 116 S.Ct. at 1941.

120. Ibid., 1972–4 (Thomas, J., concurring in the judgment).

121. Ibid., 1974.

122. Ibid., 2007 (Souter, J., dissenting).

123. Ibid., 1974–97, 1977 n. 8 (Stevens, J., dissenting).

124. Ibid., 1952 (plurality opinion) (emphasis in original).

125. As quoted in Kenneth J. Cooper and Joan Biskupic, "Unwelcome Opinion—Justice Stokes the Fires of Foes with Arguments in Voting Rights Case," *Washington Post*, 22 July 1994, A3.

126. Clint Bolick, "Bad Fences: To Preserve American Democracy, We Must Return to the Original Aims of the Voting Rights Act," *National Review*, 3 April 1995, 51.

127. Edwin M. Yoder, Jr., "Ask Why His Black Critics Are Angry at Justice Thomas," *Washington Post*, 12 August 1994, A27.

128. See Lani Guinier, "Comment: [E]racing Democracy: The Voting Rights Cases," *Harvard Law Review* 108 (November 1994): 109–37.

129. See, for example, Clint Bolick, "Quota Queen," *Wall Street Journal*, 30 April 1993, A12.

130. Lani Guinier, *The Tyranny of the Majority: Fundamental Fairness in Representative Democracy* (New York: Free Press, 1994).

131. See, for example, Richard A. Epstein, "Tuskegee Modern, or Group Rights under the Constitution," *Kentucky Law Journal* 80, no. 4 (1991–92): 869–85, 875–6.

132. Guinier, "[E]racing Democracy," 112.

133. Ibid., 118.

134. Ibid., 119 (quoting the Senate Report).

135. Ibid., 122.

136. Ibid., 121.

137. See also Andrea Bierstein, "Millennium Approaches: The Future of the Voting Rights Act after *Shaw*, *De Grandy*, and *Holder*," *Hastings Law Journal* 46 (July 1995): 1457–531, 1521 ("As a conservative Republican African-American, Thomas may feel quite strongly that being grouped with other African-Americans will not cause *him* to be better represented).

138. Guinier, "[E]racing Democracy," 122–4.

139. Ibid., 125.

140. Ibid., 126–7 (citations omitted).

141. Ibid., 128.

142. Ibid., 131.

143. Bolick, "Quota Queen."

144. Guinier, "[E]racing Democracy," 131.

145. Ibid. 131–7.

146. President Kennedy in 1961 first used the phrase "affirmative action." President Johnson four years later was responsible for the first affirmative action program. See Davis and Graham, *The Supreme Court, Race, and Civil Rights*, 246. For an insightful overview of the policy arguments for and against affirmative action, see Ellen Frankel Paul, "Affirmative Action," in *Encyclopedia of Applied Ethics*, ed. Ruth Chadwick, vol. 1 (San Diego: Academic Press, 1998), 63–80.

147. 438 U.S. 265 (1978). The Court avoided the legality question four years earlier when, in *DeFunis v. Odegaard*, 416 U.S. 312 (1974), it dismissed as moot an equal protection challenge by a White male applicant to the affirmative action admissions policy of the University of Washington School of Law.

148. "The Decision Everyone Won," *Wall Street Journal*, 29 June 1978, 1.

149. See, for example, *Pullman-Standard v. Swint*, 456 U.S. 273 (1982); *Wygant v. Jackson Board of Education*, 476 U.S. 267 (1986).

150. See, for example, *United Steelworkers of America v. Weber*, 443 U.S. 193 (1979); *Fullilove v. Klutznick*, 448 U.S. 448 (1980); *Sheet Metal Workers v. EEOC*, 478 U.S. 421 (1986); *Firefighters v. Cleveland*, 478 U.S. 501 (1986).

151. Davis and Graham, *The Supreme Court, Race, and Civil Rights*, 369.

152. 497 U.S. 547 (1990).

153. 488 U.S. 469 (1989).

154. Justice O'Connor spoke only for a plurality on this point in *Croson*.

155. 115 S.Ct. 2097 (1995).

156. Ibid., 2112–3.

157. Ibid., 2120–31 (Stevens, J., dissenting). Justice Ginsburg joined Justice Stevens's dissent. She also filed a separate dissenting opinion, as did Justice Souter. Both were joined by Justice Breyer. See ibid., 2131–4 (Souter, J., dissenting), 2134–6 (Ginsburg, J., dissenting).

158. Ibid., 2128 (Stevens, J., dissenting).

159. Ibid., 2125.

160. Ibid., 2120 (citation omitted).

161. Ibid., 2119 (Thomas, J., concurring in part and concurring in the judgment).

162. Ibid.

163. Ibid.

164. Ibid., 2122–3 n. 5 (Stevens, J., dissenting).

165. As quoted in Jan Crawford Greenburg, "Thomas' Voice Heard through His Writings," *Chicago Tribune*, 9 July 1996, 1.

166. As quoted in Joan Biskupic, "Thomas Caught Up in Conflicts; Jurist's Court Rulings, Life Experience Are at Odds, Many Blacks Say," *Washington Post*, 7 June 1996, A20.

167. As quoted in Robert Marquand, "Thomas Leads Court's Lean to the Right," *Christian Science Monitor*, 26 June 1995, 1.

168. Ralph A. Rossum, "Justice Harlan's Constitution," *Weekly Standard*, 13 May 1996, 31–3.

169. Symposium, "Race, Law, and Justice: The Rehnquist Court and the American Dilemma," *American University Law Review* 45 (February 1996). See also Symposium, *Howard Law Journal* 39 (fall 1995); Symposium, *UCLA Law Review* 43 (August 1996).

170. Angela Jordan Davis, "Keynote Address," *American University Law Review* 45 (February 1996): 636–46, 636.

171. Ibid., 642.

172. See Jeffrey Rosen, "The Color-blind Court," *American University Law Review* 45 (February 1996): 791–801.

173. Terry Eastland, *Ending Affirmative Action: The Case for Colorblind Justice* (New York: Basic Books, 1996). See also Clint Bolick, *The Affirmative Action Fraud: Can We Restore the American Civil Rights Vision?* (Washington, DC: Cato Institute, 1996).

174. Eastland, *Ending Affirmative Action*, 127.

175. 113 S.Ct. 2297 (1993).

176. See generally Charles Alan Wright, *Law of Federal Courts*, 5th ed. (St. Paul, MN: West, 1994), 67–83.

177. *U.S. ex rel. Chapman v. FPC*, 345 U.S. 153, 156 (1953).

178. *Valley Forge Christian College v. Americans United for Separation of Church and State*, 454 U.S. 464, 471 (1982).

179. 397 U.S. 150 (1970).

180. Ibid., 153.

181. See, for example, Wright, *Law of Federal Courts*, 68.

182. 112 S.Ct. 2130 (1992).

183. 896 F.2d 1283, 1319 (11th Cir. 1990).

184. 113 S.Ct. at 2305–9 (O'Connor, J., dissenting). Justice Blackmun joined Justice O'Connor's dissenting opinion.

185. Ibid., 2303.

186. Ibid.

187. See *Northeastern Florida Chapter of the Associated General Contractors of America v. City of Jacksonville*, 997 F.2d 835 (11th Cir. 1993) (remanding the case to the District Court with instructions to permit the plaintiff to amend its complaint to raise the validity of the second ordinance, if the plaintiff wished to do so). Former Jacksonville Assistant City Attorney Stephen M. Durden informed me in a February 13, 1997, conversation that the parties have "informally" resolved the dispute.

188. Linda Greenhouse, "Supreme Court Roundup," *New York Times*, 15 June 1993, A22.

189. See Girardeau A. Spann, *Race against the Court: The Supreme Court and*

Minorities in Contemporary America (New York: New York University Press, 1993).

190. See, for example, Girardeau A. Spann, "Affirmative Action and Discrimination," *Howard Law Journal* 39 (fall 1995): 1–94.

191. Girardeau A. Spann, "Color-Coded Standing," *Cornell Law Review* 80 (July 1995): 1422–97.

192. Ibid., 1425.

193. Ibid., 1437 (emphasis in original).

194. Ibid., 1468.

195. Ibid., 1424.

196. The only other law review article about *Northeastern Florida* had many positive things to say about the majority opinion. In "Standing Injuries," Cass R. Sunstein, a leading liberal law professor, praised the Court for appearing to recognize that judges must look to "legal" as opposed to purely "factual" harm when determining whether a plaintiff had pled a justiciable injury. Conspicuously absent from Sunstein's article, however, was any reference to Justice Thomas as the author of the *Northeastern Florida* opinion. See Cass R. Sunstein, "Standing Injuries," in *1993 Supreme Court Review,* ed. Dennis J. Hutchinson, David A. Strauss, and Geoffrey R. Stone (Chicago: University of Chicago Press, 1994), 37–64.

197. *Bush v. Vera,* 116 S.Ct. at 1972–4 (Thomas, J., concurring in the judgment). Justice Scalia joined Justice Thomas's concurring opinion.

198. Neil Gotanda, "A Critique of 'Our Constitution Is Color-Blind,'" *Stanford Law Review* 44 (November 1991): 1–68. See also Bryan K. Fair, *Notes of a Racial Caste Baby: Color Blindness and the End of Affirmative Action* (New York: New York University Press, 1997).

199. 163 U.S. at 559 (Harlan, J., dissenting).

200. Ibid.

201. Gotanda, "A Critique of 'Our Constitution Is Color-Blind,'" 4, 37.

202. Justice Harlan's dissent is unclear on this point. See, for example, Tinsley E. Yarbrough, *Judicial Enigma: The First Justice Harlan* (New York: Oxford University Press, 1995), 160–2. Indeed, Bryan K. Fair, himself a Critical Race Theorist, argues that Justice Harlan *opposed* the status quo. See Fair, *Notes of a Racial Caste Baby,* xxii.

203. Gotanda, "A Critique of 'Our Constitution Is Color-Blind,'" 39 n. 153.

204. 115 S.Ct. at 2119 (Thomas, J., concurring in part and concurring in the judgment).

205. See, for example, Neil Gotanda, "Failure of the Color-Blind Vision: Race, Ethnicity, and the California Civil Rights Initiative," *Hastings Constitutional Law Quarterly* 23 (summer 1996): 1135–51. See generally Derrick A. Bell, Jr., *Faces at the Bottom of the Well: The Permanence of Racism* (New York: Basic Books, 1992); Fair, *Notes of a Racial Caste Baby.*

206. No longer can Richard Delgado argue that Critical Race Theorists are ignored. See Richard Delgado, "The Imperial Scholar Revisited: How to Marginalize Outsider Writing, Ten Years Later," *University of Pennsylvania Law Review* 140 (April 1992): 1349–72; Richard Delgado, "The Imperial Scholar: Reflections on a Review of Civil Rights Literature," *University of Pennsylvania Law Review* 132 (March 1984): 561–78. Desegregation is the only area in which the traditional civil rights perspective still appears to carry some weight in scholarly discourse. See, for example, Orfield and Eaton, eds., *Dismantling Desegregation*.

207. Andrew Kull, *The Color-Blind Constitution* (Cambridge, MA: Harvard University Press, 1992). See also Kluger, *Simple Justice*; Mark V. Tushnet, *The NAACP's Legal Strategy against Segregated Education, 1925–1950* (Chapel Hill: University of North Carolina Press, 1987).

208. As quoted in Kull, *The Color-Blind Constitution*, 166.

209. See, for example, Shelby Steele, *The Content of Our Character* (New York: HarperCollins, 1990). See generally Ronald Suresh Roberts, *Clarence Thomas and the Tough Love Crowd: Counterfeit Heroes and Unhappy Truths* (New York: New York University Press, 1995).

210. See Gerber, *To Secure These Rights*, 164–75.

211. 115 S.Ct. at 2119 (Thomas, J., concurring in part and concurring in the judgment).

212. The editors of the *National Review* made the (some might say startling) pronouncement that the reelection of incumbent Blacks in Supreme Court–mandated redrawn, mostly White congressional districts suggests that racism has all but vanished in America. "The Week," *National Review*, 9 December 1996, 14. For the opposing view of one of those reelected incumbents, see Cynthia A. McKinney, "A Product of the Voting Rights Act," *Washington Post*, 26 November 1996, A15.

213. See Gerber, *To Secure These Rights*.

NOTES TO CHAPTER 4

1. Michael J. Lacey and Knud Haakonssen, "Introduction: History, Historicism, and the Culture of Rights," in *A Culture of Rights: The Bill of Rights in Philosophy, Politics, and Law—1791 and 1991*, ed. Michael J. Lacey and Knud Haakonssen (New York: Cambridge University Press, 1991), 1–18, 1. See also Scott Douglas Gerber, *To Secure These Rights: The Declaration of Independence and Constitutional Interpretation* (New York: New York University Press, 1995).

2. See, for example, *Chicago, Burlington and Quincy Railroad v. Chicago*, 166 U.S. 226 (1897); *Gitlow v. New York*, 268 U.S. 652 (1925).

3. See *Mapp v. Ohio*, 367 U.S. 642 (1961); *Robinson v. California*, 370 U.S. 660 (1962); *Gideon v. Wainwright*, 372 U.S. 335 (1963); *Mallory v. Hogan*, 378 U.S. 1 (1964); *Pointer v. Texas*, 380 U.S. 400 (1965); *Griswold v. Connecticut*, 381 U.S. 479

(1965); *Parker v. Gladden*, 385 U.S. 363 (1966); *Klopfer v. North Carolina*, 386 U.S. 213 (1967); *Duncan v. Louisiana*, 391 U.S. 145 (1968); *Benton v. Maryland*, 395 U.S. 784 (1969).

4. For a breakdown of the specific guarantees enumerated in the Bill of Rights, see Scott D. Gerber, "Roger Sherman and the Bill of Rights," *Polity* 28 (summer 1996): 521–40, especially 534–8.

5. See generally David J. Rothman, *The Discovery of the Asylum: Social Order and Disorder in the Discovery of the New Republic* (Boston: Little, Brown, 1971).

6. *Ruffin v. Commonwealth*, 62 Va. (21 Gratt.) 790, 796 (1871).

7. See, for example, Jack E. Call, "The Supreme Court and Prisoners' Rights," *Federal Probation* 59 (March 1995): 36–45; Hedieh Nasheri, "A Spirit of Meanness: Courts, Prisons, and Prisoners," *Cumberland Law Review* 27, no. 3 (1996–97): 1173–201. See generally Joseph Senna and Larry Siegal, *Introduction to Criminal Justice*, 7th ed. (St. Paul, MN: West, 1996), 667–72.

8. For one such case, see *Ex Parte Hull*, 312 U.S. 640 (1941) (holding that states could not require prisoners to submit formal legal documents to state officials for review and approval before filing those papers with the courts).

9. For the leading statement on the failure of the Burger Court to reverse many of the doctrinal innovations of the Warren Court, see Vincent Blasi, ed., *The Burger Court: The Counter-revolution That Wasn't* (New Haven: Yale University Press, 1983).

10. 418 U.S. 539, 555, 556 (1974). *Wolff* involved the question of whether prisoners had a right to maintain the "good-time credit" they had accrued. The Court held that they did.

11. 441 U.S. 520, 562 (1979). *Wolfish* involved the constitutionality of numerous conditions of confinement and practices in a federally operated short-term facility. The prisoners were unsuccessful in each of their claims. The decision was 5 to 4.

12. Melvin Gutterman, "Prison Objectives and Human Dignity: Reaching a Mutual Accommodation," *BYU Law Review* no. 4 (1992): 857–915, 898.

13. See, for example, *Wolff v. McDonnell*, 418 U.S. at 539 (procedural due process); *Vitek v. Jones*, 445 U.S. 480 (1980) (substantive due process); *Lee v. Washington*, 390 U.S. 333 (1968) (equal protection); *Cruz v. Beto*, 405 U.S. 319 (1972) (religious freedom); *Procunier v. Martinez*, 416 U.S. 396 (1974) (free expression).

14. See, for example, *In re Kemmler*, 136 U.S. 436 (1890) (hanging); *Weems v. United States*, 217 U.S. 349 (1910) (fifteen years hard labor for falsifying a government document). See also *Gregg v. Georgia*, 428 U.S. 153 (1976) (addressing the constitutionality of the death penalty itself); *Furman v. Georgia*, 408 U.S. 238 (1972) (same).

15. 429 U.S. 97 (1976). *Estelle* involved the question of whether the state was responsible for attending to the serious medical needs of its prisoners. The Court

held that it was. The Court also held, however, that the prisoner had to prove that the prison official or officials in question manifested "deliberate indifference" to his medical needs.

16. 501 U.S. 294 (1991).

17. 452 U.S. 337 (1981).

18. 475 U.S. 312 (1986).

19. 503 U.S. 1 (1992).

20. 929 F.2d 1014, 1015 (5th Cir. 1990).

21. 500 U.S. 903 (1991) (memorandum).

22. 503 U.S. at 8.

23. Ibid., 11 (citation omitted). However, Justice O'Connor also held in her opinion for the Court that, in an excessive force case such as Hudson's, the prisoner had to prove more than that the prison official acted with "deliberate indifference" to the prisoner's well-being, which was the level of mental culpability required by *Estelle*, a medical treatment case. Justice O'Connor maintained that the prisoner had to prove that the prison official exerted force "maliciously and sadistically to cause harm." Ibid., 9.

24. Ibid., 13–7, 13–4 (Blackmun, J., concurring in the judgment). Justice Stevens filed an opinion concurring in part and concurring in the judgment to make clear that he believed that even the majority's position imposed too stringent of a burden of proof on a prisoner. Ibid., 12–3 (Stevens, J., concurring in part and concurring in the judgment).

25. Ibid., 17–28, 17–8 (Thomas, J., dissenting).

26. Ibid., 20.

27. Ibid.

28. 509 U.S. 25 (1993).

29. 511 U.S. 825 (1994).

30. McKinney sued the director of the prison, the warden, the associate warden, a unit counselor, and the manager of the prison store who sold the cigarettes.

31. 924 F.2d 1500, 1508 (9th Cir. 1991).

32. 509 U.S. at 32, 33, 31.

33. Ibid., 37–42 (Thomas, J., dissenting).

34. Ibid., 37, 38.

35. Ibid., 38, 39. Justice Thomas said the following about the weight of the historical evidence: "although the evidence is not overwhelming," it nevertheless "supports the view that judges or juries—but not jailers—impose 'punishment.'" Ibid., 40.

36. That sentence was: "It suffices to note that the primary concern of the drafters was to proscribe 'torture[s]' and other 'barbar[ous]' methods of punishment." The brackets are Justice Thomas's. See ibid., 40.

37. Ibid., 40, 40–1. Those decisions were: *Gregg v. Georgia*, 428 U.S. at 153;

Wilkerson v. Utah, 99 U.S. 130 (1879); *In re Kemmler*, 136 U.S. 436 (1890); *Louisiana ex rel. Francis v. Resweber*, 329 U.S. 459 (1947); *Weems v. United States*, 217 U.S. 349 (1910); *Trop v. Dulles*, 356 U.S. 86 (1958).

38. 509 U.S. at 41 (Thomas, J., dissenting).

39. Ibid., 42.

40. 511 U.S. at 829. Marjorie Rifkin, an ACLU lawyer who represented Farmer before the Supreme Court, referred to Farmer as a woman in the article she wrote about the case. See Marjorie Rifkin, "*Farmer v. Brennan*: Spotlight on an Obvious Risk of Rape in a Hidden World," *Columbia Human Rights Law Review* (winter 1995): 273–307, 307 n. 1. I refer to Farmer in the masculine because that was what the Court did. I mean Farmer no disrespect.

41. 511 U.S. at 829.

42. Rifkin, "Spotlight on an Obvious Risk of Rape in a Hidden World," 273. The Court was not this detailed in its description of the incident.

43. 511 U.S. at 842.

44. Ibid., 851–8 (Blackmun, J., concurring). Justice Stevens also expressed concern about *Wilson* in a one paragraph concurring opinion of his own. Ibid., 858 (Stevens, J., concurring).

45. Ibid., 851 (Blackmun, J., concurring).

46. Ibid., 853.

47. Ibid., 858–62 (Thomas, J., concurring in the judgment).

48. Ibid., 859 (quoting his dissenting opinion in *Helling*).

49. Ibid., 861, 862.

50. Editorial, "The Youngest, Cruelest Justice," *New York Times*, 27 February 1992, A24; Editorial, "Was the Beating Bad Enough?" *Washington Post*, 26 February 1992, A16; Editorial, "Even Criminals Have Some Rights," *Los Angeles Times*, 1 March 1992, M4.

51. William Raspberry, "Confounding One's Supporters," *Washington Post*, 28 February 1992, A23. See also Mary McGrory, "Thomas Walks in Scalia's Shoes," *Washington Post*, 27 February 1992, A2 (calling Justice Thomas's *Hudson* dissent "disgusting").

52. Terry Eastland, "Doubting Thomas Again," *American Spectator*, May 1992, 62–3; George F. Will, "The Constitution Is Not a Cure-All," *Washington Post*, 1 March 1992, C7. See also L. Gordon Crovitz, "Justice Scalia's Ally on the Court— And Then Some," *Wall Street Journal*, 11 March 1992, A15.

53. Robert H. Bork, "Beside the Law: Failures of the U.S. Supreme Court," *National Review*, 19 October 1992, 38–44, 42, 44.

54. See, for example, Doretha M. Van Slyke, Case Note, "*Hudson v. McMillian* and Prisoners' Rights: The Court Giveth and the Court Taketh Away," *American University Law Review* 42 (summer 1993): 1727–60; Katherine L. Frazier, Case Note, "*Helling v. McKinney*: Future Risks of Harm Actionable under the Eighth Amendment," *University of Memphis Law Review* 25 (summer 1995): 1479–94;

Lisa Dibartolomeo, Case Note, "*Farmer v. Brennan*: Subjective Awareness Governs the Deliberate Indifference Standard in Cruel and Unusual Punishment Claims," *Suffolk University Law Review* 29 (spring 1995): 294–302.

55. This is not to say that prisoners' rights go unnoticed in the law reviews. See, for example, Melvin Gutterman, "The Prison Jurisprudence of Justice Thurgood Marshall," *Maryland Law Review* 56, no. 1 (1997): 149–95.

56. A. Leon Higginbotham, Jr., "The Matthew O. Tobriner Memorial Lecture: Justice Clarence Thomas in Retrospect," *Hastings Law Journal* 45 (August 1994): 1405–33, 1424–6.

57. See Thomas K. Landry, "'Punishment' and the Eighth Amendment," *Ohio State Law Journal* 57, no. 5 (1996): 1607–75. Landry also advanced a nonoriginalist theory as to why the Eighth Amendment should apply to a limited range of conditions or events in prison. I have more to say about Landry's theory later in the text.

58. See Gregory Taxin, Case Note, "The Eighth Amendment in Section 1983 Cases: *Hudson v. McMillian*," *Harvard Journal of Law and Public Policy* 15 (summer 1992): 1050–60; Jeffrey D. Bukowski, Case Note, "The Eighth Amendment and Original Intent: Applying the Prohibition against Cruel and Unusual Punishments to Prison Deprivation Cases Is Not Beyond the Bounds of History and Precedent," *Dickinson Law Review* 99 (winter 1995): 419–37. Taxin, who at the time of his essay was a member of the student editorial board of the *Harvard Journal of Law and Public Policy*, a conservative law review funded by the Federalist Society, was pleased with the policy position to which Justice Thomas's position led. Bukowski, who like Landry attempted to fashion a nonoriginalist argument to broaden the reach of the Eighth Amendment, was not.

59. See Raoul Berger, *Death Penalties: The Supreme Court's Obstacle Course* (Cambridge, MA: Harvard University Press, 1982); Anthony F. Granucci, "'Nor Cruel and Unusual Punishments Inflicted': The Original Meaning," *California Law Review* 57 (October 1969): 839–65.

60. Chief Justice Rehnquist, a noted champion of conservative originalism, is clearly a "feint-hearted originalist" in the prisoners' rights context. See William H. Rehnquist, "The Notion of a Living Constitution," reprinted in *Views from the Bench: The Judiciary and Constitutional Politics*, ed. Mark W. Cannon and David M. O'Brien (Chatham, NJ: Chatham House, 1985), 127–36. See generally Antonin Scalia, "Originalism: The Lesser Evil," *University of Cincinnati Law Review* 57, no. 3 (1989): 849–65.

61. See, for example, Don Williamson, "Justice Clarence Thomas' Cruel, Unusual Dissent," *Seattle Times*, 8 March 1992, A14.

62. Higginbotham, "Justice Clarence Thomas in Retrospect," 1426.

63. 500 U.S. at 903.

64. *Ex parte Bollman*, 8 U.S. (4 Cr.) 75, 96 (1807) (Marshall, C.J.).

65. The other five are: circumscription of the crime of treason (Article III,

Section 3), prohibition of religious tests for public office (Article VI), prohibition of ex post facto laws (Article I, Section 9), prohibition of bills of attainder (Article I, Sections 9 and 10), and prohibition of state impairment of contracts (Article I, Section 10).

66. See Clarke D. Forsythe, "The Historical Origins of Broad Habeas Review Reconsidered," *Notre Dame Law Review* 70, no. 4 (1995): 1079–171, 1083.

67. 505 U.S. 277 (1992).

68. 502 U.S. 1021 (1991) (memorandum). Justices Blackmun and Stevens dissented without opinion from the Court's writ of certiorari.

69. See generally David M. O'Brien, *Storm Center: The Supreme Court in American Politics*, 4th ed. (New York: W. W. Norton, 1996), 336 (criticizing the modern Supreme Court for failing to issue institutional opinions that speak for all of the justices).

70. Justice White issued a one-sentence concurring opinion in which he stated that there was sufficient evidence to convict West. 505 U.S. at 297 (White, J., concurring in the judgment). Justice Kennedy issued a concurring opinion in which he disagreed with Justice Thomas's interpretation of *Teague v. Lane* (1989), a key precedent. Ibid., 306–10 (Kennedy, J., concurring in the judgment). Justice Souter issued a concurring opinion in which he stated that West should be denied relief because his petition depended upon the retroactive application of a new rule, which the Court did not permit. Ibid., 310–6 (Souter, J., concurring in the judgment).

71. Ibid., 280–97 (Thomas, J., plurality opinion).

72. Ibid., 295.

73. Ibid., 285.

74. See generally *Brown v. Allen*, 344 U.S. 443 (1953).

75. 505 U.S. at 288 n. 5.

76. 474 U.S. 104, 112 (1985).

77. 505 U.S. at 289 n. 6.

78. 443 U.S. 307 (1979).

79. 505 U.S. at 291.

80. 489 U.S. 288 (1989).

81. 505 U.S. at 297–306, 297 (O'Connor, J., concurring). Justices Blackmun and Stevens joined Justice O'Connor's concurring opinion.

82. Ibid., 299. See generally *Kuhlmann v. Wilson*, 477 U.S. 436 (1986).

83. 505 U.S. at 300 (O'Connor, J., concurring).

84. Ibid., 301, 303.

85. Ibid., 303, 304.

86. Ibid., 305.

87. Ibid.

88. As quoted in Marcia Coyle and Claudia MacLachlan, "High Court Ducks Its Own Habeas Question," *National Law Journal*, 6 July 1992, 5.

89. Vivian Berger, "Axed Poised over Habeas," *National Law Journal*, 31 August 1992, S10.

90. Ibid.

91. Liebman's real opponent was the ghost of Paul M. Bator, who wrote a seminal article about habeas corpus review that Justice Thomas invoked for support. See 505 U.S. at 285. See generally Paul M. Bator, "Finality in Criminal Law and Federal Habeas Corpus for State Prisoners," *Harvard Law Review* 76 (January 1963): 441–528.

92. James S. Liebman, "Apocalypse Next Time? The Anachronistic Attack on Habeas Corpus/Direct Review Parity," *Columbia Law Review* 92 (December 1992): 1997–2097, 1998.

93. Ibid., 2015–6.

94. Ibid., 2096.

95. Ibid., 2037.

96. Justice Brennan was the most prominent proponent of this view. See, for example, William J. Brennan, Jr., "The National Court of Appeals: Another Dissent," *University of Chicago Law Review* 40 (spring 1973): 473–85. Interestingly, Justice Brennan's specific views about habeas corpus were inconsistent with his general views about the Supreme Court's unique role in the American constitutional system, something which suggests, at least to me, that he was being result-oriented about habeas corpus. See, for example, *Fay v. Noia*, 372 U.S. 391 (1963), overruled in part by *Wainwright v. Sykes*, 433 U.S. 72 (1977), abrogated by *Coleman v. Thompson*, 501 U.S. 722 (1991). The charge that Justice Brennan was result-oriented in his approach to legal questions is hardly a novel one.

97. For a detailed accounting of how and why the Supreme Court's expansionist habeas corpus precedents are wrong, see Forsythe, "The Historical Origins of Broad Federal Habeas Review Reconsidered." Congress's 1996 amendments to the Habeas Corpus Act essentially codified the interpretation Justice O'Connor advanced in her concurring opinion in *Wright*. See generally Larry W. Yackle, "A Primer on the New Habeas Corpus Statute," *Buffalo Law Review* 44 (spring 1996): 381–449.

98. See, for example, Christopher E. Smith, "Criminal Justice and the 1995–96 U.S. Supreme Court Term," *University of Detroit Mercy Law Review* 74 (fall 1996): 1–24; Christopher E. Smith and Avis Alexandria Jones, "The Rehnquist Court's Activism and the Risk of Injustice," *Connecticut Law Review* 26 (fall 1993): 53–77. See generally Christopher E. Smith, *The Rehnquist Court and Criminal Punishment* (New York: Garland, 1997).

99. Christopher E. Smith, "The Constitution and Punishment: The Emerging Visions of Justices Scalia and Thomas," *Drake Law Review* 43, no. 3 (1995): 593–613, 601.

100. Ibid., 595. See generally David A. Schultz and Christopher E. Smith, *The*

Jurisprudential Vision of Justice Antonin Scalia (Lanham, MD: Rowman and Littlefield, 1996).

101. Both of these opinions received only brief mention in the popular press and went largely unnoticed in the major academic journals.

102. 505 U.S. 42 (1992). See generally *Batson v. Kentucky*, 476 U.S. 79 (1986). A "peremptory challenge" is a legally sanctioned challenge to a juror without assigning a reason for the challenge.

103. Justice Scalia dissented. See 505 U.S. at 69–70 (Scalia, J., dissenting).

104. Ibid., 59–62, 60–1 (Thomas, J., concurring in the judgment).

105. 506 U.S. 461 (1993).

106. Ibid., 479–500 (Thomas, J., concurring).

107. 489 U.S. at 288.

108. 492 U.S. 302 (1989).

109. 506 U.S. at 493, 497 (Thomas, J., concurring).

110. See also *Dawson v. Delaware*, 505 U.S. 647, 659–70 (1992) (Thomas, J., dissenting) (arguing that membership in a White racist group supported the inference that the defendant engaged in unlawful activity in prison and thereby rebutted the defendant's evidence of good character).

111. The original "first" amendment called for a fixed schedule of apportionment for the U.S. House of Representatives. The original "second" amendment addressed altering the pay of members of Congress. The original "second" amendment was ratified in 1992 and is now the Twenty-Seventh Amendment. For a colorful accounting of the Twenty-Seventh Amendment's strange road to ratification, see William Van Alstyne, "What Do You Think about the Twenty-Seventh Amendment?" *Constitutional Commentary* 10 (winter 1993): 9–18.

112. As quoted in Gerber, "Roger Sherman and the Bill of Rights," 534.

113. Reprinted in *The Founders' Constitution*, ed. Philip B. Kurland and Ralph Lerner, vol. 5 (Chicago: University of Chicago Press, 1987), 84–5.

114. See *Everson v. Board of Education*, 330 U.S. 1 (1947).

115. See generally Henry J. Abraham and Barbara A. Perry, *Freedom and the Court: Civil Rights and Liberties in the United States*, 7th ed. (New York: Oxford University Press, 1998), chap. 6.

116. 115 S.Ct. 2510 (1995).

117. See Thomas Jefferson, Address to the Danbury Baptist Association, 1 January 1802, in *The Writings of Thomas Jefferson*, ed. Andrew A. Lipscomb and Albert E. Bergh, vol. 16 (Washington, DC: Thomas Jefferson Memorial Association, 1904–5), 281; *Everson*, 330 U.S. at 1.

118. See Walter Berns, *The First Amendment and the Future of American Democracy* (New York: Basic Books, 1976), chap. 1; *County of Allegheny v. American Civil Liberties Union*, 492 U.S. 573 (1986).

119. 115 S.Ct. at 2523, 2524.

120. 472 U.S. 38 (1985).

121. Ibid., 91–114 (Rehnquist J., dissenting).

122. 115 S.Ct. at 2528–33, 2530 (Thomas, J., concurring). As is her practice, Justice O'Connor emphasized the fact-specific nature of the case at bar in her concurring opinion in *Rosenberger*. She also discussed whether the government, as represented by the University, would have been playing favorites by endorsing or appearing to endorse the views of a specific religious group if it funded *Wide Awake*. Ibid., 2525–8 (O'Connor, J., concurring).

123. Ibid., 2528 (Thomas, J., concurring).

124. Ibid., 2529. See generally Robert L. Cord, *Separation of Church and State: Historical Fact and Current Fiction* (New York: Lambeth Press, 1982); Rodney K. Smith, "Getting Off on the Wrong Foot and Back on Again: A Reexamination of the History of the Framing of the Religion Clauses of the First Amendment and a Critique of the *Reynolds* and *Everson* Decisions," *Wake Forest Law Review* 20 (fall 1984): 569–643; Douglas Laycock, "'Nonpreferential' Aid to Religion: A False Claim about Original Intent," *William and Mary Law Review* 27, no. 5 (1985–86): 875–923. There are many other scholarly accounts of what the Framers allegedly meant by the Establishment Clause. Justice Souter discussed some of them in his dissent.

125. 115 S.Ct. at 2531 n. 4, 2532 (Thomas, J., concurring).

126. Ibid., 2533–50 (Souter, J., dissenting).

127. Ibid., 2545.

128. Ibid., 2536–7 n. 1. See generally Thomas J. Curry, *The First Freedoms: Church and State in America to the Passage of the First Amendment* (New York: Oxford University Press, 1986); Laycock, "'Nonpreferential' Aid to Religion"; Leonard W. Levy, *The Establishment Clause: Religion and the First Amendment* (New York: Macmillan, 1986).

129. See *Lee v. Weisman*, 505 U.S. 577 (1992), especially 609–31 (Souter, J., concurring).

130. As quoted in Laurie Goldstein and Joan Biskupic, "In Two Rulings, High Court Refines Relationship between Church, State," *Washington Post*, 30 June 1995, A1.

131. Ibid. Many religious magazines devoted cover stories and editorials to the *Rosenberger* decision. See, for example, Winnifred Fallers Sullivan, "The Difference Religion Makes: Reflections on *Rosenberger*," *Christian Century*, 13 March 1996, 292–5; Editorial, "The *Rosenberger* Decision: Courting Trouble," *Church and State*, September 1995, 12.

132. Jeremy Rabkin, "Common Sense v. The Court," *American Spectator*, September 1995, 26–7, 70, 26.

133. Edd Doerr, "Wobbly Wall," *Humanist*, 19 September 1995, 36.

134. See, for example, Kent Greenawalt, "Quo Vadis: The Status and Prospects of 'Tests' under the Religion Clauses," in *1995 Supreme Court Review*, ed. Dennis J. Hutchinson, David A. Strauss, and Geoffrey R. Stone (Chicago:

University of Chicago Press, 1996), 323–91. This was especially true of the student notes on the decision, something that should be expected given the emphasis in law schools on teaching legal doctrine. See, for example, Julie Madison Angus, Case Note, "Life without Lemon: The Status of Establishment Clause Jurisprudence after *Rosenberger v. University of Virginia*," *Northern Illinois University Law Review* 17 (fall 1996): 123–53; Robert L. Kilroy, "A Lost Opportunity to Sweeten the Lemon of Establishment Clause Jurisprudence," *Cornell Journal of Law and Public Policy* 6 (spring 1997): 701–51. See generally *Lemon v. Kurtzman*, 403 U.S. 602 (1971).

135. John O. McGinnis, "Original Thomas, Conventional Souter," *Policy Review*, fall 1995, 24–9, 28.

136. See, for example, People for the American Way Action Fund, Position Paper, "Judge Clarence Thomas: An Overall Disdain for the Rule of Law," 30 July 1991 (copy in my possession).

137. Elliot M. Mincberg, "The Supreme Court and the First Amendment: The 1994–95 Term," *New York Law School Journal of Human Rights* 13 (winter 1997): 223–306, 236.

138. Suzanna Sherry, "The Indeterminacy of Historical Evidence," *Harvard Journal of Law and Public Policy* 19 (winter 1996): 437–41. As I explain in the text, Sherry is exactly *wrong* about the resolution of the "indeterminacy" question by historians. See, for example, Joyce Oldham Appleby, *Telling the Truth about History* (New York: W. W. Norton, 1994); Peter Novick, *That Noble Dream: The "Objectivity Question" and the American Historical Profession* (Cambridge: Cambridge University Press, 1988).

139. See, for example, Leonard W. Levy, *Original Intent and the Framers' Constitution* (New York: Macmillan, 1988); Jack N. Rakove, *Original Meanings: Politics and Ideas in the Making of the Constitution* (New York: Alfred A. Knopf, 1996).

140. See Scott D. Gerber, "Original Intent and Its Obligations: Rediscovering the Principles of the American Founding," *Hamline Journal of Public Law and Policy* 11 (spring 1990): 1–18; Gerber, *To Secure These Rights*.

141. 115 S.Ct. at 2530 (Thomas, J., concurring) (quoting Cord).

142. Reprinted in *The Founders' Constitution*, ed. Kurland and Lerner, vol. 5, 85.

143. Justice Thomas made special reference to race in an Establishment Clause opinion he issued on the same day as *Rosenberger*, his concurring opinion in *Capitol Square Review and Advisory Board v. Pinette* (1995). Justice Thomas joined Justice Scalia's opinion for the Court in *Capitol Square* that the state of Ohio had not violated the Establishment Clause when it permitted the Ku Klux Klan to display an unattended cross on the grounds of the state capitol. He wrote separately, however, to make the point that the Ku Klux Klan erected the cross as a political act—to further its efforts "to establish a racist white government in the

United States"—not as a religious act and, consequently, the case "may not have truly involved the Establishment Clause." 115 S.Ct. 2440, 2450–1 (Thomas, J., concurring).

144. Gerber, *To Secure These Rights*, 5.

145. John Locke, "A Letter Concerning Toleration," in *Works of John Locke*, 11th ed., vol. 2 (London: Otrige, 1824), 350–1, 374–5.

146. Due in large part to the path-breaking efforts of John Dunn, contemporary Locke scholarship has tended to move away from the traditional analytical approach to Locke's political philosophy to a more historical approach in which Locke's political activities in support of England's "Glorious Revolution" of 1688 are emphasized. See, for example, Richard Ashcraft, *Revolutionary Politics and Locke's Two Treatises of Government* (Princeton: Princeton University Press, 1986). See generally John Dunn, *The Political Thought of John Locke: An Historical Account of the Argument of the Two Treatises of Government* (Cambridge: Cambridge University Press, 1969). The Founders, however, took an analytical approach to Locke's political philosophy. See Gerber, *To Secure These Rights*, 40–1 n.

147. 514 U.S. 334, 358–71 (1995) (Thomas, J., concurring in the judgment).

148. Bill F. Chamberlin, "Speech and the Press," in *The Oxford Companion to the Supreme Court of the United States*, ed. Kermit L. Hall (New York: Oxford University Press, 1992), 808–16, 810.

149. I will not reopen the incorporation debate here. The Supreme Court held in *Near v. Minnesota* (1931) that the Free Press Clause of the First Amendment applies to the states. No member of the *McIntyre* Court challenged that holding, nor did any commentator on the case. See generally *Near v. Minnesota*, 283 U.S. 697 (1931).

150. See generally Leonard W. Levy, *The Emergence of a Free Press* (New York: Oxford University Press, 1985).

151. 376 U.S. 254, 270 (1964).

152. 514 U.S. at 357, 347.

153. Ibid., 358–71 (Thomas, J., concurring in the judgment). Justice Ginsburg issued a brief concurrence to express her disagreement with the argument advanced by Justice Scalia in dissent: that Justice Stevens's opinion for the Court was inconsistent with existing case law. Ibid., 358 (Ginsburg, J., concurring).

154. Ibid., 359 (Thomas, J., concurring in the judgment).

155. See, for example, William J. Brennan, Jr., "The Constitution of the United States: Contemporary Ratification," reprinted in *The U.S. Constitution and the Supreme Court*, ed. Steven Anzovin and Janet Podell (New York: H. W. Wilson, 1988), 166–79. Justice Thomas quoted from Justice Brennan's concurring opinion in the school prayer case, *Abington School District v. Schempp*, 374 U.S. 1560 (1963).

156. See, for example, Michael J. Perry, *The Constitution in the Courts: Law or*

Politics? (New York: Oxford University Press, 1994), 213 n. 15 (referring to Justice Brennan as an originalist).

157. 514 U.S. at 360 (Thomas, J., concurring in the judgment). See generally Bernard Bailyn, ed., *Pamphlets of the American Revolution, 1750–1776* (Cambridge, MA: Harvard University Press, 1965); Paul L. Ford, ed., *Pamphlets on the Constitution of the United States* (1888; reprint, New York: Da Capo, 1968).

158. 514 U.S. at 367 (Thomas, J., concurring in the judgment).

159. Ibid., 368. The two that were not published anonymously were George Mason's "Objections to the Constitution" and Luther Martin's "The Genuine Information." Justice Thomas hypothesized that both men probably felt the need to go on the record to explain why they refused to sign the Constitution.

160. See Newt Gingrich, *To Renew America* (New York: HarperCollins, 1995).

161. 514 U.S. at 370 (Thomas, J., concurring in the judgment).

162. Ibid., 371–85 (Scalia, J., dissenting).

163. Ibid., 378. Justice Scalia also insisted that the Court's own precedents supported Ohio's position.

164. For more on Burkean conventionalism as a method of interpreting the Constitution, see Thomas W. Merrill, "Bork v. Burke," *Harvard Journal of Law and Public Policy* 19 (winter 1996): 509–23. I have more to say later in the text about Merrill's essay.

165. David S. Broder, "Bungled by the High Court," *Washington Post*, 7 May 1995, C7.

166. Linda Greenhouse, "Justices Allow Unsigned Political Fliers," *New York Times*, 20 April 1995, A20.

167. Melvin I. Urofsky, "Courts, Legislatures, and History: Having Faith in Time," *Cumberland Law Review* 27, no. 3 (1996–97): 941–9, 944. Among Urofsky's many books is *A Conflict of Rights: The Supreme Court and Affirmative Action* (New York: Scribner's 1991).

168. Merrill, "Burke v. Bork," 523 n. 22. See generally *Rubin v. Coors Brewing Co.*, 514 U.S. 476 (1995).

169. *Jones v. Opelika*, 316 U.S. 584, 608 (1942) (Stone, C.J.). See also *United States v. Carolene Products Co.*, 304 U.S. 144, 152 n. 4 (1938) (Stone, J.).

170. *Palko v. Connecticut*, 302 U.S. 319 (1937) (Cardozo, J.).

171. I am grateful to Thomas W. Hazlett for this anecdote. See generally Alex Kozinski and Stuart Banner, "Who's Afraid of Commercial Speech?" *Virginia Law Review* 76 (May 1990): 627–53, 652.

172. The theories are well chronicled in Martin H. Redish, "First Amendment Theory and the Demise of the Commercial Speech Distinction: The Case of the Smoking Controversy," *Northern Kentucky University Law Review* 24 (summer 1997): 553–83. The most famous is probably Robert Bork's theory that the Free Speech Clause protects *only* political speech. See Robert H. Bork, "Neutral Princi-

ples and Some First Amendment Problems," *Indiana Law Journal* 47 (fall 1971): 1–75.

173. See Alex Kozinski and Stuart Banner, "The Anti-History and Pre-History of Commercial Speech," *Texas Law Review* 71 (March 1993): 747–75. See generally *Valentine v. Chrestensen*, 316 U.S. 52 (1942).

174. 316 U.S. at 54.

175. 425 U.S. 748 (1976).

176. Ibid., 771 n. 24.

177. 447 U.S. 557 (1980).

178. 116 S.Ct. 1495 (1996).

179. 478 U.S. 328 (1986). The alternative analysis was that the "greater power" to ban casino gambling—which the Puerto Rican legislature possessed—included the "lesser power" to ban advertising of casino gambling. Since there are few underlying activities that the government cannot constitutionally ban, the possibility presented itself that sweeping restrictions on commercial speech would be routinely upheld.

180. 514 U.S. at 476. I say "nearly unanimous" because Justice Stevens merely concurred in the judgment and, more importantly, called into question the *Central Hudson* test. Ibid., 491–8 (Stevens, J., concurring in the judgment). Justice Stevens continued to call *Central Hudson* into question in his principle opinion for the Court in *44 Liquormart*, discussed in the text.

181. See *S and S Liquormart, Inc. v. Pastore*, 497 A.2d 729 (R.I. 1985); *Rhode Island Liquor Stores Ass'n v. The Evening Call Publishing Co.*, 497 A.2d 331 (R.I. 1985).

182. 116 S.Ct. at 1520–3 (O'Connor, J., concurring in the judgment). Chief Justice Rehnquist and Justices Souter and Breyer joined Justice O'Connor's concurring opinion.

183. Ibid., 1515 (Scalia, J., concurring in part and concurring in the judgment).

184. Ibid., 1501–15 (Stevens, J., plurality opinion). There was no majority for anything but the result. Justices Kennedy and Ginsburg joined that part of Justice Stevens's opinion that announced what test should be applied.

185. Ibid., 1515–23 (Thomas, J., concurring in part and concurring in the judgment).

186. Ibid., 1515 (Scalia, J., concurring in part and concurring in the judgment).

187. Ibid., 1515–6, 1516 (Thomas, J., concurring in part and concurring in the judgment).

188. Ibid., 1518.

189. David G. Savage, "First Amendment Rulings Are Out of Order, Liberals Complain," *Los Angeles Times*, 18 December 1996, A5. Savage himself has pub-

258 | Notes to Chapter 4

lished a book about the conservatism of the early Rehnquist Court. See David G. Savage, *Turning Right: The Making of the Rehnquist Supreme Court* (New York: Wiley, 1992).

190. Jerome L. Wilson, "A Toast to Commercial Speech," *New Jersey Law Journal*, 26 August 1996, S–14.

191. Redish, "First Amendment Theory and the Demise of the Commercial Speech Distinction," 553, 556. See generally Martin H. Redish, "The First Amendment in the Marketplace: Commercial Speech and the Values of Free Expression," *George Washington University Law Review* 39 (March 1971): 429–73. Kathleen M. Sullivan, a prominent liberal law professor at Stanford, also wrote a law review article about *44 Liquormart*. She, however, simply described the decision and the implications it may have for tobacco advertising. See Kathleen M. Sullivan, "Cheap Spirits, Cigarettes, and Free Speech: The Implications of *44 Liquormart*," in *1996 Supreme Court Review*, ed. Dennis J. Hutchinson, David A. Strauss, and Geoffrey R. Stone (Chicago: University of Chicago Press, 1997), 123–61. Sullivan took a similar tack in the popular press. See Kathleen M. Sullivan, "Muzzle Joe Camel? It May Be Illegal," *Newsday*, 30 May 1996, A51.

192. Redish, "First Amendment Theory and the Demise of the Commercial Speech Distinction," 556–7. It should be noted that Redish has served as a consultant on constitutional issues to the tobacco industry. Ibid., 553 n.

193. Ibid., 563.

194. Merrill, "Bork v. Burke," 523 n. 22.

195. 116 S.Ct. at 1517 (Thomas, J., concurring in part and concurring in the judgment); ibid., 1504 (Stevens, J., plurality opinion); ibid., 1515 (Scalia, J., concurring in part and concurring in the judgment).

196. See Charles A. Beard, *An Economic Interpretation of the Constitution of the United States* (New York: Macmillan, 1913).

197. See Learned Hand, "Chief Justice Stone's Conception of the Judicial Function," *Columbia Law Review* 46 (September 1946): 696–9, 698.

198. *The Federalist*, ed. Clinton Rossiter (New York: New American Library, 1961), No. 10, 77–84, 78 (James Madison).

199. In *The Works of John Adams*, ed. Charles F. Adams, vol. 6 (Boston: Little, Brown, 1850–59), 280.

200. See Gerber, *To Secure These Rights*.

NOTES TO CHAPTER 5

1. See Richard L. Pacelle, Jr., *The Transformation of the Supreme Court's Agenda* (Boulder, CO: Westview, 1991).

2. See Bruce A. Ackerman, *We the People: Foundations* (Cambridge, MA: Harvard University Press, 1991).

3. See, for example, *Marbury v. Madison*, 5 U.S. (1 Cr.) 137 (1803); *McCulloch*

v. Maryland, 17 U.S. (4 Wheat.) 316 (1819); *Gibbons v. Ogden*, 22 U.S. (9 Wheat.) 1 (1824); *Cooley v. Board of Wardens*, 53 U.S. (12 How.) 299 (1851); *United States v. E.C. Knight Co.*, 156 U.S. 1 (1895); *A.L.A. Schechter Poultry Corp. v. United States*, 295 U.S. 495 (1935). See generally Scott D. Gerber, "Reordering American Constitutional Law Teaching," *PS: Political Science and Politics* 27 (December 1994): 703–5.

4. This statement is a relative one. The Rehnquist Court has granted certiorari to fewer and fewer cases in recent years. See, for example, Arthur D. Hellman, "The Shrunken Docket of the Rehnquist Court," in *1996 Supreme Court Review*, ed. Dennis J. Hutchinson, David A. Strauss, and Geoffrey R. Stone (Chicago: University of Chicago Press, 1997), 403–38.

5. 115 S.Ct. 1842 (1995).

6. 115 S.Ct. 1624 (1995).

7. These two cases were decided at a time (1994–1995) that has been called "the most exciting for federal-state relations" since the New Deal and a moment when "all three national branches view[ed] the states and localities as important partners and players in democracy." Michael A. Pagano and Ann O. M. Bowman, "The State of American Federalism," *Publius: The Journal of Federalism* 25 (June 1995): 1–21.

8. See Samuel H. Beer, *To Make a Nation: The Rediscovery of American Federalism* (Cambridge, MA: Harvard University Press, 1993), 1–25.

9. 17 U.S. (4 Wheat.) at 316.

10. See, for example, *The Slaughterhouse Cases*, 83 U.S. (16 Wall.) 36 (1872).

11. See, for example, *Hammer v. Dagenhart*, 247 U.S. 251 (1918), overruled by *United States v. Darby*, 312 U.S. 100 (1941); *Carter v. Carter Coal Co.*, 298 U.S. 238 (1936).

12. See, for example, Henry J. Abraham, *Justices and Presidents: A Political History of Appointments to the Supreme Court*, 3d ed. (New York: Oxford University Press, 1992), 212, 337.

13. Linda Greenhouse, "High Court Blocks Term Limits for Congress in a 5–4 Decision," *New York Times*, 23 May 1995, 1.

14. The referendum also limited the terms of Arkansas's state executive and state legislative officials.

15. Preamble to the proposed Term Limitation Amendment, as quoted in 115 S.Ct. at 1845.

16. See, for example, George F. Will, *Restoration: Congress, Term Limits, and the Recovery of Deliberative Democracy* (New York: Free Press, 1992).

17. 395 U.S. 486 (1969). *Powell* involved the question of whether the U.S. House of Representatives could exclude a duly elected congressman for alleged misuse of public money. The Court, in an opinion by Chief Justice Warren, held that it could not.

18. *U.S. Term Limits, Inc. v. Hill*, 872 S.W.2d 349 (Ark. 1994).

19. 115 S.Ct. at 1848, 1850.

20. Ibid., 1850.

21. 395 U.S. at 547 (quoting a ratifying debate speech by Alexander Hamilton).

22. 115 S.Ct. at 1854, 1855.

23. Ibid., 1855.

24. Justice Stevens also resorted to the "arguing in the alternative" approach that is so popular among lawyers. He maintained that, even if the states possessed some control over congressional qualifications as part of their original powers, the Qualifications Clauses "were intended to preclude the States from exercising any such power and to fix as exclusive the qualifications in the Constitution." Ibid., 1856. To support this supposition, Justice Stevens repeated his earlier originalist exegesis on the states' power to add qualifications. He also resorted to originalism to reject the argument that the state amendment at issue was a permissible exercise of Arkansas's power under the Elections Clause to regulate the "manner" of elections.

25. Ibid., 1871. Justice Kennedy, the swing vote in both *Term Limits* and *Lopez* (which is discussed in the next section), also employed originalism in his *Term Limits* concurring opinion. See ibid., 1872–5 (Kennedy, J., concurring). Justice Kennedy's argument was plainly meant to rebut the arguments offered by Justice Thomas. Justice Kennedy argued that the Arkansas amendment at issue violated the "republican character of the National Government" and the "fundamental principles of federalism." He acknowledged that the policy arguments for term limits "are not lacking force," but this did not change the fact that, for him, the amendment violated the "federal right of citizenship" with which the "States may not interfere." Ibid., 1872, 1875.

26. 114 S.Ct. 2581, 2591–619 (1994) (Thomas, J., concurring in the judgment).

27. 115 S.Ct. at 1875–914 (Thomas, J., dissenting).

28. Ibid., 1875.

29. Ibid., 1876, 1875.

30. Ibid., 1876 n. 1.

31. Ibid., 1875.

32. Ibid., 1877, 1879.

33. Ibid., 1879.

34. Ibid., 1880.

35. Ibid., 1884. Justice Thomas also distinguished in his lengthy exegesis on reserved powers what he insisted were two separate concepts: (1) the selection of congressional representatives, and (2) the body they form once elected. Contrary to Justice Stevens's position, Justice Thomas maintained that the "direct link" was between the representatives from each state and that state's people, not between

the people and the nation. Ibid., 1882. Justice Thomas also insisted, again contrary to Justice Stevens's position, that the Times, Places, and Manners Clause did not restrict the people's reserved power to impose term limits on their congressional representatives.

36. Ibid., 1885 (emphasis added).

37. Ibid., 1886–7, 1885.

38. Maryland claimed that McCreery lived outside his district in violation of state law. The U.S. House of Representatives seated him anyway. To Justice Stevens, this incident illustrated "the general consensus on the lack of state power in this area." Ibid., 1861. To Justice Thomas, the House said only that McCreery was entitled to his seat and rejected proposals to declare him qualified under Maryland law or under the federal Constitution. Ibid., 1908–9 (Thomas, J., dissenting).

39. Justice Thomas also called into question whether *Term Limits* was a term limits case at all, since all Amendment 73 prohibited was listing on the ballot the names of persons who had served three terms in the House or two terms in the Senate. Such persons could, in other words, win reelection by write-in.

40. Ibid., 1909, 1913, 1914.

41. Editorial, "Right Call on Term Limits," *New York Times*, 24 May 1995, A20. The *Times* called Justice Thomas's dissent "windy" and the product of the "magic of his imagining."

42. Editorial, "Term Limits Struck Down," *Washington Post*, 23 May 1995, A14. See also Jeffrey Rosen, "Terminated," *New Republic*, 12 June 1995, 12–4 (calling Justice Thomas's opinion "Calhounian" and one that both "reopen[s] the Civil War" and "seems to imply a right of secession").

43. George F. Will, "Term Limits: This Battle Will Go On," *Washington Post*, 24 May 1995, A25. See also Will, *Restoration*. See generally Robert H. Bork, *The Tempting of America: The Political Seduction of the Law* (New York: Free Press, 1990).

44. Will, "Term Limits," A25.

45. See, for example, Lino A. Graglia, "Does Constitutional Law Exist?" *National Review*, 26 June 1995, 31–4; Stuart Taylor, Jr., "Looking Right at the Justices," *American Lawyer*, November 1995, 37.

46. See Jack N. Rakove, *Original Meanings: Politics and Ideas in the Making of the Constitution* (New York: Alfred A. Knopf, 1996). See also Jack N. Rakove, ed., *Interpreting the Constitution: The Debate over Original Intent* (Boston: Northeastern University Press, 1990).

47. Booknotes Interview, C-SPAN, 6 July 1997.

48. Jack N. Rakove, "Term Limits: Reading Today's Bias into 'Original Intent,'" *Los Angeles Times*, 28 May 1995, M2.

49. See Scott Douglas Gerber, *To Secure These Rights: The Declaration of Inde-*

262 | *Notes to Chapter 5*

pendence and Constitutional Interpretation (New York: New York University Press, 1995) (arguing for "liberal originalism").

50. Alfred H. Kelly, "Clio and the Court: An Illicit Love Affair," in *1965 Supreme Court Review*, ed. Philip B. Kurland (Chicago: University of Chicago Press, 1965), 119–58. See also Martin S. Flaherty, "History 'Lite' in Modern American Constitutionalism," *Columbia Law Review* 95 (April 1995): 523–90.

51. See, for example, Rocco Luisi, Case Note, "*U.S. Term Limits, Inc. v. Thornton,*" *Seton Hall Law Review* 26 (fall 1996): 1711–35.

52. See, for example, Harry H. Wellington, "Term Limits: History, Democracy, and Constitutional Interpretation," *New York Law School Law Review* 40 (spring 1996): 833–53.

53. See, for example, Symposium: Major Issues in Federalism, *Arizona Law Review* 38 (fall 1996).

54. See, for example, Polly J. Price, "Term Limits on Original Intent? An Essay in Legal Debate and Historical Understanding," *Virginia Law Review* 82 (April 1996): 493–533.

55. See Kathleen M. Sullivan, "Comment: Dueling Sovereignties: *U.S. Term Limits, Inc. v. Thornton,*" *Harvard Law Review* 109 (November 1995): 78–109.

56. David N. Mayer, *The Constitutional Thought of Thomas Jefferson* (Charlottesville: University Press of Virginia, 1994).

57. David N. Mayer, "Justice Clarence Thomas and the Supreme Court's Rediscovery of the Tenth Amendment," *Capital University Law Review* 25, no. 2 (1996): 339–423, 343.

58. Ibid., 407, 410, 408, 408 n. 254.

59. Sullivan, "Dueling Sovereignties," 80.

60. See, for example, Laurence H. Tribe, "'Natural Law' and the Nominee," *New York Times*, 16 August 1991, A15.

61. Sullivan, "Dueling Sovereignties," 80 n. 18, 105–9.

62. See, for example, John Paul Stevens, "Construing the Constitution," *U.C.-Davis Law Review* 19 (fall 1985): 15–21.

63. See Robert H. Bork, *Slouching towards Gomorrah: Modern Liberalism and American Decline* (New York: Regan Books, 1996).

64. See Neil M. Richards, Case Note, "Competing Notions of Federalism," *Journal of Law and Politics* 12 (summer 1996): 521–71. This was also Sullivan's point, but she then went on to make a liberal policy argument for Justice Stevens's reading of history.

65. See Gerber, *To Secure These Rights* (arguing for "liberal originalism" to resolve rights questions).

66. *The Federalist*, ed. Clinton Rossiter (New York: New American Library, 1961), No. 39, 240–6, 246.

67. U.S. Const. art. I, sec. 3, cl. 1 (amended 1913).

68. See *The Federalist*, No. 39, 246.

69. James Madison, "Vices of the Political System of the United States," in *The Papers of James Madison*, ed. W. T. Hutchinson and William M. E. Pachel, vol. 9 (Chicago: University of Chicago Press, 1962–77), 355, 358–60. See generally Merrill Jensen, *The Articles of Confederation: An Interpretation of the Social-Constitutional History of the American Revolution, 1774–1781* (Madison: University of Wisconsin Press, 1940).

70. Some of the most interesting constitutional scholarship has been devoted to the Court's Commerce Clause cases. See, for example, Felix Frankfurter, *The Commerce Clause under Marshall, Taney and Waite* (Chapel Hill: University of North Carolina Press, 1937). Readers desiring a doctrinal approach to the landmark cases are directed to Frankfurter's well-known tome.

71. 22 U.S. (9 Wheat.) at 1.

72. Ibid., 4–5, 9, 7.

73. The Marshall Court's dormant Commerce Clause cases are consistent with this reading of *Gibbons*. See, for example, *Willson v. Black Bird Creek Marsh Co.*, 27 U.S. (2 Pet.) 245 (1829).

74. *United States v. E. C. Knight Co.*, 156 U.S. at 1; *A.L.A. Schechter Poultry Corp. v. United States*, 295 U.S. at 495. See generally Howard Gillman, *The Constitution Besieged: The Rise and Demise of Lochner Era Police Powers Jurisprudence* (Durham, NC: Duke University Press, 1993).

75. See, for example, Richard C. Cortner, *The Wagner Act Cases* (Knoxville: University of Tennessee Press, 1964).

76. 301 U.S. 1 (1937).

77. See, for example, *Wickard v. Filburn*, 347 U.S. 111 (1942).

78. See, for example, *Heart of Atlanta Motel, Inc. v. United States*, 379 U.S. 241 (1964) (upholding nondiscrimination provisions of the Civil Rights Act of 1964); *Katzenbach v. McClung*, 379 U.S. 294 (1964) (same).

79. 115 S.Ct. at 1626, 1634.

80. Ibid., 1630.

81. Ibid.

82. Ibid., 1657–71 (Breyer, J., dissenting). Justice Stevens issued a short dissent of his own. He argued that guns are both commerce and articles that can be used to restrain commerce and, in contrast to his *Term Limits* opinion, he did so on nonoriginalist grounds. Ibid., 1651 (Stevens, J., dissenting). Justice Souter also filed a separate dissent. He accused the conservative majority of engaging in substantive due process analysis and urged the Court to defer to "reasonable" congressional determinations about what substantially affects interstate commerce. Ibid., 1651–7 (Souter, J., dissenting).

83. Ibid., 1657–8, 1663, 1665–71 (Breyer, J., dissenting).

84. Ibid., 1642–51 (Thomas, J., concurring). Justice Kennedy also issued a concurring opinion. His opinion was joined by Justice O'Connor. He argued for a "practical conception of the commerce power": one that was both flexible

enough to allow the Court to react to changing economic times and respectful of state sovereignty over local affairs. Ibid., 1634–42 (Kennedy, J., concurring).

85. Ibid., 1642 (Thomas, J. concurring).

86. Ibid., 1643, 1644, 1645.

87. Ibid., 1645, 1648.

88. Ibid., 1651, 1650 n. 8.

89. Editorial, "The High Court Loses Restraint," *New York Times*, 29 April 1995, 22.

90. Jeffrey Rosen, "Fed Up," *New Republic*, 22 May 1995, 13–4. See generally Richard A. Epstein, "The Proper Scope of the Commerce Power," *Virginia Law Review* 73 (November 1987): 1387–455.

91. George F. Will, "Rethinking 1937," *Newsweek*, 15 May 1995, 70.

92. Douglas W. Kmiec, "Wising Up: Supreme Court Restores the Constitutional Structure," *Chicago Tribune*, 2 May 1995, 17.

93. See, for example, Daniel A. Farber, "The Dead Hand of the Architect," *Harvard Journal of Law and Public Policy* 19 (winter 1996): 245–9; Daniel A. Farber, "The Originalism Debate: A Guide for the Perplexed," *Ohio State Law Journal* 49 (October 1988): 1085–106.

94. Daniel A. Farber, "The Constitution's Forgotten Cover Letter: An Essay on the New Federalism and the Original Understanding," *Michigan Law Review* 94 (December 1995): 615–50, 648.

95. For more on the methodological shortcomings of conservative originalism, see, for example, Gerber, *To Secure These Rights*, introduction.

96. J. Clay Smith, Jr., "Shifts of Federalism and Its Implications for Civil Rights," *Howard Law Journal* 39 (spring 1996): 737–57, 757.

97. See, for example, Raoul Berger, *Government by Judiciary: The Transformation of the Fourteenth Amendment* (Cambridge, MA: Harvard University Press, 1977). See also Raoul Berger, *Federalism: The Founders' Design* (Norman: University of Oklahoma Press, 1987) (arguing for the compact theory of federalism). The Liberty Fund published a second edition of Berger's *Government by Judiciary* in 1997.

98. Raoul Berger, "Judicial Manipulation of the Commerce Clause," *Texas Law Review* 74 (March 1996): 695–717, 715.

99. Richard A. Epstein, "Constitutional Faith and the Commerce Clause," *Notre Dame Law Review* 71 (January 1996): 167–93, 172. Epstein relied in his *Notre Dame Law Review* essay on the earlier *Virginia Law Review* essay that Rosen accused Justice Thomas of plagiarizing. Ibid., 169 n. 11.

100. Ibid., 172.

101. 115 S.Ct. at 1649–50 (Thomas, J., concurring).

102. Beer, *To Make a Nation*, 351–3.

103. See, for example, "Centinel," Number I (5 October 1787), reprinted in

The Anti-Federalist Papers, ed. Ralph Ketcham (New York: New American Library, 1986), 227–37, 232 (Samuel Bryan).

104. See, for example, *The Federalist* No. 45, 288–94, 292–3 (James Madison).

105. 115 S.Ct. at 1657 (Souter, J., dissenting).

106. 116 S.Ct. 407, 407–9, 408 (1995) (Thomas, J., dissenting). Although Justice Scalia did not join Justice Thomas's dissenting opinion in *Cargill,* he too appears to want to carry *Lopez* forward. See *United States v. Ramey,* 115 S.Ct. 1838, 1839 (1995) (Scalia, J., dissenting), denying certiorari to 24 F.3d 602 (4th Cir. 1994). But see Suzanna Sherry, "The Barking Dog," *Case Western Reserve Law Review* 46 (spring 1996): 877–83 (analogizing *Lopez* to a dog that is all bark).

107. Beer, *To Make a Nation,* vii.

NOTES TO CHAPTER 6

1. In Roy M. Mersky, J. Myron Jacobstein, and Bonnie L. Koneski-White, eds., *The Supreme Court of the United States: Hearings and Reports on Successful and Unsuccessful Nominations of Supreme Court Justices by the Senate Judiciary Committee, 1916–1991,* vol. 17A, Clarence Thomas (Buffalo, NY: William S. Hein and Co., 1995), 1431.

2. See Scott D. Gerber, "The Jurisprudence of Clarence Thomas," *Journal of Law and Politics* 8 (fall 1991): 107–41.

3. See, for example, Ruth S. Intress, "Review of Thomas's Record Shows Inconsistencies," *Richmond Times-Dispatch,* 6 September 1991, B4; Marcia Coyle, "They Hew to Script, With Some Ad-Libbing," *National Law Journal,* 23 September 1991, 8; Mersky, Jacobstein, and Koneski-White, eds., *Hearings,* 1612 (remarks of Senator Paul Simon [D-IL]).

4. See Scott Douglas Gerber, "To Secure These Rights: The Declaration of Independence and Constitutional Interpretation," doctoral dissertation, University of Virginia, 1992. My dissertation was subsequently published in revised form as *To Secure These Rights: The Declaration of Independence and Constitutional Interpretation* (New York: New York University Press, 1995).

5. See Scott D. Gerber, "Judging Thomas: The Politics of Assessing a Supreme Court Justice," *Journal of Black Studies* 27 (November 1996): 224–59; Scott D. Gerber, "Justice Clarence Thomas: First Term, First Impressions," *Howard Law Journal* 35 (winter 1992): 115–53. I also wrote an op-ed about press reaction to Justice Thomas. See Scott D. Gerber, "Bout with Justice: Clarence Thomas Gets Bashed Again," *Daily Press,* 9 July 1995, H1, cols. 2–5, and H4, cols. 1–3. See also Scott D. Gerber, "The Ideas of Justice Thomas," *Washington Post,* 28 July 1998, A15, col. 5.

6. A "judicial behavioralist" is a political scientist who studies the performance patterns of judges, typically by applying statistical methods to the judges'

opinion-writing and voting-record outputs. See, for example, Scott D. Gerber and Keeok Park, "The Quixotic Search for Consensus on the U.S. Supreme Court: A Cross-Judicial Empirical Analysis of the Rehnquist Court Justices," *American Political Science Review* 91 (June 1997): 390–408. See generally Mersky, Jacobstein, and Koneski-White, eds., *Hearings*, 1396 (where Thomas characterized himself as a "part-time political theorist").

7. See, for example, Timothy M. Hagle, "'Freshman Effects' for Supreme Court Justices," *American Journal of Political Science* 37 (November 1993): 1142–57; Eloise C. Snyder, "The Supreme Court as a Small Group," *Social Forces* 36 (March 1958): 232–8.

8. See A. Leon Higginbotham, Jr., "An Open Letter to Justice Clarence Thomas from a Federal Judicial Colleague," *University of Pennsylvania Law Review* 140 (January 1992): 1005–28; A. Leon Higginbotham, Jr., "Justice Clarence Thomas in Retrospect," *Hastings Law Journal* 45 (August 1994): 1405–33. See also A. Leon Higginbotham, Jr., "Disinvitation: Talking Back to Thomas," *National Law Journal*, 3 August 1998, A23–4.

9. See, for example, "Uncle Thomas: Lawn Jockey of the Far Right," *Emerge*, November 1996.

10. All but two of Justice Thomas's major opinions were concurring or dissenting opinions. Clearly, Justice Thomas was not the "accommodationist judge" and "coalition builder" that Justice O'Connor was during the 1991–1995 Supreme Court terms. See Nancy Maveety, *Justice Sandra Day O'Connor: Strategist on the Supreme Court* (Lanham, MD: Rowman and Littlefield, 1996). This is undoubtedly a result of Justice Thomas's unwavering commitment to first principles.

11. Cass R. Sunstein, "Supreme Caution: Once Again, the High Court Takes Only Small Steps," *Washington Post*, 6 July 1997, C1, C5. See also Cass R. Sunstein, "Foreword: Leaving Things Undecided," *Harvard Law Review* 110 (November 1996): 4–101. In my view, Justice Scalia has become more of a conventionalist in recent years (see Chapter 4), whereas Justice Thomas has remained an originalist (more on this in the text).

12. See, for example, Richard A. Brisbin, Jr., *Justice Antonin Scalia and the Conservative Revival* (Baltimore: Johns Hopkins University Press, 1997); Christopher E. Smith, "The Constitution and Punishment: The Emerging Visions of Justices Scalia and Thomas," *Drake Law Review* 43, no. 3 (1995): 593–613.

13. See *Adarand Constructors, Inc. v. Peña*, 115 S.Ct. 2097, 2119 (1995) (Thomas, J., concurring in part and concurring in the judgment); *Rosenberger v. University of Virginia*, 115 S.Ct. 2510, 2528–33, 2530 (1995) (Thomas, J., concurring).

14. There are, of course, exceptions to every rule. Justice Thomas's position on the First Amendment issue of anonymous political writing was, for instance,

quite liberal. However, his conservative originalism led him there. See *McIntyre v. Ohio Elections Commission*, 514 U.S. 334, 358–71 (1995) (Thomas, J., concurring in the judgment).

15. See Mersky, Jacobstein, and Koneski-White, eds., *Hearings*, 1601; *United States v. Lopez*, 115 S.Ct. 1624, 1642–51 (1995) (Thomas, J., concurring).

16. Clarence Thomas, "Toward a 'Plain Reading' of the Constitution—The Declaration of Independence in Constitutional Interpretation," *Howard Law Journal* 30 (fall 1987): 983–95, 990–2; Clarence Thomas, "The Higher Law Background of the Privileges or Immunities Clause of the Fourteenth Amendment," *Harvard Journal of Law and Public Policy* 12 (winter 1989): 63–8, 68. See generally *Brown v. Board of Education*, 347 U.S. 483 (1954).

17. 115 S.Ct. 2038, 2061–73 (1995) (Thomas, J., concurring).

18. Ibid., 2065.

19. See, for example, Bernard Grofman, Lisa Handley, and Richard G. Niemi, *Minority Representation and the Quest for Voting Equality* (New York: Cambridge University Press, 1992), 1.

20. Clarence Thomas, "The Modern Civil Rights Movement: Can a Regime of Individual Rights and the Rule of Law Survive?" Tocqueville Forum, Winston-Salem, NC, 18 April 1988, 1–26, 17 (copy in my possession).

21. 114 S.Ct. 2581, 2591–619 (1994) (Thomas, J., concurring in the judgment). See generally *Thornburg v. Gingles*, 478 U.S. 30 (1986).

22. 114 S.Ct. at 2597 (Thomas, J., concurring in the judgment).

23. Ibid.

24. Clarence Thomas, "Affirmative Action Goals and Timetables: Too Tough? Not Tough Enough!" *Yale Law and Policy Review* 5 (spring–summer 1987): 402–11, 403 n. 3.

25. 115 S.Ct. at 2119 (Thomas, J., concurring in part and concurring in the judgment).

26. 115 S.Ct. 1842, 1875–914, 1880 (Thomas, J., dissenting).

27. *Hudson v. McMillian*, 503 U.S. 1, 17–29, 19 (1992) (Thomas, J., dissenting); *Helling v. McKinney*, 509 U.S. 25, 37–42, 39 (Thomas, J., dissenting).

28. See 115 S.Ct. at 1850 n. 9, 1854, 1855.

29. Legal realism is a school of legal thought that took root during the New Deal era. (Realism's origins trace to Oliver Wendell Holmes, Jr.) Realists insisted that the outcomes of cases were not "predetermined" by the law and that law was not the "science" described by legal formalists such as Christopher Columbus Langdell during the late nineteenth century. Rather, the realists argued, each case provided a range of discretion within which a judge could pursue his own policy goals. See, for example, Laura Kalman, *Legal Realism at Yale* (Chapel Hill: University of North Carolina Press, 1986).

30. See Clarence Thomas, "Judging," *University of Kansas Law Review* 45 (November 1996): 1–8. Justice Thomas's most controversial speech was his July 1998

speech to the National Bar Association. See Clarence Thomas, Speech to the National Bar Association, Memphis, TN, 29 July 1998, broadcast on C-SPAN.

31. See, for example, *West Virginia Board of Education v. Barnette*, 319 U.S. 624, 646–70, 647 (1943) (Frankfurter, J., dissenting). My research about the political nature of Supreme Court decisionmaking starts with the first Supreme Court. See Scott Douglas Gerber, ed., *Seriatim: The Supreme Court before John Marshall* (New York: New York University Press, 1998).

32. Letter from Felix Frankfurter to Franklin D. Roosevelt, 18 February 1937, in *Roosevelt and Frankfurter: Their Correspondence, 1928–1945*, ed. Max Freedman (Boston: Little, Brown, 1967), 383.

33. Clarence Thomas, Speech to the National Center for Policy Analysis, 6 September 1996, rebroadcast on C-SPAN on 19 October 1996.

34. Clarence Thomas, Speech to the Savannah, Georgia, Bar Association, Savannah, GA, 1997, broadcast on C-SPAN.

35. See, for example, Maya Angelou, "I Dare to Hope," reprinted in *Court of Appeal: The Black Community Speaks Out on the Racial and Sexual Politics of Clarence Thomas vs. Anita Hill*, ed. Robert Chrisman and Robert L. Allen (New York: Ballantine Books, 1992), 33–5.

36. Anita Hill, *Speaking Truth to Power* (New York: Doubleday, 1997).

37. What follows in the text is adapted from Scott D. Gerber, "Narrative within a Framework," review of Anita Hill, *Speaking Truth to Power* (1997), *Washington Times*, 22 November 1997, C3, reprinted in *Washington Times Weekly*, 14 December 1997, 27.

38. Hill, *Speaking Truth to Power*, 118.

39. Robert H. Bork, *The Tempting of America: The Political Seduction of the Law* (New York: Free Press, 1990).

40. John C. Danforth, *Resurrection: The Confirmation of Clarence Thomas* (New York: Viking, 1994).

41. See, for example, Adrien Katherine Wing, ed., *Critical Race Feminism: A Reader* (New York: New York University Press, 1997).

42. Hill, *Speaking Truth to Power*, 178–9.

NOTES TO APPENDIX I

1. The pioneering study is Eloise C. Snyder, "The Supreme Court as a Small Group," *Social Forces* 36 (March 1958): 232–8. See also Timothy M. Hagle, "'Freshman Effects' for Supreme Court Justices," *American Journal of Political Science* 37 (November 1993): 1142–57. *Judicature* frequently publishes freshman effect analyses.

2. See, for example, Snyder, "The Supreme Court as a Small Group;" S. Sidney Ulmer, "Toward a Theory of Sub-Group Formation in the Supreme Court," *Journal of Politics* 27 (February 1965): 133–52.

3. Christopher E. Smith and Scott P. Johnson, "Newcomer on the High Court: Justice David Souter and the Supreme Court's 1990 Term," *South Dakota Law Review* 37, no. 1 (1992): 21–43, 22.

4. See, for example, Hagle, "'Freshman Effects' for Supreme Court Justices;" Snyder, "The Supreme Court as a Small Group."

5. See, for example, Hagle, "'Freshman Effects' for Supreme Court Justices;" J. Woodford Howard, Jr., "Mr. Justice Murphy: The Freshman Years," *Vanderbilt Law Review* 18 (March 1965): 473–505; Snyder, "The Supreme Court as a Small Group;" Ulmer, "Toward a Theory of Sub-Group Formation in the Supreme Court."

6. Clarence Thomas, "Freedom: A Responsibility, Not a Right," *Ohio Northern University Law Review* 21, no. 1 (1994): 5–12, 5 (stating that it takes "five years to become fully adjusted to the Court"); Clarence Thomas, Speech to the National Center for Policy Analysis, 9 September 1996, rebroadcast on C-SPAN, 19 October 1996.

7. William J. Brennan, Jr., "The National Court of Appeals: Another Dissent," *University of Chicago Law Review* 40 (spring 1973): 473–85, 484.

8. Felix Frankfurter, "The Supreme Court in the Mirror of Justices," *University of Pennsylvania Law Review* 40 (April 1957): 781–96, 789. See also William O. Douglas, *The Court Years, 1939–75: The Autobiography of William O. Douglas* (New York: Random House, 1980), 45 ("It is always difficult, especially so for a newcomer, to withdraw his agreement to one opinion at the last minute and cast his vote for the opposed view. A mature Justice may do just that; a junior is usually too unsure to make a last-minute shift.").

9. See, for example, Albert P. Melone, "Revisiting the Freshman Effect Hypothesis: The First Two Terms of Justice Anthony Kennedy," *Judicature* 74 (June–July 1990): 6–13, 7; Thea F. Rubin and Albert P. Melone, "Justice Antonin Scalia: A First Year Freshman Effect?" *Judicature* 72 (August–September 1988): 98–102, 99; John M. Scheb II and Lee W. Ailshie, "Justice Sandra Day O'Connor and the 'Freshman Effect,'" *Judicature* 69 (June–July 1985): 9–12, 10.

10. Melone, "Revisiting the Freshman Effect Hypothesis: The First Two Terms of Justice Anthony Kennedy," 6–7 (noting Justice Kennedy's prior service on a U.S. Court of Appeals); Rubin and Melone, "Justice Antonin Scalia," 98–9 (discussing Justice Scalia's prior experience on a U.S. Court of Appeals); Scheb and Ailshie, "Justice Sandra Day O'Connor and the 'Freshman Effect,'" 10 (noting Justice O'Connor's background as a state trial and appellate judge). But see Scott P. Johnson and Christopher E. Smith, "David Souter's First Term on the Supreme Court: The Impact of a New Justice," *Judicature* 75 (February–March 1988): 238–43, 243 (remarking that Justice Souter's prior experience on the New Hampshire Supreme Court "did not expose him to the range of issues presented to the U.S. Supreme Court"). See generally Scott D. Gerber and Keeok Park, "The Quixotic Search for Consensus on the U.S. Supreme Court: A Cross-Judicial Em-

pirical Analysis of the Rehnquist Court Justices," *American Political Science Review* 91 (June 1997): 390–408.

11. Tony Mauro, "Thomas Laments Loss of Anonymity," *USA Today*, 11 September 1992, 2A (quoting *The Docket Sheet*, an internal newsletter for Supreme Court employees).

12. Melone, "Revisiting the Freshman Effect Hypothesis," 7.

13. See Elliot E. Slotnick, "Judicial Career Patterns and Majority Opinion Assignment on the Supreme Court," *Journal of Politics* 41 (May 1979): 640–8.

14. Ibid., 642 n. 7.

15. Harold J. Spaeth, "Distributive Justice: Majority Opinion Assignments in the Burger Court," *Judicature* 67 (December 1983–January 1984): 299–304, 303.

16. Because Justices O'Connor, Kennedy, and Souter jointly penned the opinion for the Court in the landmark abortion case, *Planned Parenthood of Southeastern Pennsylvania v. Casey*, 505 U.S. 833 (1992), each is credited with one-third of the opinion.

17. Glendon A. Schubert, *Quantitative Analysis of Judicial Behavior* (Glencoe, IL: Free Press, 1959), 91.

18. See, for example, Christopher E. Smith, *Justice Antonin Scalia and the Supreme Court's Conservative Moment* (Westport, CT: Praeger, 1994).

19. See, for example, Sue Davis, *Justice Rehnquist and the Constitution* (Princeton: Princeton University Press, 1989); Peter H. Irons, *Brennan vs. Rehnquist: The Battle for the Constitution* (New York: Alfred A. Knopf, 1994).

NOTES TO APPENDIX II

1. See, for example, Lee Epstein, Jeffrey A. Segal, Harold J. Spaeth, and Thomas G. Walker, *The Supreme Court Compendium: Data, Decisions, and Development*, 2d ed. (Washington, DC: CQ Press, 1996).

2. See, for example, Scott D. Gerber and Keeok Park, "The Quixotic Search for Consensus on the U.S. Supreme Court: A Cross-Judicial Empirical Analysis of the Rehnquist Court Justices," *American Political Science Review* 91 (June 1997): 390–408. See generally Jeffrey A. Segal and Harold J. Spaeth, *The Supreme Court and the Attitudinal Model* (New York: Cambridge University Press, 1993).

3. Epstein et al., *The Supreme Court Compendium*, 455.

4. The only exception was Justice Thomas's first term, where Justice Scalia was slightly more conservative.

Index

Abortion: and Declaration of Independence, 48, 55, 56; and Lehrman, 48–9, 55, 56; and *Roe v. Wade*, 55, 56; and Thomas's legal philosophy, 194 n; and Thomas's political philosophy, 48–9, 55–7, 194 n

Accommodationism (nonpreferentialism): and Establishment Clause, 60, 60 n, 140

Adams, John: on property, 161

Adarand Constructors, Inc. v. Peña (1995): and affirmative action, 99–104; Critical Race Theory on, 71; reaction to Thomas's opinion in, 102–4; and Thomas's *Bush* opinion, 93; and Thomas's legal philosophy, 99–104; and Thomas's natural law views, 42; Thomas's opinion in, 102, 110, 193, 196

Advice and Consent (1992): on Thomas-Hill, 220 n.20

Affirmative action: definition of, 98; history of, 98–9, 241 n.146; reaction to Thomas's position on, 32–3; and Thomas's legal philosophy, 98–109, 194, 196; and Thomas's personal success, 12, 34, 102; and Thomas's political philosophy, 12, 51–3, 51 n, 98, 194, 196; and Thomas's U.S. Court of Appeals opinion, 52 n

African American Women Speak Out on Anita Hill-Clarence Thomas (1995): on Thomas-Hill, 19

A.L.A. Schechter Poultry Corporation v. United States (1935): and Commerce Clause, 177, 178, 180

Allen v. State Board of Elections (1969): Thomas on, 88, 90, 240 n.109; and voting rights, 84, 90, 91–2, 239 n.93

American Founding: and individual rights, 113; and individualism, 64; Thomas on, 45–7, 64, 150–1

American Spectator: and Thomas, 20

Anderson, Myers: influence on Thomas, 11, 53, 53–4, 218 n.1

Angelou, Maya: on Thomas, 19

Anger: and Thomas, 30, 38, 224 n.78

Appointment process: and Thomas hearings, 63–5

Articles of Confederation: and commerce, 177, 185

Association of Data Processing Service Organizations, Inc. v. Camp (1970): and standing, 105

Bailyn, Bernard: and freedom of the press, 150

Banner, Stuart: on commercial speech, 155

Batson v. Kentucky (1986): and criminal justice, 138; Thomas on, 138

Beard, Charles A.: on Constitution, 161

Beer, Samuel H.: on federalism, 164, 185, 186

Bell, Derrick A., Jr.: on *Brown v. Board of Education*, 72, 236 n.44; and Critical Race Theory, 71

Bell v. Wolfish (1979): and prisoners' rights, 115

Berger, Raoul: on Eighth Amendment, 128; on Thomas's *Lopez* opinion, 183–4

Berger, Vivian: on Thomas's *Wright* opinion, 134–5

Biden, Joseph R., Jr.: and Hill, 200; on Thomas's natural law views, 36, 43; and Thomas's views about economic freedom, 54

Bierstein, Andrea: on Thomas's voting rights jurisprudence, 241 n.137

Bill of Rights: and criminal justice, 114; importance of, 113–4; and Thomas, 113–4

Biography: Posner on, 5, 198 n; Thomas's, 11–3, 69–70; varieties of, 4–5

Black, Hugo: on freedom of the press, 148

About the Author

Scott Douglas Gerber received both a Ph.D. and J.D. from the University of Virginia, and a B.A. from the College of William and Mary. He is a former law clerk to a federal judge. He is author of *To Secure These Rights: The Declaration of Independence and Constitutional Interpretation* (1995) and editor of *Seriatim: The Supreme Court before John Marshall* (1998), both from New York University Press.